*Biblical Foundations*
*&*
*Contemporary Strategies*

# MISSIONS

*Biblical Foundations*
*&*
*Contemporary Strategies*

# MISSIONS

GAILYN VAN RHEENEN

ZondervanPublishingHouse
*Grand Rapids, Michigan*

*A Division of HarperCollinsPublishers*

*Missions*
Copyright © 1996 by Gailyn Van Rheenen

Requests for information should be addressed to:

**≝Zondervan Publishing House**
*Grand Rapids, Michigan 49530*

**Library of Congress Cataloging-in-Publication Data**

Van Rheenen, Gailyn.
    Missions : biblical foundations and contemporary strategies / Gailyn Van Rheenen.
        p.    cm.
    Includes bibliographical references and index.
    ISBN: 0-310-20809-2 (hardcover)
    1. Missions—Theory.    2. Christianity and culture.    I. Title.
BV2063.V35 1996
266'.001—dc20                                                           96-15860
                                                                             CIP

This edition printed on acid-free paper and meets the American National Standards Institute Z39.48 standard.

*Edited by Gerard H. Terpstra*
*Interior design by Tammy Johnson*

*Printed in the United States of America*

06 07 08 09 10 • 19 18 17 16 15 14 13 12 11

# CONTENTS

# FOREWORD

It is clear that we live in a rapidly changing world. What is sometimes overlooked is that in such times, the central missionary vision of the church must be constantly renewed, lest its foundations become lost in the confusion of change or its practices trapped in missionary models of the past. In this book, Dr. Van Rheenen challenges us to renew our missionary vision, rooted in God's call on our lives, and to proclaim the Gospel in new ways in our changing times. We need to do both if we want to remain central in God's mission to a lost and broken world.

After laying solid theological foundations for our call and motivation to mission, Van Rheenen gives us a brief overview of missionary life. He then deals with the critical issues that confront all those in intercultural ministries, such as identifying with the people, learning new languages and cultures, dealing with feelings of superiority, communicating cross-culturally without distorting the Gospel, and strategizing for planting living, reproducing churches. Finally, Van Rheenen looks at the newer models of mission outreach based on partnerships between churches in different cultures. I found this section particularly useful since most missionaries talk about partnership without effectively understanding it. The difficulties are immense because they bring all the issues of cross-cultural communication into the heart of the ministry team.

Throughout the text, Van Rheenen's illustrations based on his experience in intercultural teaching and church planting help make missions a living reality in our minds. His balanced assessment of the strengths and weaknesses of past and present mission theories helps us learn from what God has done so mightily through his people in the past, and to go beyond them to address the global issues we face in missions today.

PAUL G. HIEBERT
Trinity Evangelical Divinity School

# PREFACE

The study of missions is a *journey* that expands our horizons and broadens our understanding in at least four directions. First, the study of missions is a *journey into the world* to see the world *as it really is*—as God sees it—as a culturally diverse, pluralistic world torn between the opposing forces of Satan and God. Second, it is a *journey above* to perceive the purposes of God—what he is about in his world and what he desires of us. Third, the study of missions is a *journey into Christian community*. The Christian servant realizes that Christians cannot live autonomous lives disconnected from the church but must unite as a community of faith for the purposes of God. The initial desire for mission, nurturing of new believers, and training for missions most effectively occurs within intimate Christian community. Fourth, it is *journey within*—a journey of spiritual formation. This is a journey of prayerful reflection during which Christians ask, "Who am I in God's world? What is God calling me to be and become?" Thus the study of missions can never be a cerebral, academic exercise but a transforming experience in which the heart and head are actively engaged in determining the will of God in the world and in our lives. This text, *Missions: Biblical Foundations and Contemporary Strategies*, is a basic equipping tool for this journey. Each section provides a new building block to missions to stretch monocultural horizons and equip Christian leaders to become effective cross-cultural communicators of God's message.

Reading a significant introductory missions text should be the first task of the future missionary. This experience serves to form the conceptual infrastructure on which all subsequent studies and analyses of missions are based.

Some prospective missionaries, however, assume that general life training in their culture is adequate. Others realize their inadequacy to evangelize, nurture new Christians, and train leaders in a foreign culture and humbly seek training from those who in years past have effectively carried the mission of God. For example, Jim and Julie went on a campaign to Eastern Europe, their first trip outside the United States. For the first time they realized how many people do not know the way to God in Jesus Christ and how this immense world is, to a large extent, socially broken

9

and spiritually alienated from God. They decided that they must do something about it. Which pattern were they to follow?

*Pattern #1*: Jim and Julie's immediate impulse was to seek support of an agency or church and immediately return to Eastern Europe as missionaries. Had they not taught people while they were there in a short term venture? Were they not greatly respected as American teachers? Could they not make significant differences in people's lives by serving them? Within a year they were able to raise support through their local church and began serving as missionaries in Eastern Europe. Because of lack of training, however, they never learned the language, developed the tools to learn the culture, or acquired the understanding to construct long-term strategies. Although they desired to *Christianize* rather than *Americanize*, they did not have the basic training to understand the difference.

*Pattern #2*: Although Jim and Julie were tempted to return to Eastern Europe as soon as possible, they humbly realized their inadequacies. They realized how little they knew about the Gospel and how to serve in a foreign context as missionaries. They reasoned, "How can we teach what we do not yet know? What do we know about learning a language and culture and converting unbelievers to Jesus Christ in a foreign land?" Therefore, they decided to get the best training available before returning to Eastern Europe. In subsequent years Jim and Julie were used by God not only to convert hundreds of unbelievers but also to develop a process of nurturing new Christians and training leaders that launched a growing movement of God in that part of Eastern Europe.

In the first case study, the missionaries ministered in Eastern Europe as monocultural Americans without developing a conceptual infrastructure to develop and evaluate their ministries. They served as Americans who transplanted their language, culture, and message.

*Missions: Biblical Foundations and Contemporary Strategies* was written for people who have chosen the second course of action. The purpose of this text is to equip present and future missionaries with an understanding of the theological, cultural, and strategic foundations on which effective missions is based. The book guides missionaries (1) to understand purposes of God that empower mission, (2) to discern personal motives for carrying the mission of God, (3) to learn how to be learners as they enter a new culture, (4) to confront personal feelings of ethnocentrism so that they might communicate to those of another culture as equals, (5) to communicate God's eternal message in cultural categories that are both meaningful and effective, (6) to develop understandings of priorities in strategy formulation, (7) to grasp basic understanding of principles of planting churches, nurturing new believers, and training leaders, and (8) to determine fundamental criteria for selecting sites for missions.

Finally, a word of appreciation is appropriate for those who have significantly helped in preparing this book. The major contributor has been my wife, who read and reread the manuscript, reflected on the content, and made suggestions. She has provided both inspiration and wisdom for the formation of content of this text. With great insight, Delno Roberts has conscientiously proofed each chapter for wording, style, clarity, and grammar. I also thank my co-workers both in and outside of the Department of Missions at Abilene Christian University for their continued insight and encouragement. Philip Slate, Richard Chowning, Ed Mathews, Ian Fair, Reg Cox, and Ted Presley are among those who have had significant influence on my mission thinking, practice, and writing. Two graduate assistants—Chris Flanders, who is currently a missionary in Ching Mai, Thailand, and Alan Diles, serving in Prague in the Czech Republic—have helped greatly in organizing, proofing, and editing. Finally, I thank my many mentors and teachers whose courses and models formed my missiology. These include Dr. George Gurganus, past mission educator at Abilene Christian University; Drs. David Hesselgrave and Timothy Warner, under whom I studied at Trinity Evangelical Divinity School; and Dr. Paul Hiebert, whose writings and courses continue to stimulate my thinking.

GAILYN VAN RHEENEN
Abilene Christian University

# LIST OF FIGURES

# THEOLOGICAL FOUNDATIONS OF MISSIONS:
## Biblical Undergirdings of God's Mission

When a ship is in harbor, it must be anchored firmly. If it is not securely moored, it is moved by the constant ebb and flow of the sea. Likewise, the Christian faith must be theologically anchored. Without such anchors theology shifts with the ebb and flow of social and political currents.

Several examples illustrate how the Christian missionary movement has frequently drifted with the ebb and flow of cultural currents. After the Vietnam war the American people retreated militarily and politically from the world. During this period many churches mirrored this national isolationism by greatly reducing their foreign evangelistic commitments. The "social gospel" movement of the 1930s and 1940s de-emphasized evangelism and stressed social service. This movement was based on the theology that all world religions contain truth about God. Rather than introducing unbelievers to the way of God in Jesus Christ, religious leaders entered into dialogue with those of other religions to learn their truths. These concepts, set forth at the Jerusalem Missionary Conference of 1928, grew out of the social currents of the day rather than from a strong theological anchorage. Western secularism has also impacted the missionary movement. People were thought to be self-sufficient, able to solve all human problems empirically. This gospel of self-help became part of the cultural baggage of the Western missionary. The Bible, however, pictures people without God as unable to direct their own steps (Jer. 10:23). Humans, it avers, are not regenerated by realizing the poten-

**Mission does not originate with human sources, for ultimately it is not a human enterprise. Mission is rooted in the nature of God, who sends and saves.**

tial within themselves but by believing in the saving actions of God, who stands above them. Despite the ebb and flow of human cultures, Christians must stand firm, anchored by a God-ordained, biblically inspired worldview.

This chapter is written with the hope that it will provide theological anchorage to the student of missions. Mission is shown, not as a temporary historical phenomenon passing away for social and political reasons, but as eternally rooted in the will and nature of God.

God's mission might be pictured as an effervescent spring of pure water cascading down a mountainside and flowing into the sea. In this analogy God himself is the spring—the source from whom all living water flows. Christ is the living water that God has poured out upon the world. The Holy Spirit is the power, like gravity, driving forward the living water of God. The church is the receptacle, the waterway, that partakes of the living water and also conveys it to the world. The world, the target of mission, is those in need of the pure, life-giving water of God.

# God: The Source of Mission

Mission does not originate with human sources, for ultimately it is not a human enterprise. Mission is rooted in the nature of God, who sends and saves. When Adam and Eve acquiesced to Satan's temptations in the Garden of Eden, God came searching for them, calling, "Where are you?" (Gen. 3:9). This question testifies to the nature of God throughout all generations. He continually seeks to initiate reconciliation between himself and his fallen creation. God demonstrated his nature by sending his one and only Son into the world. The emphasis of John 3:16 is on God, who loved the world so much that he *gave*. . . . This is the very nature of God. He is always giving, relating, reconciling, redeeming! He is the spring that gives forth living water—the source of mission! From the very foundation of the world God has been the great initiator of mission, as vividly portrayed by the acts of God in both the Old and New Testaments.

### The Deliverance: A Great Old Testament Illustration of God's Mission

The Israelites defined God's mission by his actions in delivering them from Egyptian captivity. His actions became foundational for his continued interaction with Israel. God's covenant, for instance, was based on what God had done in Egypt when he carried Israel "on eagles' wings" and brought them to himself (Ex. 19:4). The Law was also prefaced by "I am the LORD your God, who brought you out of Egypt" (20:2). On the basis of God's activities in Egypt the Ten Commandments were given (vv. 3–17). During their feasts Jews recited a declaration of what God had done in Egypt (Deut. 26:5–9). This confessional statement affirmed that the Israelites went down into Egypt few in number but there grew to a mighty nation. When they suffered, God "heard" their cries, "saw" their misery, and "brought them out" with miracles, wonders, and signs. This confession, repeated throughout the ages, testified of God's mighty mission of deliverance in Egypt.

God's mission of deliverance was based on his eternal attribute of love (Ex. 34:6–7). The deliverance account reveals that the Israelite cry of desperation was "heard" by God, who "remembered" his covenant with Abraham and "looked on" the Israelites and "was concerned" about them (2:23–25). These verbs portray a compassionate God. God's love motivated him to call Moses to deliver the Israelites from captivity. God is therefore seen as the originator of the mission. The mission was not instigated by the Israelites' cries but by the ever-present God who responded to these groanings.

God, the originator of the mission of deliverance, then sought a person to carry out his mission. At the burning bush Moses was given the commission to be God's missionary of deliverance (Ex. 3:10). This call itself shows that the mission was God's; it was not a deliverance improvised by human ingenuity.

Forty years previous to God's call, Moses had attempted to take the salvation of the Israelites into his own hands. Although he was the adopted son of Pharaoh's daughter, Moses identified the Israelites as "his own people" and felt the injustice of their bondage. He slew an Egyptian slavemaster, expecting that they would realize that "God was using him to rescue them" (Acts 7:25). God's timing, however, did not run according to Moses' schedule. The discovered insurrectionist fled to Midian.

After forty years in Midian Moses feared God's call. He felt insufficient, afraid that he could not accomplish what God desired. He failed to realize that *the mission was not his; it was God's.* He was to be only the emissary to carry out the mission of God. Because he misunderstood, Moses initially objected to God's mission.

Moses objected to God's call in four ways. First, Moses asked, "Who am I that I should go. . .?" (Ex. 3:11). In this question Moses was emphasizing the egocentric "I." He was placing too much emphasis on himself and his own capabilities. God answered this first objection by saying, "I will be with you" (v. 12). Moses was to rely on God rather than on himself. In essence, God was telling Moses that the mission was greater than the missionary. The mission was God's, and he would be with those who carry his mission.

Moses' second objection had to do with the Israelites' understanding of Yahweh. Moses asked, "Suppose I go to the Israelites and say to them, 'The God of your fathers has sent me to you,' and they ask me, 'What is his name?' Then what shall I tell them?" (v. 13). The question implies polytheistic thinking. Moses assumed the Israelites would want to know which of the many gods of Egypt he represented. God responded by describing himself as "I AM WHO I AM" (v. 14), a name by which he would always be known (v. 15). This title defines God to be the ever-present deity who is consistently faithful to his promises and is sovereign over all. He was present as the God of the Israelite fathers—Abraham, Isaac, and Jacob (v. 15). He was even present during Israel's distress in Egypt. God's presence during suffering reveals compassion: Even in their distress God watched over them, heard their cries, and remembered his promises (vv. 16–17). Moses could rest assured that God, the great I AM WHO I AM, was present in the mission.

Moses' third objection was "What if [the Israelites] do not believe me or listen to me and say, 'The LORD did not appear to you'?" (Ex. 4:1). Moses' objection was once again on himself; he wondered if the Israelite people would believe him and listen to him. God responded by saying that he would work mightily through Moses to enable him to create belief (v. 5). God gave Moses the ability to perform three miracles: (1) His staff would be changed into a serpent (vv. 2–5); (2) his hand, when put into his cloak, would become leprous (vv. 6–8); and (3) water from the Nile would become blood on dry land (v. 9). In other words, *God, the Source of mission, would provide the power to help the missionary fulfill the mission.* God would not leave his messenger without the means to create belief in the hearts of those to whom he would minister.

Moses' fourth objection was that he had "never been eloquent" but was "slow of speech and tongue" (4:10–11). God responded by saying that he had made man's mouth (v. 11). Therefore, he said, "I, even I, will be with your mouth, and teach you what you are to say" (v. 12 NASB). When Moses continued to object, God became angry and chose Aaron to become Moses' spokesman (vv. 13–14).

Moses' objections demonstrate the human tendency to make God's mission a mission of self. Each objection was based on human deficiencies or misunderstandings, but God always responded by showing that the mission was greater than the missionary. The ever-present I AM WHO I AM was behind it.

In the following verses God uses the first person pronoun to describe his involvement in the deliverance of the Israelites from Egyptian captivity:

> I will lay my hand on Egypt and with mighty acts of judgment I will bring out my divisions, my people the Israelites. And the Egyptians will know that I am the LORD, when I stretch out my hand against Egypt and bring the Israelites out of it. **Ex. 7:4–5**

Israel's deliverance from Egypt was not based on human resources. The Israelites had no army; they had no weapons with which to fight; they had no expertise in guerilla warfare. God was the sole power behind this mission of deliverance.

Moses' message to Israel also emphasizes God's *action* in redeeming and delivering Israel. He begins and ends the message with the declaration "I am the LORD," demonstrating his sovereignty in his mission. The verbs are highlighted to demonstrate the mighty acts of God.

> Therefore, say to the Israelites: "I am the LORD, and I will bring you out from under the yoke of the Egyptians. I will free you from being slaves to them, and I will redeem you with an outstretched arm and with mighty acts of judgment. I will take you as my own people, and I will be your God. Then you will know that I am the LORD your God, who brought you out from under the yoke of the Egyptians. And I will bring you to the land I swore with uplifted hand to give to Abraham, to Isaac and to Jacob. I will give it to you as a possession. I am the LORD." **Ex. 6:6–8**

In this passage God says, "I am; therefore I will." Moses and Aaron, instruments used to facilitate God's mission, could stand before Pharaoh and say, "Thus says the LORD. . . ." This Lord was the source of mission.

That God is the source of mission is beautifully expressed in the covenant passage of Exodus 19:4, where God recounts his redemptive work of deliverance:

> You yourselves have seen what I did to Egypt, and how I carried you on eagles' wings and brought you to myself.

The declaration "I carried you on eagles' wings and brought you to myself" describes God's reconciling mission in all generations. Mission springs forth from God. He is the source of it.

### Jesus Christ: The Great New Testament Illustration of God's Mission

Mission is also the central theme of the New Testament. In earlier periods God transmitted his mission to humanity in many diverse ways. When Jesus became human, the mission of God began to flow to humanity through Jesus Christ (Heb. 1:1–2).

The consistent theme throughout the New Testament is God, because of his great love, fulfilling his mission through Jesus Christ:

> When the kindness and love of God our Savior appeared, he saved us. . . . **Titus 3:4–5** God demonstrates his own love for us in this: While we were still sinners, Christ died for us. **Rom. 5:8** This is love: not that we loved God, but that he loved us and sent his Son as an atoning sacrifice for our sins. **1 John 4:10**

These verses show God, through Jesus, initiating his mission of reconciliation. The mission was not based on human works. God initiated the mission while we were still enemies, alienated from his presence, living in sin.

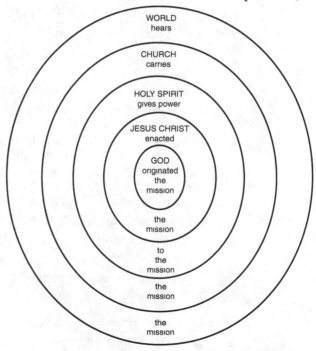

**Figure 1. The Flow of the Mission of God**

The mission of God, as illustrated in figure 1, originated in the mind of God. The mission flowed from him to Christ, who proclaimed God's kingdom message and in his death enacted God's kingdom plan. He prayed that the Father would send the Spirit. This Spirit empowered the church for mission. The message flowed, then, from God to Christ to the church, who, empowered by the Spirit, carries the mission to the world.

### Applications of the "Mission of God"

At least five specific applications of the "Mission of God" can be made:

First, if mission flows from the character and nature of God, it cannot be neglected by the church. Mission, because it is of God, cannot be aborted!

Second, since the mission is of God, God will equip people for the task. If God's messengers are afraid to speak, God will be with their mouths. If they feel inadequate, he will empower them to become capable communicators. If they are afraid of the response of the world, they must remember God's power to reshape people in his image.

Third, the "Mission of God" enables Christian missionaries to understand themselves under God's sovereignty. Christians should not undertake God's mission for self-glorification but for the glorification of God. Paul wrote to Christian leaders in Philippi concerning dissension there: "Do nothing out of selfish ambition or vain conceit, but in humility consider others better than yourselves" (Phil. 2:3). The missionary must not preach "to gain honor for himself, but . . . for the honor of the one who sent him" (John 7:18). Such an other-centered, God-oriented perspective leads the Christian communicator to realize that the mission is greater than self. It is God's enterprise! He is the spring of mission pouring forth living water upon the world.

Fourth, the "Mission of God" implies sacrifice. It is a mission worth living for and dying for. Consequently, many missionaries have entered fields knowing that their life expectancy would be severely affected. One missionary in Eastern Europe was told by the people there that because he had come to Eastern Europe his life span would probably be shortened by five years because of pollution, radiation, and ecological mismanagement.

Finally, this perspective enables the Christian communicator to recognize that because the mission is God's, it will succeed. Even though messengers fail and people reject the message, the mission of

God continues. God, the source of mission, will raise up new people like Moses to carry his message.

### Definition of "Mission" and "Missions"

With an understanding of the role of God in mission, the terms "mission" and "missions" can be better understood. As described in this chapter, mission is *the work of God*. Any understanding excluding God and perceiving mission as some type of human endeavor is, therefore, erroneous. Mission is also rooted in God's desire to reconcile sinful humanity to himself. As God worked in Egypt to bear the Israelites "on eagles' wings" and bring them to himself (Ex. 19:4), he continues to work through human ambassadors to reconcile sinful humanity to himself (2 Cor. 5:18–20). God, who initiated his mission through prophets, priests, and judges during Old Testament times and later through Jesus Christ, continues to initiate his mission through his people today. "Mission," therefore, is *the work of God in reconciling sinful humankind to himself*.

The term "missions" should not be confused with "mission." Missions is *the plans of committed believers to accomplish the mission of God*. Mission is the theological anchor of missions. Missions is the practical implementation of the mission of God. Missions without mission is empty—like a body without its spirit.

# Christ: The Message of Mission

### Proclaiming the Kingdom of God

Christ's ministry reflected two interrelated purposes. First, Christ *proclaimed the message of the kingdom of God*. John prepared the way for Jesus by teaching, "Repent, for the kingdom of heaven is near" (Matt. 3:2). Christ's message paralleled that of John (Matt. 3:11). A fuller summary of Christ's message is given in Mark's Gospel: "The time has come. . . . The kingdom of God is near. Repent and believe the good news" (1:15). The term "near" has both present and future connotations. It means "'drawing near,' 'breaking in,' 'in process of becoming'" (Ferguson 1989, 24). In this passage "the time has come" is synonymous with "the kingdom of God is at hand." The first phrase "looks backward, while the second looks to the present and future; the first announces the end of the old era, the second proclaims the beginning of the new" (Ambrozic 1972, 21–22). Beasley-Murray interprets this passage to mean, "If the time before the kingdom is finished, the time of the kingdom has begun" (1986, 73). The coming of Jesus Christ, therefore, formed the watershed of the ages, a turning point in history, a time for the breaking in of the mighty reign of God in his Messiah.

The biblical concept of *kingdom*, however, predates the coming of Christ. The word means the "rule, reign, or sovereignty of God." The synonymous parallelisms of Psalm 145:11–13 define the nature of the kingdom of God:

> *They will tell of the glory of your kingdom*
> *and speak of your might,*
> *so that all men may know of your mighty acts*
> *and the glorious splendor of your kingdom.*
> *Your kingdom is an everlasting kingdom,*
> *and your dominion endures through all generations.*

God's kingdom is one of glory and splendor. The synonymous parallelisms equate the kingdom with *power, mighty acts*, and *dominion*. God "does not merely sit on a throne, but he reigns by performing mighty deeds . . . expressed in acts of power" (Ferguson 1989, 7).

God's right to rule is established at creation. Because God is creator, he must be acknowledged as sovereign over all of his creation. This is the implied meaning of the psalmist who wrote, "The earth is the LORD's, and everything in it, the world, and all who live in it; for he founded it upon the seas and established it upon the waters" (Ps. 24:1–2). God, therefore, is incomparable; no other gods are like him. After God had delivered the Israelites from Egyptian captivity, Moses praised him, saying, "Who among the gods is like you, O LORD? Who is like you—majestic in holiness, awesome in glory, working wonders?" (Ex. 15:11). God's rule is demonstrated throughout the Old Testament in his raising up *judges* to deliver the Israelites (Judg. 2:10–19), instituting *priests* to intercede for the people of Israel (Ex. 28–29; Lev. 8–9), and sending *prophets* to proclaim his message to kings and the people (Jer. 1:5–6; 15:19; Ezek. 3:17; Amos 7:16). God, the creator, reigns as Lord over his universe.

From the very beginning, Satan has challenged the rule of God. Satan tempted Adam and Eve to seek their own solutions independent of God (Gen. 3:1–5). Israel consistently made God jealous by abandoning him as the rock of their salvation in favor of the gods of nations (Deut. 32:15–18). Because of Israel's proclivity for the gods, God disowned his elected people and sent them into captivity to Assyria and Babylonia (2 Kings 17:7–23; Jer. 5:19).

With the coming of Jesus Christ the word "kingdom" took on a new meaning. Kingdom began to connote God's ultimate, decisive reign through his Son.

Christ proclaimed the kingdom in both word and deed. He preached "the good news of the kingdom" (Luke 4:43). His parables described the nature of the kingdom. During these last days, the kingdom of God and the kingdom of Satan would coexist—like tares and wheat, only to be separated in the final harvest. Christ gave a rationale for the continuance of the kingdom of Satan even though the ultimate reign of God in his Messiah had been consummated (Matt. 13:24–30, 36–43). This kingdom is like a pearl of great price, so precious that a merchant would give all that he has to possess it (vv. 45–46). The Sermon on the Mount was descriptive of the qualities of the kingdom of God in contrast to the earthly messianic expectations of the Jews. The casting out of demons was a demonstration of the kingdom. Jesus explained the healing of a demon-possessed man who was blind and mute by saying, "If I drive out demons by the Spirit of God, then the kingdom of God has come upon you" (Matt. 12:28). Jesus described the casting out of demons as the entering of a strong man's house, binding the strong man, and carrying off his possessions (v. 29). Christ, the implied stronger man, entered the domain of Satan and claimed what Satan possessed. This defeat of Satan during Jesus' ministry was a foretaste of his disarming of Satan's power on the cross (Col. 2:15).

The essence of Christ's kingdom proclamation is summarized by the first three petitions of the Lord's Prayer. They are synonymous parallelisms describing various aspects of the kingdom:

> *Hallowed be your name,*
> *your kingdom come,*
> *your will be done*
> *on earth as it is in heaven.*
>
> Matt. 6:9–10

The first phrase reflects the awe with which people of the kingdom should regard the name of God. God's reputation was not to be defiled by sin and acts of disbelief but glorified by obedient, holy living. This reflects God's remarkable words through Ezekiel: "I will show the holiness of my great name, which has been profaned among the nations. . . . Then the nations

*With the coming of Jesus Christ the word "kingdom" took on a new meaning. Kingdom began to connote God's ultimate, decisive reign through his Son.*

will know that I am the LORD, declares the Sovereign LORD, when I show myself holy through you before their eyes" (Ezek. 36:23). The phrase "your kingdom come" is a petition that the messianic expectations of God's rule would occur. Similarly, the phrase "your will be done" is a prayer that God's purposes in the world might be accomplished. The phrase "on earth as . . . in heaven," applying to all three statements, signifies the universality of God's rule (Beasley-Murray 1992, 23–24).

*Kingdom*, therefore, is like a "scarlet thread" interwoven "through the biblical testimonies" (Moltmann 1981, 95). People of God have always proclaimed the kingdom of God. The concept of kingdom, however, took on special meaning with the coming of Christ. In Christ, God acted decisively to defeat the powers of Satan and bring his own rule into the world. The message of Christ, therefore, became the theme of kingdom proclamation.[1]

### Becoming the Message of Mission

But Christ did more than merely *proclaim the message of the kingdom*. Because of who he is—the Son of God—and his willingness to die for sinners, he became the very *message of mission*. The message taught by the early church was that Jesus was "the Christ," the anointed one of God (Acts 5:42). In the book of Acts Christian proclamation was described as "preaching Christ." Philip "proclaimed the Christ" in Samaria (8:5) and began with the passage of the suffering Servant to tell the Ethiopian "the good news about Jesus" (v. 35). The preaching of "the good news about the Lord Jesus" led to the beginning of the first Gentile church (11:20). Athenians accused Paul of being a "babbler" because they could not understand his message "about Jesus and the resurrection" (17:18). The phrase "preaching Jesus," therefore, came to summarize the fundamental message of the early church.

The message of Christ was not distinct from the message of the kingdom but parallel to it. Philip, for instance, "preached the good news of the *kingdom of God* and *the name of Jesus Christ*" in Samaria (Acts 8:12). Paul related to the Ephesian elders how he had "gone about preaching the kingdom" (20:25).

---

[1] For a more comprehensive treatment of the kingdom of God, read *Communicating Christ in Animistic Contexts* (Van Rheenen 1991, 131–42). Everett Ferguson's *The Everlasting Kingdom* (A.C.U. Press, 1989) is an excellent introduction for the beginner. Beasley-Murray's *Jesus and the Kingdom of God* (Eerdmans, 1986) is a definitive, comprehensive treatment of the topic.

Early sermons in Jewish contexts all presented the work of God in Jesus Christ. On the Day of Pentecost Peter presented Christ as a man affirmed by God by miracles, foreordained by God's purposes and knowledge, slain on the cross, raised from the dead by God's mighty hand, and exalted to God's right hand. When they understood God's work in Jesus Christ, the Jews asked, "What shall we do?" The fundamental message in this sermon was God's work in Jesus Christ (Acts 2:14–39).

Paul's preaching centered on Jesus. Luke gives this summary of Paul's sermons in Jewish synagogues:

> As his custom was, Paul went into the synagogue,. . . reasoned with them from the Scriptures, explaining and proving that the Christ had to suffer and rise from the dead. "This Jesus I am proclaiming to you is the Christ," he said. **Acts 17:2–3**

In 1 Corinthians 15:1–4 Paul defined the *gospel* he *preached*, the message the Corinthians had *received*, on which they *had taken their stand* and by which they *were saved*. This message is described to be of *first importance*.

> Now, brothers, I want to remind you of the gospel I preached to you, which you received and on which you have taken your stand. By this gospel you are saved, if you hold firmly to the word I preached to you. Otherwise, you have believed in vain. For what I received I passed on to you as of first importance: that Christ died for our sins according to the Scriptures, that he was buried, and he was raised on the third day according to the Scriptures.

The gospel, according to Paul's definition, is the death, burial, and resurrection of Jesus Christ from the dead.

This fundamental message of the Christian faith rests on the foundation of the kingdom of God. One cannot comprehend the significance and work of Christ without first understanding God who creates, sustains, and acts. Whenever Paul preached in non-Jewish contexts, he first laid the foundation of the kingdom of God. His failure to do so in the Athenian marketplace led some Epicurean and Stoic philosophers to ask, "What is this babbler trying to say?" Others remarked, "He seems to be advocating foreign gods" (Acts 17:18). They could not understand the message of Christ without a basic understanding of the creator God who sends and saves. Therefore, Paul in the Areopagus attempted to define God who sent Jesus Christ (vv. 22–31). Likewise, when Barnabas and Paul healed the crippled man in Lystra, the people thought they were gods in human form. These missionaries had to lay the foundation of the person and working of the creator God before the people could understand the message of Christ (14:8–18).

Thus the fundamental message of Christian proclamation is Jesus Christ. Paul wrote, "No one can lay any foundation other than the one already laid, which is Jesus Christ" (1 Cor. 3:11). And again, "I resolved to know nothing while I was with you except Jesus Christ and him crucified" (2:2). The New Testament shows that Christ became the fundamental message preached by the early church.

### Messages Usurping the Foundational Message of Mission

Frequently, the first message proclaimed to unbelievers is a *side issue*. The issue may be important to the ongoing of the kingdom of God, but it is not the fundamental saving message of the gospel. Such secondary issues often displace the gospel message as the dominant topic of religious discussion. For example, the Seventh-day Adventists began working with the Kisii people of Kenya in 1906. Today a third of the Kisii tribe consider themselves Seventh-day Adventists. New missionaries working with the Kisii are invariably asked, "Should we worship on Saturday or Sunday?" Although a large proportion of this ethnic group is unchurched, the issue of the day of worship has supplanted the core message of "Jesus Christ and him crucified" as the major topic of religious discussion.

For others *the church* has become the fundamental message communicated to the unbeliever. The church, as the corporate body of believers, is a *result* of the message of Jesus. It is an outgrowth of the mission of God through Christ. But the church, in and of itself, is not the message; it is the fellowship of believers that results when people respond to the fundamental message of Jesus Christ.

Others preach *the Holy Spirit* as the fundamental message of the gospel. Their teaching usually emphasizes the possession of spiritual gifts such as speaking in tongues as evidences of the presence of the Holy Spirit. But Paul admonished the church to desire "the greater gifts" or "the most excellent way" of love (1 Cor. 12:31–13:7) over temporal spiritual gifts (13:8). The Holy Spirit is a gift bestowed on those who respond to the central message of Christ (Acts 2:38). The Holy Spirit is not the core message; he is the helper of those who follow the core message.

Others present *baptism* in such a way that it appears to be the core message of the gospel. Baptism, in fact, is *related* to the fundamental Christian message because it is a likeness of the death, burial, and resurrection of Jesus (Rom. 6:3–6). Nevertheless, no action of believers can supplant

Jesus Christ as the foundation of the gospel. Truly, "no one can lay any foundation other than the one already laid, which is Jesus Christ" (1 Cor. 3:11).

The above discussion deals with the problem of theological emphases. Surely no Christian would deny the importance of the biblical doctrines of the church, the Holy Spirit, and baptism. But these doctrines are not the foundational message of the gospel, and they cannot be understood without a knowledge of the fundamental message of God's work through Jesus Christ. For example, if evangelists begin by preaching the doctrine of the Holy Spirit, this doctrine will almost surely supplant Jesus Christ and his death and resurrection. Therefore, initial teaching must bring the hearers to a belief in Jesus Christ. Only then will the foundation be laid for broader theological teaching.

Wendell Broom, seeking to clarify theological priorities, asks, "Is Christianity more like bowling or archery?" In bowling, each pin is of equal importance; special bonuses are given for perfection. In archery the focus is on hitting the bull's-eye. When Christianity is viewed as bowling, all Christian beliefs are held to be equally important. But when Christianity is understood as archery, Jesus Christ is the bull's-eye, the center of the target, and all other Christian beliefs and values are understood in relation to this foundational doctrine.

In drawing his target, Broom argues that the Bible shows some aspects of the Judeo-Christian tradition to be more significant than other aspects and that the Bible must be allowed to set the theological agenda. Love is the foundation of the law—the greatest commandment of all (Matt. 22:34–40), the fundamental attribute of God and Christ. Jesus accused the scribes and Pharisees of emphasizing tithing while neglecting "the more important matters of the law—justice, mercy and faithfulness." He said that they "should have practiced the latter, without neglecting the former" (23:23). In comparison to the spiritual gifts of miracle working, healing, and tongue speaking, Paul considered love to be "a greater gift" and "the most excellent way" (1 Cor. 12:31). God desires heartfelt obedience rather than sacrifice (1 Sam. 15:22). Observing outward rituals in feasts, offerings, and prayer rites is meaningless if one is not showing compassion to the oppressed, the fatherless, and the widowed (Isa. 1:10–17).

Broom states that the Christian communicator must not start on the periphery of his target—with the least important items—and work inward toward the bull's-eye. Fundamental Christian teachings of the sovereignty of God and his distinctive work in Jesus Christ are foundational

**Initial teaching must bring the hearers to a belief in Jesus Christ. Only then will the foundation be laid for broader theological teaching.**

to all other Christian beliefs and must, therefore, be given priority in the initial presentation of the gospel to unbelievers.

# The Holy Spirit: The Power of Mission

Gravity is an almost imperceptible power; yet it is vital to the flowing of water. Likewise, the Spirit of God is the power (sometimes perceived only by the spiritually discerning) driving forward the mission of God. In the analogy of a spring the Holy Spirit is God's empowering agent, propelling the living water to the world.

Luke described the work of the Holy Spirit in the mission of God to such an extent that the book of Acts might be called Acts of the Holy Spirit. The topic of the Holy Spirit is introduced in Christ's pre-ascension discussion with his apostles (Acts 1:5–8). Instead of the political power formerly sought by those of a first-century Jewish heritage, Christ promised them a far greater and nobler power. Jesus said:

> *You will receive power when the Holy Spirit comes on you; and you will be my witnesses in Jerusalem, and in all Judea and Samaria, and to the ends of the earth.* **Acts 1:8**

God's Spirit is behind his mission! Led by the Holy Spirit, the witnesses will be empowered to evangelize even "to the ends of the earth" (Acts 1:8). This power is not of the apostles alone: The statement demonstrates that the witnesses will evangelize not only in Jerusalem and in all Judea and Samaria but even "to the ends of the earth."

The concept of God empowering his mission through the Spirit is parallel to the words of the Great Commission in Matthew. Christ said, "I am with you always, to the very end of the age" (28:20). In John 14 Jesus revealed that he would soon depart (vv. 2–3), but he would not leave his children as orphans (v. 18). He would come to them as the Spirit to abide in them and be with them (v. 17). This indwelling Spirit makes the people of God temples of the Holy Spirit (1 Cor. 3:16–17; 6:19–20). The Spirit, therefore, is *God with us* just as Christ was Immanuel, "God with us" (Matt. 1:23).

In the book of Acts the Spirit of God guided evangelists to those seeking the way of God. The "Spirit told Philip" to flag down a chariot in which a searching Ethiopian was reading a prophecy about the suffering servant (8:29). The Spirit was active in the conversion of Cornelius. The Spirit directed Peter to go with the three servants from Cornelius (10:19–20). Newbigin, in commenting on Cornelius' conversion, says:

It is certainly true that this story shows how God's mission is not simply an enterprise of the Church. It is a work of the Spirit who goes ahead of the Church, touches the Roman soldier and his household, prepares them for the message, and teaches the Church a new lesson about the scope of God's grace. **1989, 168**

These passages show God arranging divine encounters so that people seeking him are able to find him.

According to the testimony of Acts, the Spirit sets aside leaders for ministry. After fasting, praying, and laying their hands on Barnabas and Saul, the church in Antioch sent them to become the first Gentile missionaries (Acts 13:1–4). This sending was no human endeavor. The Holy Spirit had spoken, saying, "Set apart for me Barnabas and Saul for the work to which I have called them" (v. 2). The church's sending (v. 4) and the Spirit's speaking (v. 3) were not incompatible. The church commissioned and sent out those selected by a praying and fasting fellowship of believers.

The Spirit also opens and closes doors. In Acts 16 the Spirit closed the doors of Asia (v. 6) and Bithynia (v. 7) but opened the door to Macedonia (v. 9). My family and I experienced God's closing the door of Uganda by forcing us to leave during the persecutions of Idi Amin in 1972, but God opened the door for us to work for thirteen years among the Kipsigis people of Kenya. God has broken the yoke of atheistic communism, thus opening Eastern Europe and Russia and other previously Marxist countries such as Mozambique, Benin, Angola, and Ethiopia to Christian proclamation.

These examples from Acts demonstrate that mission is not a human endeavor. God, who is the source of mission, continues to guide his mission through his divine Spirit.

# The Church: The Embodiment of God's Mission

Few Christians are able to describe vividly in biblical terms what God desires the church to be. Without biblical undergirdings, the church is swept along by the ebb and flow of culture and in various forms degenerates into a social fraternity. When this happens, the church more nearly reflects the world than the nature of God and has little that is distinctive to offer the world. Consequently, during this age of cultural accommodation, the church must reinterpret her very nature. In this section the church will be seen as the result of mission; God's distinctive, set-apart people in the world; and his instrument for mission.

## The Result of Mission

The church is not a human organization. It is the result of a mission or a sending that began with God. The mission of God, initiated through Jesus Christ and continued through his disciples, led to the formation of the church. Christ prayed about this sending in John 17:18: "As you sent me into the world, I have also sent them into the world." He reiterated the statement after his resurrection: "As the Father has sent me, I am sending you" (John 20:21). In other words, both Christ and his disciples were ambassadors sent by God, the source of mission. The Christian community reproduces this sending by sending those called and empowered by God into the world. Disciples are expected to lead others to believe in Christ (17:20). The church, then, should conceive of itself as "the outcome of the activity of God who sends and saves" (Vicedom 1965, 80).

Had God not sent his Son, there would be no church. Since God's mission through Christ conceived the church, it must be thought of as his institution, under his jurisdiction, set aside to fulfill his purposes in the world. In no way should his body be considered a social fraternity without a relationship to him who initiated it.

## God's Distinctive People in the World

Too often Christians see little difference between their values and ethics and those of the world. The church is so permeated by the world that biblical analogies of its separateness are no longer recognized. How are disciples of Christ in the world but not of the world (John 17:14–16)? How can people of God live in the heavenlies while dwelling in the "earthlies" (Eph. 1:3; 2:6; 3:11–12)? What does Paul mean when he says that the believers' "citizenship is in heaven" (Phil. 3:20)? Why do two Christian scholars define the church as "a colony, an island of one culture in the middle of another"? "In baptism," they say, "our citizenship is transferred from one dominion to another" (Hauerwas and Willimon 1989, 12).

Israel illustrates a nation's struggle to be God's distinctive people. God's covenant with Israel set them aside to be "a kingdom of priests and a holy nation" within God's world (Ex. 19:5–6). Their designated purpose was to become God's light to the nations (Isa. 42:6; 49:6), to mediate God's purposes as his priests. Unfortunately, Israel forgot the God who chose them and imitated the nations around them by going after their gods (Deut. 32:15–18). As a result, God sent them into captivity (2 Kings 17:7–23). The church, like Israel, is called to be a distinctive, separate people, personally relating to the God who chose them.

Peter defines the church's separateness from the world in words that call to mind God's election of Israel. The church, God's new Israel, was to be "a chosen people, a royal priesthood, a holy nation, a people belonging to God. . ." (1 Peter 2:9). Such separation from the world led Peter to describe Christians as "aliens and strangers in the world" (v. 11; cf. 1:1, 17). They have entered into Christ through a fundamental change of life, called a *new birth*, which gives them an eternal inheritance with God (1:3, 23). As strangers in a world not their own, they must be holy because their God is holy (v. 15), and they must not imitate the vain ways of their forefathers (vv. 13–19). Because they are God's distinct people, they are able to suffer as Christians without shame, knowing that they are participating in the sufferings of Christ (4:12–16).

Unfortunately, the church today frequently loses its identity as God's distinct people. Vicedom has written that the greatest problem with Christians today is that "they do not know that they are Christians" (1965, 80). Instead of permeating the world with its eternal message, the church is being permeated by the world.

Without a distinctiveness it becomes almost impossible for the church to call unbelievers into a relationship with God and into the body of Christ. How can those permeated by the world call others out of the world? Peter writes, "You are a chosen people, a royal priesthood, a holy nation, a people belonging to God, that you may declare the praises of him who called you out of darkness into his wonderful light" (1 Peter 2:9). The last part of this verse is contingent on the first part. If the church is distinct from the world as "a people belonging to God," then it can call sinners to holiness in God. If the church partakes of the world, it has no right to call people out of the world. Distinctiveness as God's people is, therefore, closely tied to Christian witnessing.

### God's Witness to the World

The church is God's people called out from the world to be his witness in the world. As an institution, it appears fallible and weak, but paradoxically it has outlasted states, nations, and empires (Newbigin 1989, 221). The church reflects the eternal nature of the kingdom that cannot be destroyed (Dan. 2:44; 7:13–14). Its continuance is rooted in its being God's people under his eternal sovereignty.

> Without a distinctiveness it becomes almost impossible for the church to call unbelievers into a relationship with God and into the body of Christ. How can those permeated by the world call others out of the World?

Those redeemed by God's mission and incorporated as his distinctive people become witnesses to his nature and mighty acts. How can those who have been delivered from the bondage of Satan and reconciled to God in Jesus Christ remain silent? They "believe and therefore speak" (2 Cor. 4:13). They have been given the "ministry of reconciliation" and become ambassadors sent by God. Through these emissaries God makes his appeal for unbelievers to be reconciled to him (5:18–20).

Within the context of describing the lostness of Israel and a recognition that "everyone who calls on the name of the Lord will be saved," Paul describes the significance of mission (Rom. 10:1–17). His rhetorical questions show the role of mission in the church:

> *How, then, can they call on the one they have not believed in? And how can they believe in the one of whom they have not heard? And how can they hear without someone preaching to them? And how can they preach unless they are sent? As it is written, "How beautiful are the feet of those who bring good news!"* **Rom. 10:14–15**

The basis of all mission is sending. Unbelievers cannot call on God until they first believe; they cannot believe until they hear; they cannot hear without a preacher; and preachers will not go unless they are sent. The messenger's feet appear "beautiful" to those hearing and receiving the word of Christ.

In a real sense mission is the very lifeblood of the church. As the body cannot survive without blood, so the church cannot survive without mission. Without blood the body dies; without mission the church dies. As the physical body becomes weak without sufficient oxygen-carrying red blood cells, so the church becomes anemic if it does not express its faith. The church most frequently establishes its rationale for being—its purpose for existing—while articulating its faith. An unexpressed faith withers. A Christian fellowship without mission loses its vitality. Mission is the force that gives the body of Christ vibrancy, purpose, and direction. When the church neglects its role as God's agent for mission, it is actually neglecting its own lifeblood.

How, then, should the church be defined from a biblical perspective? The church is *the distinctive people of God called by him through his mission and set aside for his mission.* The purpose of the church is not merely to interpret history but to become a passionate and articulate "history-making force." It is through the church that "God brings history to its goal, and only because this is so does it provide the place where the goal

**The church most frequently establishes its rationale for being—its purpose for existing—while articulating its faith.**

of history can be understood" (Newbigin 1989, 131). The church embodies the very essence of the mission of God.

# The World: The Target of Mission

In communicating the Christian message to the world, Christian ministers must understand both the nature of the world and the nature of Christian communication to the world.

The intrinsic character of the world is shocking to Christians who have grown up in the church without having actively ministered in the world. The world consists of people broken by sin, suffering because of depraved cravings, and alienated from a personal, intimate relationship with God. Christ calls them "harassed and helpless, like sheep without a shepherd" (Matt. 9:36).

The Bible describes the status change that occurs when unbelievers leave the world and come to Christ. Those *dead* in sin are made *alive* in Christ (Eph. 2:1–6). The *old self* has been taken off and a *new self* replaces it (4:22–24; Col. 3:9–10). Paul was sent to the Gentiles to turn them from "*darkness* to *light*, and from the *power of Satan* to *God*" (Acts 26:18). God "has rescued us from *the dominion of darkness* and brought us into the *kingdom of the Son. . .*" (Col. 1:13). These contrasts illustrate the radical change that occurs at conversion. Conversion is a new birth, a change of ownership. Negatively, conversion is a radical turning from self and from idolatries that are in rebellion to God; positively, it is turning to God through faith in Jesus Christ and coming into union with him through baptism.

Although God and his nature are unchanging, the world in which Christian communicators find themselves is ever-changing. How does the church communicate God's unchanging message in an ever-changing world? The unchanging gospel must be presented in such a way that unbelievers will listen and not be alienated. Christian communicators must emulate Paul and Barnabas, who "spoke so effectively that a great number . . . believed" (Acts 14:1). They must "become all things to all men" so that all people—Jews and Gentiles, weak and powerful, poor and rich—will grasp a Christian worldview (1 Cor. 9:22). They must not, however, change significant elements of the gospel to increase Christianity's appeal to the unbeliever. On the other hand, a person must seek powerful communication models so that the gospel is not lost in the ideological menus of a pluralistic age.

# Conclusion

The church of the first century grew rapidly out of the theological perspectives discussed in this chapter. Christians understood that God was behind the mission. Peter could courageously stand before the Sanhedrin and say to those who had had the Savior killed, "We must obey God rather than men!" (Acts 5:29). The mission was worth dying for because it was of divine, not human, origin. Christians preached Christ as the fundamental message. All other topics either prepared the way for or built upon this central teaching. The message, in a nutshell, was "that the Christ had to suffer and rise from the dead" and that Jesus of Nazareth was the Christ (17:3).

The early church, as people of the Spirit, learned to rely on the Spirit of God. God was in them actively guiding his mission. The early Christians believed themselves to be God's messengers carrying his mission.

The church, the result of God's mission in Christ, perpetuated and extended itself by mission. Jesus commissioned his followers to be his "witnesses in Jerusalem, and in all Judea and Samaria, and to the ends of the earth" (Acts 1:8). Luke records the fulfillment of this commission in the book of Acts. The message was proclaimed in Jerusalem (Acts 1–7), in Judea and Samaria (Acts 8–12), and "to the ends of the earth" (Acts 13–28). Paul was able to tell the church in Rome that he had preached the gospel from Jerusalem to Illyricum, in present-day Croatia (Rom. 15:19). He was planning a trip to Rome en route to Spain (v. 24), where the message of Christ had not been proclaimed (v. 20). The church felt the urgent mission of God to evangelize the world.

The world, torn by sin and living under the dominion of Satan, desperately needs reconciliation to God in Jesus Christ. Paul wrote to the Colossians that God "has rescued us from the dominion of darkness and brought us into the kingdom of the Son he loves, in whom we have redemption, the forgiveness of sins" (1:13–14). The task for these redeemed, forgiven ones is to evangelize and fulfill the mission of God. This task is crucial, and the end "is nearer than when [they] first believed." The ultimate purpose of the mission of God is to reestablish an intimate relationship of sinners to God so that they may live under his sovereignty both in this world and in the world to come.

# BUILDING ON THE THEOLOGICAL FOUNDATIONS

## QUESTIONS:

1. How does the understanding that God is the source of mission prepare our hearts for missions?
2. How do Moses' four objections to God's call to mission help us understand the mission of God? In your answer give all four objections and God's responses to these objections. Apply each response to the nature of the mission of God in the world.
3. Contrast the meaning of the terms *mission* and *missions*. What occurs when missionaries do *missions* without *mission*?
4. Describe what the message of mission is and give at least three biblical references that specifically express what this message is.
5. What other messages have displaced this core message? Why do you think this has occurred?
6. Why may we call the book of Acts the *Acts of the Holy Spirit*? Give specific ways in which the Spirit of God guided the mission of God in the book of Acts.
7. Why do you think that many Christians molded by secular culture fail to understand the role of the Holy Spirit in missions and evangelism?
8. What is meant by each of the following statements concerning the relationship of the church and mission?
   a. "The church is *the result of mission*."
   b. "For the church to effectively minister it must be *God's distinctive people in the world*."
   c. "The church most frequently establishes its rationale for being— its purpose for existing—while articulating its faith. An unexpressed faith withers."
   d. "The purpose of the church is not merely to interpret history but to become a passionate and articulate 'history-making force.'"
9. Contrast how the world sees itself and how the church molded by the mission of God sees the world. How does the Christian live *in* the world yet not be *of* the world (John 17:14–16)?

## Basic Texts in Theology of Missions:

Gnanakan, Ken R. 1993. *Kingdom Concerns: A Biblical Approach Towards Theology of Mission*. Downers Grove: InterVarsity Press.

Hedlund, Roger. 1991. *The Mission of the Church in the World: A Biblical Theology*. Grand Rapids: Baker.

Niringiye, David Zac. 1996. The nature and character of God's mission. *Evangelical Missions Quarterly* 32 (January): 60–68.

Piper, John. 1993. *Let the Nations Be Glad: The Supremacy of God in Missions*. Grand Rapids: Baker.

Shenk, Wilbert R., ed. 1993. *The Transfiguration of Mission: Biblical, Theological and Historical Foundations*. Scottdale, Pa: Herald Press.

Steyne, Philip. 1992. *In Step With the God of the Nations: A Biblical Theology of Missions*. Houston: Touch Publications.

Van Engen, Charles, Dean S. Gilliland, Paul Pierson, eds. 1993. *The Good News of the Kingdom: Mission Theology for the Third Millennium*. Maryknoll, N.Y.: Orbis.

## Personal Application Question:

Contrast a missionary (or North American pastor) who does not have a well-defined theology of mission to a missionary (or North American pastor) guided by a theology of mission. How differently would they minister?

## Special Activity:

Write a script for a drama comparing the nature of the church and of the world. Use the contrasts of Ephesians 2 in your script.

# CHAPTER

# 2

# MOTIVES OF MISSIONS:
## Reasons for Participating in God's Mission

The recognition that God is the source, Christ the message, the Holy Spirit the power, and the church the embodiment of mission should lead to personal reflection. What motives spur participation in the mission of God? Are these motives fundamental, secondary, or defective? Do they flow from the mind of God or do they flow from human desires and egos? Are they primary or secondary to the heart of God?

Motives are heart allegiances that lead missionaries and ministers into action and sometimes result in inaction. Most frequently the human psyche is made up of impulses that battle against each other. Prayerful consideration of motives enables those who carry the mission of God to overcome or at least compensate for defective motives and deepen the foundations of fundamental Christian motivations.

For example, Isaiah indicted the Israelites because they were offering burnt offerings and sacrifices, attending convocations and assemblies, and spreading out their hands in prayer while mistreating their fellowman (Isa. 1:10–17). They were like silver that had become dross (v. 22). God was to "purge away [their] dross and remove all [their] impurities" (v. 25). This process occurs when Christians evaluate their motives. God works to purge defective motives and make those who are his "as white as snow" (v. 18). God, who weighs all motives (Prov. 16:2), desires to purify, not destroy. In this process of reflection fundamental motives become more fully the driving force of the missionary's life.

# Fundamental Motives: Reflecting the Will of God

Fundamental motives of mission mirror the mind of God; they reflect his attributes and will. In prioritizing motives, Christian ministers must search the heart of God and make his motives their motives. They do this by diligently studying the Word, fasting and praying, and meditating on God and his message. As they practice these Christian disciplines, the creator God works in their lives to form fundamental motives and reform negative ones. Motives change as they reflect inward and upward.

Fundamental motives of mission include the compelling love of God incarnate in human life, a living acknowledgment that God is sovereign over time, and an outpouring of thanksgiving to God for what he has done.

### God's Love and Compassion

God's dominant attribute is love. The Old Testament Hebrew captures this quality in the word *hesed*, "steadfast love." God describes himself before Moses as "compassionate and gracious,... slow to anger, abounding in love and faithfulness, maintaining love to thousands, and forgiving wickedness, rebellion and sin" (Ex. 34:6–7; cf. Num. 14:18; Neh. 9:17; Pss. 86:15; 103:8; 145:8; Joel 2:13; Jonah 4:2). God can, therefore, be described by the one term "love" (1 John 4:7–8). Love motivated God to minister within human cultures: He raised up *judges* to deliver the Israelites (Judg. 2:10–19), instituted *priests* to intercede for the people of Israel (Ex. 28–29; Lev. 8–9), sent *prophets* to proclaim his message to kings and the people (Jer. 1:5–6; 15:19; Amos 7:16; Ezek. 3:17), and gave his Son *Jesus Christ*, the Messiah, to die for humankind (John 3:16). God chose Israel, not because they were a great people, but because he loved them (Deut. 7:7–8). He loved Israel as a father loves his son (Hos. 11:1–11). He compassionately taught Israel to walk (v. 3), and led them with "cords of human kindness, with ties of love" (v. 4). Even when Israel's disobedience forced God to forsake them, God shed divine tears. He cried:

> *How can I give you up, Ephraim?*
>    *How can I hand you over, Israel? . . .*
> *My heart is changed within me;*
>    *all my compassion is aroused.*
> *I will not carry out my fierce anger,*
>    *nor will I turn and devastate Ephraim.*
> *For I am God, and not man—*
>    *the Holy One among you.*
>
> Hos. 11:8–9

God's steadfast love motivated him to send Jesus to die for humankind: "God so loved the world that he gave his one and only Son" (John 3:16). "God demonstrates his own love for us in this: While we were still sinners, Christ died for us" (Rom. 5:8). "This is how God showed his love among us: He sent his one and only Son into the world that we might live through him" (1 John 4:9).

Jesus, sent from God, reflected the love of God. Jesus touched the untouchable (Mark 1:40–45), cried with the crying (John 11:32–37), and died for those dying in sin.

Christian compassion also motivates the missionary for ministry. Paul describes Christ's love, which "compels us." Acknowledging that all people must die to self because Christ died for all, they can "no longer live for themselves but for him who died for them and was raised again" (2 Cor. 5:14–15). Just as love compelled God to reconcile sinners to himself, his love propels Christians to minister to those broken by sin, alienated from him, and living without hope in the world. Like parents entering a burning house to save their children, Christians urgently enter human contexts, compassionately seeking the lost. The dominant characteristic of God in Scripture becomes our fundamental motivation for mission: "We love because he first loved us" (1 John 4:19)!

In my living room hangs a picture that depicts the mission of God. At the top are two hands—relaxed, compassionate, inviting—gently reaching down. Other hands—shackled, tense, desperate—are urgently reaching up. This portrait symbolizes God's loving hands reaching down to grasp the anxious hands of the world. Or, it connotes Christian hands, toned by a loving Father, reaching down to the lost of the world. According to the *hands* metaphor, missions is the loving hands of God reaching through compassionate Christian hands to release the shackled hands of the lost.

### God's Sovereignty Over Time

Before Christ's ascension the apostles asked him when God would restore the kingdom to Israel. Jesus responded by declaring that *God is in charge of time:* "It is not for you to know the times and dates the Father has set by his own authority" (Acts 1:6–7).

Scripture affirms that time is in the hand of God. The Bible begins with God's initiating human time (Gen. 1:1) and ends with Christ's promising to come soon to conclude time (Rev. 22:20). God brought the world into existence and will bring it to an end. Although God is "from

> Jesus, sent from God, reflected the love of God. Jesus touched the untouchable,... cried with the crying,... and died for those dying in sin.

everlasting to everlasting," that is, beyond time, he is to be praised because he "brought forth the earth and the world" (Ps. 90:2). He sent Christ to the earth at the appointed time (Gal. 4:4) and will determine the time for his second coming (Matt. 24:36). The duration of nations, the span of kings, and the length of lives are all in the hand of God.

God does set the boundaries of time in terms of his dominant attribute of love: He is waiting patiently for sinners to repent before bringing judgment (2 Peter 3:9), and he will change his mind about punishment if there is repentance (Jonah 3:10). Christians today live in the *in-between times*—the age between the first and second comings of Christ. God's kingdom came into the world in the person of Jesus of Nazareth, who was anointed by God to be the Savior of the world. Those who believe in Christ have come to live under God's sovereignty and have access to his power and blessings. But, paradoxically, Satan continues to be active in this age. The parable of the wheat and tares teaches that even though the kingdom of God has come into the world, the dominion of Satan continues to exist (Matt. 13:24–30, 37–43). The tares and the wheat represent two different kingdoms: The tares are "the sons of the evil one," and the wheat "the sons of the kingdom" (v. 38). Since the roots of the tares have mingled with those of the wheat, removing the tares would endanger the harvest. The focus of the parable is on the command "Let both grow together until the harvest" (v. 30). Jesus teaches that the good and the bad are not separated in the present age. This separation will be the final work of God when he consummates his kingdom with judgment: The tares will be separated from the wheat, and "the righteous will shine forth . . . in the kingdom of their Father" (Matt. 13:43). This parable gives a reason for the continuance of Satan's kingdom even though God's kingdom in Christ is in the world.

How does belief that Christ is sovereign over time become a motivation for mission? During this in-between period Christians are called to prepare both themselves and the world for Christ's second coming. Christ calls Christians to "watch" (Matt. 24:42–43; 25:13) and "be ready" (24:44). The reason for this watchfulness or readiness is that we "do not know the day or the hour" that Christ will come (24:42, 44; 25:13). Peter reiterates and expands this theme of watchfulness in anticipation of Christ's second coming: "You ought to live holy and godly lives," he writes, "as you look forward to the day of God. . . . Since you are looking forward to this, make every effort to be found spotless, blameless and at peace with him" (2 Peter 3:11–12, 14).

The realization of the end of time also motivates Christ's followers to teach those broken by sin and alienated from God. All people will ultimately stand before the judgment seat of God and be judged by their Creator for what they have done while living in the body. Cognizant of this reality and knowing "what it is to fear the Lord," Christians must make every attempt to persuade people to be reconciled to God (2 Cor. 5:10–11). The Christian missionary movement has also struggled with the meaning of Matthew 24:14: Did Christ teach that preaching to the whole world will coincide with the time when the end will come? Does how Christians live and reach out to the world, in some way, "speed its coming" (2 Peter 3:12) of Christ? Regardless of the meaning of these difficult passages, it is evident that the ultimate work of Christians is to be prepared and to prepare the world for Christ's second coming.

Modern "Christians" may reject this eschatological plea because they are living for the present and not preparing the world for Christ's second coming. The consequences of a Christianity lived for the here and now are frightening. Christianity should not be merely a way to meet temporal human needs but be based on a heart-to-heart, intimate relationship with the sovereign God who sets the boundaries of time.

### An Outpouring of Thanksgiving to God

Mission in its essence is an outpouring of thanksgiving to God for what he has done in human lives. The psalmist sang:

> Give thanks to the LORD, call on his name;
>     make known among the nations what he has done.
> Sing to him, sing praise to him;
>     tell of all his wonderful acts.
> Glory in his holy name;
>     let the hearts of those who seek the LORD rejoice.
>                               Ps. 105:1–3

This passage indicates the function of praise literature. Praise speaks not only to God but also to the nations. They hear of God's mighty acts and glorify his name. Those who praise God cannot refrain from speaking of him. Thus Paul writes that those who speak because they believe will "cause thanksgiving to overflow to the glory of God" (2 Cor. 4:13–15).

# Secondary Motives: Preaching Christ for Humanitarian and Personal Reasons

Many secondary motives, although neither deficient nor fundamental, lead people to the mission field. These motivations are most frequently humanitarian and personal. Often they include a desire to help people physically, a yearning for adventure, and a desire for a deeper faith.

### Desire to Help People Physically

Westerners are frequently touched by the poverty of the world in comparison to their own wealth. They are drawn to missions as a response to human poverty. They desire to use their medical, technical, and teaching skills to upgrade the physical and socioeconomic conditions of people. This response may be rooted in the compassion of God and reflect the mind of God, thereby becoming a fundamental motive for Christian mission; sometimes, however, this response is no different from that of philanthropists who desire to improve the world.

If the desire to help the poor is rooted in God's compassion, Christian medical practitioners will seek to minister to the human soul as well as to the body. Prayer and reflection on evil will be coupled with medical missions. Building Christian lives and the Christian church will be part of lessons on carpentry. Helping the world run under the sovereignty of God will be part of mechanics. The church, God's distinctive people in the world, will be emphasized over human organizations. Compassion will lead missionaries to make their ministry holistic—integrating the message of God and prayer to God into social ministry. If such integration does not occur, these social ministries are no different from those performed by governments and social organizations.

Thus, being touched by poverty is a Christian motivation only when it is related to God's compassion for the poor and reaches beyond the physical to touch the spiritual.

### Desire for Adventure

It is not at all uncommon for prospective missionaries to feel the excitement of seeing the world and experiencing new and unusual customs and foods. Many of those inclined toward missions have a sense of curiosity that propels them beyond the boundaries of their own culture to

> Compassion will lead missionaries to make their ministry holistic—integrating the message of God and prayer to God into social ministry. If such integration does not occur, these social ministries are no different from those performed by governments and social organizations.

learn why people of other cultures think and act as they do. While people should not become missionaries simply because they are adventuresome, this spirit of curiosity is present in those used by God to carry his mission. They are enthralled by the challenge of learning a new language, visiting in the homes of people of the land, and questioning the traditional spiritual leaders of the culture. Many good missionaries have a sense of adventure.

### Building a Deeper Faith

Still others enter the mission field because of a desire to build a deeper faith. They view missionaries as spiritual giants who have learned to rely totally on God. Wanting to surrender totally to God but feeling that their faith is insufficient, they are drawn to the mission field to increase their faith and reliance on God. They view missions as a faith-builder. Again the emphasis is on self, not on others. Although such faith building as a motivation for missions may be defective, it inevitably *is* a spin-off of missions. John Wesley made this entry in his diary: "I went to America to help the Indians get converted but what have I discovered meanwhile? That I myself need to be converted to God." Most other missionaries could make similar statements.

## Defective Motives: Preaching Christ for Selfish Purposes

Ultimately, secondary motives are not adequate to sustain missionaries on the field. Their motives, to some degree, must reflect the mind of God in order to carry the mission of God.

Almost all Christian missionaries and ministers have defective motives that do not reflect the heart of God. These motives are intermingled with secondary and primary motives. The existence of defective motives, however, should not reduce Christian servants to inaction. God, because of his great mercy, sees these motives within the hearts of his servants and helps to develop new ones, which more clearly reflect his nature. Paul reflects on the radical changes that occur in those who are in Christ. He describes Moses, who reflected God's radiance after communing with God on Mount Sinai. Christians, like Moses, are being transformed into the image of God as they intimately commune with him (2 Cor. 3:18). Defective motives are in need of transformation under the molding hand of God.

### Making a Name for Oneself

Paul acknowledged that not all who preach do so from pure motives. Some preach Christ "out of selfish ambition, not sincerely" (Phil. 1:17). They have concern for the lost of the world, but they also desire to make a name for themselves, to be recognized for their accomplishments. Paul contrasts preachers with selfish motives and those who preach "out of goodwill" (v. 15). The former are motivated by ego, the latter by love (vv. 16–17). Becoming famous means little to those motivated by love; they unselfishly desire to lead the lost to the Redeemer, to glorify God, not themselves.

Paul further exhorted the Philippians to "do nothing out of selfish ambition or vain conceit" (Phil. 2:3). They were not to look only to their "own interests, but also the interests of others" (v. 4). This other-directedness is portrayed by Christ's becoming human. In his incarnation he "humbled himself"; he gave up equality with God and "made himself nothing" (vv. 6–8). Paul states that this attitude of humility, this willingness to seek others' interests, should become our nature (v. 5). Harrell writes:

> The hinge on which this section of the letter turns is the contrast between the empty glory of man who willfully grasps at what he does not have and the glory of Christ who willingly emptied Himself of that which was always His. **1969, 85**

Just as Christ emptied himself and became a lowly human, Christian ministers and missionaries must strive to empty themselves of "selfish ambition" and acknowledge that they are only "jars of clay" empowered by God (2 Cor. 4:7).

Jesus encountered this problem even with his apostles (Mark 10:35–45). James and John came to Jesus asking to be given places of importance in his kingdom—one on his right hand and one on his left. The other ten were indignant: Why should James and John expect to be given significant positions of authority? Upon hearing of their indignation, Jesus called the apostles together and described the nature of Christian leadership. He contrasted leadership in the world to his model of servant leadership: The greatest in the kingdom of God is not one who rules but one who *serves!* Jesus himself reflected this servant leadership. He said, "For even the Son of Man did not come to be served, but to serve, and to give his life as a ransom for many" (v. 45). Thus Christian leaders are not to "preach [themselves] but Christ Jesus as Lord, and [themselves] as bond-servants for Jesus' sake" (2 Cor. 4:5 NASB).

### Building Personal Kingdoms

Similarly, a feeling of superiority causes some to use missions as a means to create "little kingdoms" where they are in control. They dominate a new work and establish their own rules and regulations that must be followed. In effect, they become "rulers" over their own kingdom. Charles Landreth recounted such motives when describing certain ministers in inner-city North America: "Sometimes people go down to the very poor because they can have power over them. They set themselves up as *gods* to these people. They intimidate them" (Lamascus 1989, 2).

### Escaping from One's Own Culture or Church Situation

Some view missionary work as an escape from conservative or lukewarm churches within their own country or from a culture that they consider less than perfect. Their dissatisfaction with the church in their home country prompts them to leave behind a disappointing situation with plans to establish a "perfect" Christian movement in some other area of the world. Or perhaps their disdain for their own homeland provokes them to seek a more congenial society.

Rejecting one's culture and church situation is both highly idealistic and selfish. Most likely the problems one is escaping will reappear in the new culture, since propensities for nominalism and sin are universal. And no missionary can, in reality, escape the culture that has had a significant molding influence on his life.

Healthy missionaries do not desert their own culture when going to another. They strive to become bicultural—able to relate to both their home culture and their adopted culture. They realize that both cultures have strengths and weaknesses—that the dominion of Satan and the kingdom of God are present in each. Paul, for example, was a Jewish leader called at the time of his conversion to be an apostle to the Gentiles. However, he was not seeking to escape his culture. Before going on the first missionary journey, he and Barnabas visited Peter and John in Jerusalem. These pillars of the Jerusalem church gave Paul and Barnabas "the right hand of fellowship," agreeing that they "should go to the Gentiles" (Gal. 2:9). Later, to show the unity of the Christian church, Paul took up a contribution to help Jewish Christians during a time of famine (Rom. 15:25–28). After the final missionary journey Paul purified himself in the temple to demonstrate that he was walking orderly as a Jew and that he was not teaching Jews of the dispersion to forsake the law of Moses (Acts 21:17–26). Despite being chosen by God as an apostle to the Gentiles, he continued to feel "great sorrow and unceasing anguish" in his heart because of the lost condition of his own people (Rom. 9:1–3). Paul did not reject the Jewish church but attempted to bridge the cultural and theological gaps between the Christian fellowships in the two cultures.

### Reacting to Guilt

Other people enter missions as a reaction to guilt. One missionary was obsessed with his parents' failure as missionaries and desired to succeed where they had failed. Achieving an unfulfilled parental dream may be viewed as erasing a failure and bringing honor to the family. However, this motivation increased the already great pressures of adapting to another culture. Another missionary was strongly aware of his sinfulness before God—the utter brokenness of his own life—and committed his life to missions as recompense. *I'll become a missionary to try to atone for my sins*, he felt. This motive is depicted by Robert DeNiro, a sinner turned priest, in the movie *The Mission*. He repeatedly stated that he would endure any hardship that God put before him in order to "buy" atonement for his many sins.

Paradoxically, these defective motives for missions may be used by God to produce great good. Joseph's brothers certainly had defective motivations when they sold Joseph into Egyptian slavery. But God turned the evil that was done into good so that Joseph's being in Egypt saved his family from the famine that followed (Gen. 50:20). Likewise, God may use ministers with faulty motives to carry his message. And frequently faulty motives are transformed as ministers themselves are changed into the image of God.

> Ministers and missionaries can be effective only if their personal spiritual motives are well defined. Conflicting motives will ultimately reduce them to inaction.

## Conclusion

Ministers and missionaries can be effective only if their personal spiritual motives are well defined. Conflicting motives will ultimately reduce them to inaction. This chapter calls future ministers and missionaries to evaluate their motives overtly before God and to allow him to refine them.

# BUILDING ON THE MOTIVATIONAL FOUNDATIONS

## QUESTIONS:

1. What is meant by these statements: "Motives are heart allegiances that lead missionaries and ministers into action and sometimes result in inaction. Most frequently the human psyche is made up of impuls-

es that battle against each other"? Why is the evaluation of motives important in the preparation for Christian ministry?

2. What is the relationship between compassion and action?

3. In what way is *God's sovereignty over time* a fundamental motive of mission?

4. Describe three secondary motives of missions. Which is most descriptive of your motivation?

5. What are four deficient motives of missions?

## Personal Application Question:

What motives of mission were present in my life prior to reading this book? How have these motives hindered or aided God's mission through my life? To what extent do these motives reflect the mind of God?

## Reflections on Motive Transformations:

1. Read Philippians 1:15–2:8 and make a list contrasting godly and deficient motives.

2. What do Romans 12:1–8, 2 Corinthians 3:18–4:6, and Colossians 2:6–12 teach about motive transformation? How does God change our motives?

3. Imagine God in his role as the pruner of his vineyard (John 15:1–4; cf. Isa. 5:1–7). What is your emotional reaction to God's being the pruner who trims your branches?

4. Do you allow God to shape your motives? Are you able to say, "God, I will do what you want me to do and be what you want me to be"?

## Case Study:

Imagine that you have served as a missionary in a certain country of the world for 23 years—years that were the prime working years of your life. During these years, you struggled to learn the language, raise your children away from their grandparents, and nurture the initial Christians. When you were ready to return to the States, the church was still small and struggling. You remember thinking, *I wonder if these churches will be able to continue without me.* Five years later, Biwott, who was converted under your ministry, began a revival movement among the weak churches of this country. While you lived and worked there, Biwott had been weak, frequently a thorn in your flesh. His own revival began after he had experienced a time of prayer, fasting, and reflection. Then the church, after a period of intense revival, began to grow rapidly. When you visit, everyone praises Biwott but seems to have forgotten that you were instrumental in Biwott's conversion and that you initiated the church in this part of the world.

1. As the missionary in this case study, what emotions would you struggle with?
2. Why might you have a difficult time recognizing the hand of God and praising God for what he has done through Biwott?
3. Would you be satisfied if God used your life as he did that of the missionary in this case study?

# THE MISSIONARY CYCLE:
# Predeparture Through Reentry

All people experience trauma and tension during major transitions in their lives. Beginning a new job or moving to a new city or state creates stress. Getting married or having a new baby causes a disruption of the norm and requires an adjustment of lifestyle. During these times of transition, people struggle with their identities. They ask, "Who am I in the midst of all these changes? What does the future hold for me?"

Missionaries go through the trauma of transition both when they enter other cultures and when they reenter their own cultures. This chapter describes the stages through which missionaries and missionary families pass from the time of their decision to become missionaries, through their years of experience on the mission field, until their reentry into their home culture. The cycle may be recurring because many missionaries and their families enter mission fields more than once.

It is important during these transitions to realize that the struggles are normal and are experienced by all who have made such transitions. Intensive self-examination is common and healthy because a more accurate knowledge of self brings acceptance.

The cycle of missionary service can be divided into seven stages: commitment to go to the mission field, general training, field selection, focused training, initial adjustment, long-term missionary service, and reentry to the home culture. Each of these stages has its own distinctive struggles.

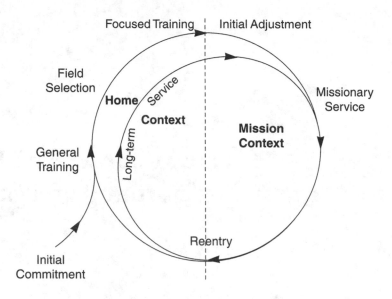

**Figure 2. The Missionary Cycle**

# Initial Commitment

The first step in the missionary cycle is initial commitment to carry God's mission. This involves both receiving and accepting God's call to go. During this stage missionaries-to-be frequently are questioned by friends, family, and coworkers about the need to go so far away. They ask, "Why go overseas or to another part of our continent? Is there not much work to do close to home?" Parents want their children and grandchildren close enough for frequent visits. They also fear disease and political instability in the country or place chosen for ministry. Before we went to Uganda with our ten-month-old son, several friends told us, "We understand your wanting to go, but is it fair to take a baby to Africa?" We were encouraged, if we really wanted to be missionaries, to select a mission area in the United States. Such remarks lead prospective missionaries to question whether they have indeed received the call of God.

# General Training

Commitment to go leads missionaries to seek training to better prepare themselves for the task of evangelizing in a new context. At this point their preparation is general, exploring what is involved in the work of a missionary. They will study classes that give foundations for their chosen work as well as basic textual courses to better ground them in the Bible. Families will learn what is involved in keeping house and raising children in another culture. Women will explore their opportunities in ministry, including teaching unbelievers, training women for Christian service, developing curriculum for youth education, and offering seminars in family health and nutrition. During this stage future missionaries are frequently torn between the need to prepare and the urgency to begin their work. They can only partially fathom the role of training in missions preparations. "Why do I need training?" they ask. "Why can I not just go?" Frequently the value of training becomes apparent later in the maturing process.

## Field Selection

**During this stage future missionaries are frequently torn between the need to prepare and the urgency to begin their work. They can only partially fathom the role of training in missions preparations.**

During these early stages in the missionary cycle a decision will be made concerning where the future missionaries will serve. Frequently missionary candidates are certain of God's call but unsure of where God is leading them. Short-term campaigns give them exposure to different types of peoples and their cultures. In this international age missionary candidates frequently go on a number of these exposure-level trips. Other future missionaries feel called to a certain continent but have not decided the specific area where they hope to minister. An internship of two to three months helps future missionaries see mature missionaries in action. They also begin to learn a new language and thus overcome their fears of language learning; live with national Christians for short periods and begin to learn a new culture; and experience from national Christians and missionaries the processes of planting churches, nurturing Christians, and training leaders. A more lengthy apprenticeship of approximately two years serves to equip them to become effective missionaries in a specific field under the guidance of experienced missionaries.

Before, during, and after campaigns, internships, and apprenticeships, missionaries should begin to develop prayer-support groups. Prayer warriors ultimately become the supporters of the long-term mission endeavor. The raising of financial support comes naturally when God's ambassadors dream God's dreams with God's people. Support raising is much more than the finding of funds to be able to work on a mission field. One missionary author called this entire process *friend raising* (Barnett 1991).

God frequently puts a burden for a certain city or ethnic group on hearts of future missionaries during campaigns, internships, and apprenticeships. Missionary candidates begin to ask themselves, "Could we carry out the mission of God in this context?" They also come face-to-face with questions concerning the selection of a place to serve: "How do we select a place from all these possibilities? Where does God desire that we minister?"[1] They also attempt to determine how God desires that they serve on the mission field. They ask, "What will be my ministry there?" Seeking answers to these questions leads the future missionary to begin more focused training.

# Focused Training

During the focused-training stage future missionaries are engaged in both formal and informal preparation. Their formal training includes classes geared exclusively for those involved in long-term missions. Class assignments address specific issues that missionaries will encounter in their new cultural contexts. Future missionaries begin to ask focused questions, such as, "How do we go about learning this particular language and culture? How do the people view reality? How will we communicate God's eternal message so that these people can both understand and accept it? What strategy models will we use to plant the church, nurture new Christians to become mature, and train leaders?" Informal training will include frequent meetings and/or correspondence with those familiar with one's chosen field. Consulting with missionaries on furlough or recently returned missionaries gives much insight into the missionaries' future work.

Developing a team frequently occurs during this stage. In other words, a group of committed Christians with various gifts and ministries purpose together to begin a movement of God in some part of the world. This group works together to become a listening, caring, ministering team. The team develops patterns of decision making, seeks support of local churches or mission agencies, and applies mission principles to the specific culture in which it plans to work. Mature teams seek the counsel and advice of mission resource people during this stage of focused training and during their time of missionary service.

# Initial Adjustment

After months of planning and preparation, missionaries bid farewell to family and friends and board a plane for their new home. There

[1] Chapter 8 provides specific guidelines for such selection.

is sadness because of separation from their family but also excitement because the missionary endeavor is beginning. The first weeks are partially consumed with setting up house, opening a bank account, buying a car, determining where to buy groceries, and learning to get from place to place. Missionaries also begin language and culture learning immediately upon arrival in the host culture. It is exciting—meeting new people, eating new foods, hearing a new language. Everything is great!

New missionaries, after several weeks (or even months) of glamorizing the new culture, suddenly find themselves annoyed that people cut in front of them at the bank or post office, frustrated that shopping takes so long (going to one shop for meat, another for canned goods, and still another for vegetables), irritated that people stare at them when they walk down the street, and downright angry because a beggar asks them for money. "These are the most inconsiderate, disorganized, rude people I've ever met," they say to themselves. "Why can't they be like people ought to be?" For a time they reject their new culture and want everything to be like their own culture. They may withdraw and go into their new culture only when necessary. They see very little good in their host culture and no wrong with their home culture. During this stage of adjustment some missionaries, deciding that they can never adapt to this new lifestyle, return home. Others begin looking for positive elements in the host culture and learn to accept the differences as part of life. They begin to adapt their lifestyle to their host culture and become active participants in the community where they live. They learn the language, visit in nationals' homes, eat the nationals' food, make friends, and share the saving grace of Jesus with their host culture. They begin to feel at home in the new culture.[2]

# Long-Term Missionary Service

The goal of this period is to plant churches that become able, with God's help, to stand by themselves. Missionaries first struggle to make initial contacts with people in their new host culture. They then strive to learn how to effectively teach those who desire to know God's way. As new believers emerge from these initial contacts and the first churches are established, missionaries struggle to determine how to nurture new Christians and eventually train them to become leaders. When the national leadership matures and a number of vibrant churches have come into existence,

[2]Chapter 5 specifically defines three stages of a typical missionary acculturation process.

missionaries are ready to "commit them to the Lord" (Acts 14:23). This process may take ten years in some fields and thirty in others, but it must be accomplished in all for stable movements to occur. Ideally, church-planting missionaries should stay until they have accomplished their task of planting a movement that "builds itself up in love" (Eph. 4:16).[3]

During the missionary-service stage, missionaries progressively learn to minister in their new cultures. Occasions that were dreaded in the early days of missionary service soon are seen as wonderful times of fellowship. For example, in our early years working in Kipsigis I would return from a three-day period of working with some national Christians in establishing a church. These people came back with me, planning to go on to their destination the next day but expecting to spend the night at my house first. This was at first very frustrating to both my wife and me. After all, I had been gone for three days and wanted to come home and relax. I wanted to speak English and eat American food! We felt that our privacy was being invaded. Later when we had been with the Kipsigis for some time, we began to view those evenings as unexpected pleasures. Sharing our lives with nationals in our own home became a joy rather than something to be endured. Missionary families slowly develop friends among the nationals and feel blessed in the time they spend with them. They learn to rejoice with them, cry with them, grow with them.

> Ideally, church-planting missionaries should stay until they have accomplished their task of planting a movement that "builds itself up in love" (Eph. 4:16).

## Reentry

Missionaries enter their area of service expecting to experience the difficulty of learning a new language and adjusting to a new culture. They go knowing they are entering a new world. They expect little trouble, however, when they complete their time of service and return to their home country. Are they not returning *home?* They soon find that the *home* they had known no longer exists (Thompson 1992, 52). Excitement sometimes turns to frustration. They experience reentry shock—the trauma of learning to readapt to their own culture.

Why do returning missionaries feel like strangers in their own culture? In reality they are not the same people who left their culture several years before. They have been changed by their experience in another culture and return *home* looking at their own culture with different eyes. And over the years their home culture has also significantly changed.

[3]Chapter 10 gives guidelines for planting churches, nurturing new Christians, and training leaders.

**Why do returning missionaries feel like strangers in their own culture? In reality they are not the same people who left their culture several years before.**

A color analogy may help readers grasp the changes that occur in missionaries while they are overseas. Their home culture may be pictured as *blue* and their host culture as *yellow*. After years in the foreign culture, the missionaries' own culture has been blended—in their lives and in their personalities—with the host culture, making them different people. A new color, *green*, emerges. Green missionaries do not identically match with either their own or their adopted culture. The home culture has also changed while the missionary has been gone; it is no longer the same shade of blue. Returning missionaries have difficulty reconciling the new shade of blue with the old.

During times of reentry, very flexible missionaries flourish because they are able to move equally well in two or more cultures and use the perspectives of one culture in the other. Some of the greatest Christian writers, evangelists, and teachers have developed maturity for Christian service in mission contexts. The less flexible, however, struggle and adapt only over a long period of time.

Reentry has two phases: the *farewell* phase and the *hello* phase. The "farewell" phase includes last visits to churches with which missionaries have worked, family vacations to favorite places, selling belongings, and packing. Before our return to the U.S. in 1986 we had a *chaikab saisere* ("a tea to say farewell"), a Kipsigis tradition when people move from one location to another. Three hundred Christians from numerous churches spent most of one day with us, singing, praying, and exhorting us to remain true to God in our new place and new ministry. Of course, the actual good-byes in churches, friends' homes, and the airport were also part of this phase. The "hello" phase begins with greeting family and friends in the early days of returning to the home culture. It continues as children begin school, new jobs are found, a house and furnishings procured, and a new ministry developed.

Missionaries must make adequate preparation for reentry. Realizing that they have been changed by their years on the mission field and that their home culture has also changed is part of this preparation. Our family memorized Psalm 37:5: "Commit your way to the LORD; trust in him and he will do this." We defined the word "this" as God's helping us to readapt to North American culture. Supporting churches and mission agencies must also make adequate preparation for their missionaries' reentry. They must listen attentively to reports of God's work in the missionaries' lives and praise God for his work in other world contexts; they must help the returned missionaries find ministries fitting their gifts; and they must provide counseling and time for readjustment into the home context.[4]

---

[4]*Cross-Cultural Reentry* (1986), a reader edited by Clyde Austin, provides valuable information on reentry.

# Conclusion

Clyde Austin says, "The formidable challenge confronting the missionary and the sending organization is to keep our missionaries whole through the international cycle" (1986, 123). By understanding the missionary cycle and the struggles associated with each stage, returning missionaries are better able to cope with readapting to their home culture.

# BUILDING ON THE UNDERSTANDINGS OF THE MISSIONARY CYCLE

## QUESTIONS:

1. Describe each of the seven stages in the missionary cycle. What distinctive struggles occur during each stage?
2. During which stages do *culture shock* and *reentry shock* occur? Briefly compare these two types of cultural disorientation.
3. Contrast two different levels and types of training in the missionary cycle.
4. Ideally, how long should church-planting missionaries stay in an area?
5. How will understanding the missionary cycle help the missionary?

## Personal Application Question:

Answer *one* of the following two questions: (1) How will understanding the missionary cycle help you nurture a foreign missionary whom your local church is sponsoring? (2) How will understanding the missionary cycle help you prepare for missionary life in a foreign or domestic context during each part of the cycle?

# IDENTIFICATIONALISM VERSUS EXTRACTIONISM:
## Two Philosophies in Conflict

## Beginning Illustrations

### Inner-City Ministries—Dallas, Texas

In July 1989, Charles Landreth spent five days on the streets of Dallas, Texas, living with and dressing like the homeless. He wore an old T-shirt, remained unshaven, and carried only a toothbrush in a plastic bag. During his time on the streets, he moved from shelter to shelter in an effort to empathize with homeless people. He wanted to understand them on a level that is rarely grasped by those who have the security of family and finances. Later, wearing a suit and tie, he returned to the same shelters to speak with inner-city religious leaders about their philosophies of ministry.

Landreth's findings were even more shocking than his methodologies of learning street culture. He found a wide disparity between the services that shelter administrators claimed they offered and what actually occurred in the shelters.

> They said they provided counseling or spiritual help to each client. But I had eaten and slept there and no one ever said a word to me about my needs and what could they do to help. They didn't even ask my name. It seems to me like they're just warehousing people. **Lamascus 1989, 10**

Landreth felt the conditions were frequently dehumanizing. In one shelter all people admitted were forced to undress, put all belongings into a numbered box, take a shower, and be issued clean clothes on the other side of the shower. The homeless felt trapped, unable to leave until a designated time, with supervisors impersonally controlling time and environment.

Although people with good intentions had started the shelters, those supervising the institutions were now "just going through the motions." To Landreth the "people who work there are not very sensitive," and he feels that these once vibrant institutions have become impersonal (Lamascus 1989, 10).

Landreth comments that, like the Lord Jesus, we must be "interested in reaching out to the real sinners—the homosexuals, drug addicts, alcoholics. But we must *go to* these people and not wait for them to *come to us*" (Lamascus 1989, 1). This statement reflects identificational ministry. Christian ministers must personally and compassionately relate to sinners where they are. The shelters Landreth describes, where food and lodging needs are met without compassionate interaction, illustrate extractionistic ministry.

## Church Planting in Uganda

As part of my research for a master's thesis,[1] I interviewed leaders of various religious groups in Uganda for the purpose of correlating their philosophies of ministry with the growth of their movements. In this research I discovered the tendency for missionaries to create foreign institutions through which they attracted Ugandans into their movements. Missionaries felt extremely uncomfortable ministering where they did not know the language and culture of the peoples. They therefore created training schools to teach the Bible in their own language in an urban context. In some cases the building of these institutions preceded the conversion of national Ugandans and the beginning of a local church. I termed this method of pulling people out of their cultures and into the missionaries' arena *extractionism*. Few missionaries chose the difficult process of learning the local language and culture, personally teaching people the way of God, nurturing them to minister effectively within a body of Christ, and training them as Christians leaders. I began to call this

---

[1] Gailyn Van Rheenen, *Church Planting in Uganda* (Pasadena, Calif.: William Carey Library, 1976).

process *identificationalism*. A direct correlation was always found between the growth of religious movements and the personal relationship of their leaders with specific national peoples.

# Contrasting Identificationalism and Extractionism

The two philosophies of ministry presented in this chapter, identificationalism and extractionism, are general frameworks devised to enable Christian ministers to examine how they relate to unbelievers within their communities. They are introductory analytical categories to help Christian ministers evaluate present evangelistic ministries and plan future ones.

Few missionaries or missionary programs are exclusively identificational or totally extractionistic. Rather, these descriptions are extremes on a continuum bound by identificationalism at one end and extractionism at the other.

Identificationalism and extractionism will be contrasted in five different areas.

### Perspective on Learning

Recognizing that they know only their own culture, identificational missionaries enter a field humbly, taking the role of learners. They accept the fact that they must be learners before they can be teachers. Extractionistic missionaries, on the other hand, expect to be teachers without first learning. They assume that because they have graduated from American universities, they have the qualifications for ministry. They enter the new culture thinking that they have the answers, when, in reality, they do not yet know the questions.

### Perspective on Relating to People

**Identificational missionaries regard nationals as equals. They have a reciprocal relationship with them. Not only do they eat their food, sleep in their homes, and understand local problems, they also welcome nationals into their homes and their lives.**

Identificational missionaries regard nationals as equals. They have a reciprocal relationship with them. Not only do they eat their food, sleep in their homes, and understand local problems, they also welcome nationals into their homes and their lives. In contrast, extractionistic missionaries prefer that the local people come to them to learn from them within their context. They rarely, if ever, eat local food, sleep in homes of local people, or perceive local problems.

### Perspective on Language

Identificational missionaries learn the language of the local people. They know that culture is communicated by verbal symbols and consider language learning the most important tool of culture learning. Extractionistic missionaries, however, feel little need to learn the local language but assume that they can adequately communicate the gospel through translators or by teaching nationals who know English. They assume that these English-speakers will become Christian leaders and eventually launch the Christian movement. They naively rationalize, "All world cultures are learning English and becoming like ours anyway." Consequently, they expect their students to know their language, or they use a translator.

### Perspective on Use of Indigenous Thought Forms

Identificational missionaries teach in ways people can understand. Realizing that different cultures conceive reality differently, they use indigenous categories of thought. They struggle to adjust their teaching methodologies to fit local patterns of learning and reasoning. But extractionistic missionaries fail to perceive differences in cultures and continue to use Western thought categories. They assume people can understand them if they teach exactly as they do in their own culture. They seldom perceive cultural dilemmas, because they have shunned intimate relationships with nationals, who could become their cultural tutors.

### Perspective on Ministry

Identificational missionaries personalize their ministry. Language learning and cultural understandings enable them to develop personal relationships with nationals. They are not against institutions, but they believe that national leaders should help organize and oversee these institutions. Because of linguistic and cultural limitations, extractionistic missionaries are able to relate to nationals only through institutions. These institutions either provide translators to help missionaries bridge language and cultural barriers, or they express the expectation that, as a prerequisite to study, the nationals must speak the language and know the culture of the missionary. Extractionists can neither study the Scripture personally with the local people in their language nor work with local Christians to implement appropriate programs and institutions for their locality.

Extractionists, consequently, superimpose American perspectives of thinking and organizational programs on local people.

# A Comprehensive Look at Extractionistic Thinking

Extractionistic missionaries generally *assume that all people are alike*. They wrongly assume that people who wear Western clothes and speak English are just like them. They deduce that similar externals correlate to similar internals. People think as *they* think, feel as *they* feel, and communicate as *they* communicate.

Quite often new or short-term missionaries express the belief that people all over the world are basically alike. They see a child's fascination with balloons, or a mother's tender care for her baby, or a man wearing a Chicago Bulls shirt and quickly judge that people everywhere are similar. They may initially write home to their friends: "People are people are people! We can use English here, and everyone knows what we are talking about." These new missionaries fail to understand that *nationals are forced to identify with them!* And they are able to reach only those who have the formal education and international contact to use English effectively and understand American categories of thought!

Extractionistic approaches to missions *seldom focus on specific audiences*. In tribal societies extractionistic missionaries do not distinguish between specific ethnic entities. Local people are identified as Kenyans, Ugandans, and Rwandese rather than Kikuyu, Kipsigis, Luo, and Kamba of Kenya; the Acholi, Baganda, Ankole, and Bachiga of Uganda; and the Batusi and Bahatu of Rwanda. Kenya has forty such tribes, Uganda twenty-two, and Rwanda three. In Africa south of the Sahara there is more a mosaic of cultures than a national culture.

People of India are divided into castes. Castes are hierarchical rankings of people based on purity and pollution, two "pivotal concepts of South Asian thought" (Kluck 1985, 219–37). *Brahmans* are at the top of the scale because of their purity and abstinence from pollution. They must remain ritually pure in order to intercede with the gods on behalf of all the people. *Untouchables* are at the bottom because they have been born into castes that do polluting tasks. Numerous locally defined castes exist between the upper and lower ends of the scale. Lower castes perform more polluting tasks than higher castes. Maintaining purity of caste and family is central to social relations in the Indian subcontinent. This social arrangement is the "unifying feature" of Indian society; it "transcends religious, linguistic, and regional boundaries" (Kluck 1985, 221). Extractionists tend to see all types of people as "Indians" and fail to recognize caste differences.

Because of the multicultural nature of most world-class cities, they are even more difficult to understand. In Singapore socioeconomic status overlays ethnic differences. Chinese make up 77 percent of the population of this world-class city, with Malays and Indians being principal minorities. Receptivity to the gospel, however, depends more on socioeconomic class than on ethnicity. The rapidly growing Christian community is primarily composed of the young, educated, English-speaking upper-middle-class people. Large parachurch organizations that evangelize among students are responsible for much of this growth. Christian churches, however, have very few working-class members—the 65 percent of the population without secondary school education (Hinton 1985; cf. Hall 1986, 2).

North American cities are undergoing radical social transition. Once American cities, like American culture in general, were great melting pots where people of various national and ethnic heritages slowly merged into the mainstream American culture. Until the end of World War II cities were the domain of the white middle class. After the war affluent whites began moving to the suburbs as Southern blacks migrated to the cities. These blacks and destitute whites remaining in the city were soon joined by immigrants from throughout the world. These new immigrants, however, tended to live in enclaves and retained their own languages and cultures. By 1983 the Population Reference Bureau saw the United States developing into "a multicultural society, which while still predominantly English speaking, would tolerate and even accept other languages and cultures" (Chaze 1983, 49). New York, for example, became "a patchwork of thriving ethnic pockets . . . with the arrival of thousands of Haitians, Jamaicans, Vietnamese, Koreans, Indians and others. Nearly 1 in 4 New Yorkers . . . is foreign born" (1983, 49). A Dallas journalist described how he could "walk four blocks and move through five cultures—upscale white, low-income white, black, Hispanic and Asian" (1983, 51).

Since extractionistic approaches do not typically differentiate between types of people, extractionists are not equipped to focus on specific cultural problems. They consider all people within their host context as "peas out of the same pod" rather than as distinctive types of people.

Extractionistic approaches to missions *almost invariably create national churches and institutions dependent on the outside for support and guidance.* Typical of Western-sponsored mission enterprises in the Third World is the mission compound. Mission compounds are initiated when missionaries select an area and enclose it for privacy. They build Western houses for their accommodations and construct hospitals and schools to serve the community. Typically the missionaries' houses are separated from the rest of the mission station by a hedge or a fence. Almost all contact with nationals occurs within the mission compound. The missionaries train leaders by bringing nationals to the compound for formal schooling and attempt to evangelize by sending compound-trained leaders back to their villages. Naturally, leadership training is limited to those who are able to speak the missionaries' language and understand their cultural framework. The cost of maintaining the compound makes it very difficult to turn the mission enterprise over to the national church without continued financial subsidy. The mission compound is an arena where the foreigner can feel at home in the midst of a foreign culture.

This mission-station approach was first used by early missionaries who knew little about the indigenous people among whom they had come to minister. No prefield training and orientation was available. They knew little about the new culture or the best way to reach the people with the gospel. Early missionaries, therefore, created environments that provided them with cultural security in a foreign environment. Often later missionaries automatically accepted the method of ministering and training within a mission compound and failed to consider identificational options.

Extractionistic approaches to missions *have secularized non-Western societies*. Although extractionistic missionaries desire to Christianize society, they do not have the language skills and cultural understandings to meaningfully communicate a Christian view of reality and to contrast allegiance to the sovereign God with whatever allegiances the people have traditionally held. Communication about how to accomplish certain tasks is on a functional level. Consequently, a vast disparity exists between what the missionaries intend to communicate and what they actually do communicate.

For example, although most medical missionaries intend to communicate the caring love of God, they often communicate the idea that spiritual beings (including God) have no power to overcome disease. They give pills and suggest therapy without praying with the patient and helping him work through his beliefs concerning who or what caused the illness. Often people begin to trust in medicine and therapy without relying on the Great Physician. Extractionistic missionaries (together with other forces of secularization) thus unconsciously undercut spiritual concepts that may have been directed toward faith in God's working through

Jesus Christ. If medical missions are to be holistic, missionary doctors and nurses must integrate teaching and prayer ministry with medical practice.

Likewise, Western schools, church-related and otherwise, frequently instruct students how to understand the physical causes of the phenomena of the ecological system but fail to teach about the Giver of rain and the One who holds the ecological system together (Col. 1:17; Heb. 1:3). This can lead to the belief that humanity, with its scientific understanding, is self-sufficient, is able to handle all obstacles in life, and does not need God.

Extractionistic approaches to missions *require a high degree of indoctrination and a long period of dependence on the missionary because the frame of reference is foreign to the national.* Christian concepts seem foreign because they are encased in foreign illustrations and language, and they cannot be quickly integrated into past experience. Extractionistic missionaries frequently feel that lengthy indoctrination is necessary, not because of cultural and linguistic barriers, but because of the years the people have been rooted in paganism. They fail to grasp the life-changing power of the gospel that motivated Ephesian Christians to burn their books of magic (Acts 19:18–20) and motivated the Thessalonians to turn "from idols to serve the living and true God" (1 Thess. 1:9–10). Many years of indoctrination are required when missionaries feel that the nationals must be taught to believe and act in the missionaries' accustomed ways. Missionaries must be willing to train nationals to think for themselves and to answer theological questions on their own.

> **Missionaries must be willing to train nationals to think for themselves and to answer theological questions on their own.**

# Qualities of Identificational Thinking

### Compassion Leading to Intimate Relationships

The compassion of God is central to identificational ministry. The word *compassion* literally means "feeling or suffering with [another]." As God wept over the sin of Israel and expressed his love for her (Hos. 11:1–8), so identificational missionaries, who have internalized God's love, cry over the brokenness and alienation of this sinful world.

This compassion is demonstrated in Christ's ministry. Continually Christ was "*moved* or *yearned* with compassion" (NKJV) as he considered the condition of people in the world. He yearned with compassion when he saw that the multitudes were "harassed and helpless, like sheep without a shepherd" (Matt. 9:36). This compassion led Christ to touch the untouchable leper (Mark 1:40–42), feed the hungry multitudes (Matt. 15:32), and give sight to two pleading blind men (20:29–34).

Compassionate love characterized Jesus' interpersonal relationships with the family of Lazarus. John records how Jesus "loved" Lazarus and his family (John 11:5). When Lazarus became sick, his sisters sent for Jesus, saying, "Lord, the one you love is sick" (v. 3). When Lazarus died and Jesus saw Mary and her friends weep, Jesus was "deeply moved in spirit and troubled" (v. 33); and he himself wept (v. 35). Jesus was not weeping because Lazarus had died; he had just acknowledged himself to be "the resurrection and the life" (v. 25). He was empathetically feeling the pain of those he loved.

The love of Jesus Christ is demonstrated in his incarnation. Christ personally related with humanity by giving up life in holy heaven to dwell on sinful earth (John 1:14). He came as the great physician healing the sick and ministering to the poor and outcast. Christ defined his ministry by quoting Isaiah:

> *The Spirit of the Lord is on me, because he has anointed me to preach good news to the poor. He has sent me to proclaim freedom for the prisoners and recovery of sight for the blind, to release the oppressed, to proclaim the year of the Lord's favor.* **Luke 4:18–19**

It is difficult for humans to fathom divine compassion. Christ so loved the world that he entered into the human arena of sin and brokenness. He became the Savior who dared to enter a burning house and rescue his children. By his love, his children have been saved!

God's compassion was re-created in Paul's ministry. He wrote to the church at Philippi: "I have you in my heart" (Phil. 1:7), and "I long for all of you with the affection of Christ Jesus" (v. 8). He trusted that God would work in their lives to bring them to maturity. He was confident that God "who began a good work in [them would] carry it on to completion" (v. 6). Paul and his co-workers wrote to the Thessalonians:

> *We loved you so much that we were delighted to share with you not only the gospel of God but our lives as well, because you had become so dear to us. . . . We dealt with each of you as a father deals with his own children, encouraging, comforting and urging you to live lives worthy of God.* **1 Thess. 2:8, 11–12**

Paul's core motivation was Christ's compelling love (2 Cor. 5:14).

Fielden Allison, my co-worker for thirteen years among the Kipsigis of Kenya, epitomizes such compassionate love in his life. Although Fielden was not the greatest teacher or strategist on our team, Kipsigis

Christians knew they could call on him to carry their dead from the hospital to their compound for burial. They knew he desired to pray with and minister to their sick. They knew he would help them with their livestock and crops. They knew he would accept them as guests in his home. They knew he would love them even after they fell away. They knew his life was committed to helping them in the love of God.

In each of these examples the compassion of God led Christian missionaries to enter into the suffering of people. One great measure of identification is the degree to which missionaries enter into the suffering of their people. Such identification is not an external façade designed to create some kind of artificial congeniality; it is the heart of God incarnate in the missionary.

### Interpersonal Rapport

Interpersonal rapport is a second characteristic of identification. This characteristic was evident in Christ's participation in the day-to-day struggles of his apostles and in Paul's training of new evangelists like Timothy.

Christ's central teaching ministry consisted of taking twelve different individuals, as diverse as a tax collector and a Zealot, revamping their perceptions of the reign of God, and molding them into a cohesive group. His first contact with any of these men illustrates the nature of his personalized training ministry (John 1:35–42). Upon hearing from John that Jesus was the "Lamb of God," two disciples, one being Andrew, followed Jesus. When they asked Jesus, "Teacher, where are you staying?" he answered, "Come, and you will see." That evening they stayed with Jesus, who was willing to give his time in an unstructured, noninstitutional way. Andrew, like any other person who meets Jesus, felt the need to witness. He found his brother Peter and brought him to Jesus. Jesus immediately began a dialogue with Peter about his name, thus establishing a personal bond between them. This type of personalized interaction, vividly pictured in John's Gospel, is typical of the Master Teacher's relationship with people.

The transforming influence of Christ's identificational ministry can be illustrated by John, who was changed from a "son of thunder" to the "apostle of love." Early in his ministry, Christ named John and his brother James "Sons of Thunder" (Mark 3:17). Jesus was perhaps anticipating the storm that would arise when the brothers asked to be elevated to positions of authority over fellow apostles in the kingdom of God. He patiently taught them that the greatest among them would become a servant (10:35–45). On another occasion John wanted to call down fire from heaven to destroy Samaritans who would not receive Jesus (Luke 9:51–55). Nevertheless, John, who described himself in the Gospel as "the disciple whom Jesus loved," soon began to reflect this quality in his writings. John records how God's essential nature is love (1 John 4:7–8). The love of the Father for the Son is a model for all Christian love. This love is made visible by the sending and sacrifice of his Son (John 3:16; 1 John 3:1, 16). Salvation is seeing and knowing the love of God. "Parallel ideas such as *dikaiosyne* (righteousness) and *charis* (grace) and *eleos* (mercy)," prevalent in Pauline literature, "recede somewhat in favour of *agape*" in John's writings (Gunther and Link 1986, 546).

Peter's life was also transformed by the ministry of Jesus. When Jesus first met Simon, he gave him the name "Cephas" or "Peter," which means "rock" (John 1:41–42). Yet the gospel accounts frequently portray him as rash, confused, impetuous—anything but a "rock." After acknowledging Christ as the Son of God, Peter impetuously took Jesus aside to rebuke him for saying that the Messiah should die (Matt. 16:13–23). He denied Jesus three times during his trial (26:69–75). After the crucifixion he returned to fishing (John 21:3), but Jesus called him back to apostolic ministry and exhorted him to "feed [his] sheep" (vv. 15–17). Under the hand of the divine potter this struggling fisherman became the rock of the early Christian church, and he was given the keys of the kingdom of heaven (Matt. 16:18–19). Christ's ministry was a three-year struggle of personally helping twelve men understand the true nature of the kingdom of God as they ministered to the masses.

Paul's ministry also reflects the characteristic of interpersonal rapport. Paul's personal relationship with specific churches and individuals is demonstrated by the numerous greetings he sent to those he knew. At the end of the letter to the Romans Paul included personal greetings to twenty-five individuals, three churches, and two households (16:3–16). In addition, he conveyed the greetings of eight brothers working with him (vv. 21–24). He also recorded his prayers for these churches and individuals (Rom. 1:8–10; 1 Cor. 1:4–9; Eph. 1:15–23; 3:14–21; Phil. 1:3–5; 3:8; Col. 1:3–8; 1 Thess. 1:2–4; 2:13; 2 Thess. 1:3; 2:13; 2 Tim. 1:3). These greetings and prayers showed Paul's intense concern for people and his desire to maintain long-term relationships with them.

Paul, like Christ, trained leaders interpersonally. Many were chosen as helpers to travel with him as he planted new churches. John Mark (Acts 13:5) and Timothy (16:3) were two such missionary apprentices.

Training took place within a community of evangelists. On one occasion seven evangelists accompanied Paul (20:4) and on another occasion eight (Col. 4:7–14). These evangelists were left behind at newly established churches. Silas and Timothy remained at Berea (Acts 17:14), Aquila and Priscilla in Ephesus (18:18–19), and Luke in Philippi (contrast the "we" in Acts 16:10–18 with the "they" in verses 19–39). These co-workers often went back and forth between Paul and the churches as Timothy served as Paul's substitute in Philippi (Phil. 2:19). Training seems to have occurred within the context of a community of evangelists traveling and ministering together.

Paul's training of Timothy is thoroughly documented. Paul mentored Timothy as a father teaching his son (1 Tim. 1:2, 18; 2 Tim. 1:2). After sending him to Corinth, Paul reflected on the similarity of their ministries: "He will remind you of my way of life in Christ Jesus, which agrees with what I teach everywhere in every church" (1 Cor. 4:17). These two developed a kindred spirit, genuinely caring for the welfare of Christians. Timothy "proved himself, because as a son with his father he [had] served with [Paul] in the work of the gospel" (Phil. 2:20–22). As Timothy's spiritual father, Paul instructed him concerning what to teach (1 Tim. 4:11; 5:7; 6:17–19; 2 Tim. 1:13; 3:10), where to teach (1 Tim. 1:3; cf. Phil. 2:19; 1 Thess. 3:2), how to teach (1 Tim. 1:5; 3:15; 6:20; 2 Tim. 1:13–14; 2:14–18, 23–26), and how to live (1 Tim. 4:12–16; 5:23; 2 Tim. 3:14–17).

In contrast to the interpersonal identification of Christ and Paul, many contemporary evangelists relate impersonally with people. Some of this is due to the urban crunch; they fence themselves off from the masses of people who infringe on their privacy. They no longer live in a face-to-face culture, interacting personally with those living close at hand. They have "built cultural devices for keeping people close by from being neighbors" unless for some reason they choose to include them, a phenomenon that Smalley termed "proximity with neighborliness" (1967, 302). This cultural distance between people leads many missionaries to organize programs of work that reach people through mass media but they have little intimate heart-to-heart interaction with them. However, the church of Jesus Christ by its very nature must be the *community* of God, and a community requires personal relationships.

### Reciprocity

In addition to compassion and interpersonal rapport, identification also implies reciprocity. Reciprocity is mutual respect, mutual sharing, and mutual giving of one to another. This relationship is described in the "one another" passages in Scripture such as "Be kind and compassionate *to one another,* forgiving *each other. . .*" (Eph. 4:32; cf. Rom. 12:10, 15–16; Col. 3:13).

**An identificational missionary realizes that people will respond to him the way he responds to them. He must learn in order to teach, appreciate in order to be appreciated, love in order to be loved, forgive in order to be forgiven.**

An identificational missionary realizes that people will respond to him the way he responds to them. He must learn in order to teach, appreciate in order to be appreciated, love in order to be loved, forgive in order to be forgiven. He must share his joy in order for others to share their joy (Phil. 2:17–18).

Reciprocity requires transparency—an opening of one's life and personality. Reticence to openly portray inner feelings, struggles, hopes, and temptations hinders identification. The now-deceased Anglican Bishop of Uganda Festo Kivengere, at the Inter-Varsity Missionary Convention in 1961, said, "How can I open my 'box' when the missionary's 'box' is not only closed, but has a lock on it?" (Kivengere 1962, 27–29). When communicants open their souls to one another sharing their feelings, struggles, hopes, and temptations, tremendous power is unleashed. Those who share—though different in culture and background—become one in heart and soul (Acts 4:32). For example, the Great Revival began in East Africa after missionaries and nationals began confessing their faults to one another (Van Rheenen 1976, 64).

In the very early stages of our work in Kenya, while I was still learning the language and trying to understand new cultural perceptions, I shared my frustrations with a group I was teaching. They were from the Luo tribe but were working in the Kipsigis tribal area. As I told of my struggles, these Luo brethren also began to express the temptations and problems they faced while living away from home and working in a different tribal area. This time of fellowship and sharing created an empathy that drew the Christian community together.

The three characteristics —compassion, interpersonal rapport, and reciprocity—define the qualities of genuine missionary identification. Such identification enables missionaries to enter empathetically into human relationships, guided by the nature of God and attuned to his purposes.

# Definition of Identification

Missionary identification, then, is *an empathy between communicants involving a compassionate, interpersonal, reciprocal sharing of feelings and concepts.*

Empathy means that the missionary *understands* the local culture and can *feel* the people's struggles, triumphs, defeats, and temptations. Christian empathy, however, is not the blind acceptance of the local culture. Christian missionaries must approach a new culture knowing that God must be sovereign over every facet of culture in spite of the fact that significant elements of culture have been distorted by Satan. In every human culture there is friction between eternal elements reflecting the nature of God and distortions introduced by Satan. Although missionaries are frequently called to introduce radical worldview changes, they do so with empathy and love for the people.

> Empathy means that I understand why my people are what they are no matter what they are. . . . Without approving polygamy the missionary must understand why his people are polygamists, and without tolerating fetishness or promiscuity he must understand why his people venerate fetishes and are promiscuous. . . . Although empathy is internal, it is nonetheless clearly perceptible to the local people, and it is a prerequisite for genuine apostolic identification. **Luzbetak 1970, 96–97**

Missionaries, therefore, feel the struggles of the people as they grapple with Christian teachings and rejoice with them as they make Jesus a part of their culture. The struggles and successes of the people become the missionaries' struggles and successes.

Identification is characterized by "sharing." Such sharing is defined by Nida as an active "participation in the lives of people, not as benefactors but as co-workers" (1990, 230). It necessitates standing *with* new Christians, not standing *over* them. Identification involves active social participation. Identificational evangelists learn about building a traditional house by participating in the building. They learn about death by ministering to the dying and to the families of those who have died. They learn the significance of a rite of passage by witnessing the event and conversing with participants about its function in society.

Identification involves both the sharing of feelings on a personal level and the sharing of concepts on a philosophical level. On the one hand, identification implies empathy about personal problems, temptations, and triumphs. On the other hand, it implies an empathy between communicants while they search for truth about how God works, who man is, and how man responds to God.

During my thirteen years of working with the Kipsigis tribe in Kenya, I developed an empathy with Samuel arap Koske and his wife,

Mary. We shared many personal struggles about their inability to have a baby and later suffered together as we buried their stillborn baby in the corner of our yard. Together we prayed seemingly unanswered prayers for a child, sought to understand why their first child was born dead, and asked God for even greater faith. Sharing these struggles with Samuel and Mary opened to me a whole new realm of cultural understanding concerning procreation in an African setting. As is usually the case, personal identification opened the door to cultural understanding.

# Inner and Outer Identification

The type of identification discussed in this chapter is more than physical conformity. One can live among a people—eating like them, living in houses like theirs, and making a living as they do—without truly identifying. For example, a European construction worker and his family lived among the Banyoro people of Uganda for economic reasons, in order to save money, but they never learned to communicate with their neighbors. They rather ridiculed Banyoro customs and lifestyle. People can mimic a Third World lifestyle without understanding the people among whom they are living. Physical conformity, sometimes called "outer identification," should therefore not be equated with "inner identification," the heartfelt empathy discussed in this chapter. Nida rightly comments that "in themselves things are only things—it is only when people attach values to them that they acquire meaning and serve to hinder effective evangelism" (1990, 213).

Sometimes such *outer identification* does impede *inner identification*. After one of our children began to crawl, we bought a large rug to spread over the floor. Many Kipsigis visitors, however, had walked only on bare floors. When coming to our house, they would try to walk around the edges of the room and jump to a chair so that they would not have to step on the carpet. We soon replaced the large rug with a smaller one that we could easily take up when visitors came. Another mission team in a remote area spent their first four years building houses and a compound. During a political campaign, the opposition party accused them of being spies:

> The families have built four large luxury houses in the same compound surrounded by a high wall. Within the wall the "missionaries" have erected a huge radio ... installation complete with its own diesel generator. Each day they send messages. . . . Each house is luxuriant plush with computers and all. Each family runs a brand new

4x4 Toyota and they generally live very well. In the four years of their stay the "missionaries" have not built a church, have not made any conversions, and hardly ever hold services. **Keineetse 1989**

This mission team was shocked, sometimes refuting these charges and sometimes attributing the attack to Satan. One introspective team member, however, confessed, "It is possible that we have been accused of being CIA agents because people perceive us as rich, selfish, impatient white Americans rather than as ambassadors of Christ" (Walker 1989, 2).

It is wise for Western missionaries ministering in poorer areas of Asia, Africa, Latin America, and Eastern Europe to have simple (or modest) lifestyles. This is fitting for Christians who are dedicating their resources to Christian ministry, and it also minimizes the economic gap between them and those among whom they are ministering. When we were living among the Kipsigis, we lived in a block house with a concrete floor and tile roof. The house had both running water and electricity. Although this house was substantially better than the thatch-roofed, mud-walled houses of most Kipsigis, it portrayed neither excessive affluence nor cultural separation.[2] If a missionary's house is of such luxury that nationals feel uncomfortable visiting, or if unusual elements of the house dominate conversation when nationals come, then some changes should be made. In most parts of our modern world, it would be naive for missionaries to live in thatch-roofed houses when people around them are saving money to build houses roofed with tiles or corrugated iron.

# Christ: The Great Illustration of Identificational Ministry

The incarnation of Christ is the great example of identificational ministry. Christ existed in the form of God but gave up his godlike existence in order to identify with humanity. He humbled himself by becoming human and dying in a human way for human sins (Phil. 2:6–8). Christ—God himself, the One and Only Son—the Word, "became flesh and made his dwelling among us" (John 1:14). He became *like* humanity in order to communicate with humanity. By becoming human, Jesus Christ became the presence of God among his people and the supreme example of how Christians relate to the world.

[2]In this discussion I have only briefly dealt with relationship between inner and outer psychological identification. For further consideration read Viv Grigg's *Companion to the Poor* (1990) and Jonathon J. Bonk's *Theory and Practice of Missionary Identification, 1860–1920* (1989).

**By becoming human, Jesus Christ became the presence of God among his people and the supreme example of how Christians relate to the world.**

The message of God must become incarnate in us. We must become God's message in human flesh dwelling among people. According to Paul, we become Christ's living letters written "not on tablets of stone but on tablets of human hearts" (2 Cor. 3:3). Because we are human incarnations of Christ, we are not perfect as Christ was perfect. The fact that God uses human "jars of clay" to transmit his message demonstrates that the "all-surpassing power is from God and not from us" (2 Cor. 4:7).

Our incarnational nature helps define our relationship with the world. We are *in* the world but not *of* the world (John 17:14–16); we live in the earthlies but belong to the heavenlies (Eph. 2:6); we are "aliens and strangers" in a foreign world (1 Peter 2:11). We are separate people, not belonging to this realm, calling people "out of darkness into his wonderful light" (v. 9).

Like Christ, the living Message in flesh, we must not separate ourselves from people by means of impersonal programs and institutions. As ambassadors of Christ, we must become the Word in flesh dwelling in the midst of people.

## Conclusion

Identificational missions is the most demanding yet most rewarding type of ministry. It is most demanding because it requires learning new languages, speaking the eternal message in cultural terms that may be understood by diverse societies, and personally interacting with people where they live, rather than expecting them to come to the missionary. It is most rewarding because interpersonal relationships with Christians of other cultures enrich spiritual perceptions and broaden horizons. Above all, God works through evangelists to bring the lost to him through Jesus Christ. Those who are receptive are found, taught of Jesus, baptized into Jesus Christ, nurtured in faith, and molded into spiritual fellowships awaiting the coming of the Lord. No other vocation can surpass this one! May God raise up thousands of identificational ministers and missionaries to plant churches in receptive soil throughout the world!

> *When he saw the crowds, he had compassion on them, because they were harassed and helpless, like sheep without a shepherd. Then he said to his disciples, "The harvest is plentiful but the workers are few. Ask the Lord of the harvest, therefore, to send out workers into his harvest field."* **Matt. 9:36–38**

# BUILDING ON THE UNDERSTANDINGS OF IDENTIFICATIONAL MISSIONS

## QUESTIONS:

1. On the basis of this chapter make a chart contrasting identification-alism and extractionism in five different areas.
2. Describe five general characteristics of extractionistic thinking according to this chapter.
3. How have extractionistic approaches to missions led to secularization of Third World societies? Be specific.
4. What is the *unifying feature* of the Indian society? Into what type of groups are people of India divided?
5. Briefly describe the current change in American cities. Are cities now *melting pots* or *groupings of people having ethnic and socio-economic identities*?
6. Define the term *mission compound*. Why were mission compounds originally created?
7. Describe the role of compassion in identificational missions.
8. Describe how Jesus used interpersonal rapport in his ministry. Give an example.
9. Define the term *identification*. Why is empathy important to identificational missions?
10. Discuss the relative importance of both *inner* and *outer identification* to missionary life.
11. Describe the life of Jesus Christ as the great illustration of identificational ministry.

## Personal Application Questions:

1. Is the church of which you are a part (or mission work with which you are familiar) extractionistic, identificational, or some mixture of the two? After considering both the identificational and the extractionistic tendencies of your own Christian ministry, how might you improve?
2. From your experience describe a domestic or foreign missionary whom you consider identificational.

# Case Study:

Make a chart contrasting the approaches of the two missionaries who have gone to minister in the country of Zinzin. Each interchange illustrates one major contrast.

MISSIONARY 1: When I went to Zinzin, I knew that I had much to learn. I wondered, "How will God use me as a Bible teacher and as a nurse?" I praise God that he gave me Basuben as my language and culture teacher. After a short period of time, he became not only my teacher but also my brother in Christ. God has been teaching me so much, especially through Basuben.

MISSIONARY 2: I came to Zinzin to be a medical missionary. Shortly after arriving I found this man called Basuben. I hired him as my translator. Since I was trained as a teacher and a nurse, I opened my clinic to make contacts and then asked all contacts to come for Bible studies in the evenings. It is great to be a teacher!

MISSIONARY 1: I have enjoyed visiting Basuben's house and talking and eating with his family. At first the food and surroundings seemed strange, but now I am getting used to them. Eating with chopsticks has been especially difficult to learn. My family and I have decided to live with Basuben and his family for a month to learn their culture. Of course, I find that I cannot stay there without teaching those who do not know the gospel and treating any who are sick. It is also a joy to involve my family. I guess you could say that life has become ministry.

MISSIONARY 2: Generally I feel it is best for those interested in the gospel to come to visit me in my clinic and Bible study center. I like to separate my work time and my personal family time. Otherwise, these people will consume all my time and energy. We must not lose our privacy. I have instructed my children not to eat the food, and I will not eat it except on special occasions. My surroundings are very primitive, and I am frightened for the health and well-being of my family.

MISSIONARY 1: The most difficult task for me is learning the local language. You see, I am not good at learning a language. However, I am thankful that my wife and children are gifted. Basuben has also been an exceptional teacher. While teaching us the language, he has also taught us how people think. I have discovered a most amazing fact: The words we use and how we think are intimately related! I am learning the Zinzini culture by learning their language!

MISSIONARY 2: There is no need for me to learn the Zinzini language. Their young people are learning English, and English is the language of the future! Also time is so limited. Should I delay working for a year and learn this language when they are learning mine?

MISSIONARY 1: I am attempting to teach the people of Zinzin in ways that they can understand. Because they believe in a number of gods and evil spirits, I am teaching them that Christ has defeated the evil powers on the cross; he has put them to open shame! Colossians 2:15 has become a significant verse in my teaching. I still have much to learn, but my new brothers and sisters in Christ have become my teachers. How could I possibly minister without them?

MISSIONARY 2: People are people are people. What has amazed me is how similar people are around the world. I am teaching basically as I have always taught in the United States, and people seem to understand what I am saying. So Basuben says.

MISSIONARY 1: The way I minister among the Zinzini is very simple. I am developing friendships, showing compassion through ministering to the sick, and teaching the gospel to people who have become my friends. Then they take me to their friends. I have more teaching opportunities than I can handle. However, Basuben and others are quickly becoming teachers themselves. They will soon be better teachers than I am.

MISSIONARY 2: I have come to Zinzin to be a medical missionary. I have first established my clinic in the town. Constructing the building and getting licensed with the government has taken a considerable amount of time. My next project is the construction of a Bible study center to train church leaders next to the clinic. Maybe Basuben and others might even become preachers. Basuben sure is a good translator and might even become a Christian with some encouragement. I guess I need to study with him sometime.

# CHAPTER
## 5

# ENTERING A NEW CULTURE:
## Learning to Be Learners Where Worldviews and Customs Vary

Human beings—whether they are Kipsigis of Kenya, Kalingas of the Philippines, urbanites of Caracas, or middle-class suburbanites of Kalamazoo—are influenced and shaped by their culture both before and after they come into a relationship with God. Missionaries must therefore understand the culture concept and how they must minister in terms of, and frequently in opposition to, human customs and worldviews. This chapter helps equip the beginning missionary to understand the nature of culture.

## The Character of Culture

On a popular level cultures may be defined as *different perceptions of reality*. Defining culture in terms of diversity equips new students of missions to overcome the tendency to interpret all realities of the world in terms of their own perception of reality.

Nonverbal aspects of culture, especially gestures, illustrate this cultural diversity. Different cultures frequently use the same form to convey two entirely different messages. For example, it is very common in Africa to see men holding hands with men and women holding hands with women. New missionaries frequently interpret this custom through American eyes and label it homosexuality.

Two newly arrived Americans responded to this African custom in totally different ways. One saw a national leader holding my hand and inquired, "What are you doing!" I attempted to describe the African meaning: "Holding hands has an entirely different meaning here. It means *friendship or personal communication with a confidant.*" His retort spontaneously sprang out of the resources of his culture: "Well, if a man holds my hand, I'll hit him!" The other American also saw men holding hands with men and women holding hands with women but asked, "What does this mean? Does holding hands have the same meaning here as in the United States?" His questions reflected his expectation that cultures are different and demonstrated that he was ready to enter the culture as a learner.

A gesture instinctively used by an American within his own cultural milieu may be an insult to a person of another culture. An Abilene Christian University student describes how she used American gestures within a Thai context:

> In the U.S., one curls the index finger upwards when summoning another person. In contrast, Thais summon one another by placing the palms down and bringing the fingers to touch the palms. I happened to forget this fact upon one occasion in Thailand. While sitting in Patinya Thitathan's living room, I beckoned his two-year-old to come to me in the American fashion. Looking at me with a shocked face, she toddled to me and promptly punched me on the arm! Confused for one moment, I realized that I had motioned to her as one would motion to an animal. **Cox 1990, 1–2**

Languages also reflect cultural diversity. Languages are composed of arbitrary symbols. Symbols reflecting a particular idea in one language may represent a completely different idea in another language. When Americans see the word "anyone," they understand it to be an indefinite pronoun meaning "no person in particular." Kipsigis, however, read this word in their own language to mean, "I am coming." The combination of letters is the same but the meaning and pronunciation are different. People's interpretation of the letters depends on which system of written symbols they are using.

The Kipsigis of Kenya frequently tell a story about a white farmer who owned land in Kipsigis during colonial days. Because he and his sons spoke only English and their Kipsigis field laborers spoke only Kipsigis, the farmer hired an educated Kipsigis man as assistant farm manager. His job was to translate the owner's orders for the day and see that all assignments were carried out. One day the Kipsigis manager was ill and could not come to work. The farmer himself was forced to give orders. He walked to where the Kipsigis were waiting for their work assignments and began with the words, "I want *six boys.*" The farm hands heard the Kipsigis words *siks bois*, which literally meant "kick the old men." Offended, the Kipsigis workers left, thinking, *That is just like white people! They have no respect for old people!* The colonial farmer, on the other hand, thought, *That is just like Africans! If there is work to do, they run away!* The colonist and the Kipsigis workers reacted differently because they had different perceptions of the same reality.

A new missionary, struggling to learn the Kipsigis language, was invited to visit a Kipsigis home. While he and the host were waiting for a meal to be served, others from the village came to greet the visitor. After exchanging greetings with the visitors, he repeatedly heard remarks using the word *tondet*, or "visitor." The new missionary, very sensitive to his inability to hear the words, thought they were saying the English words "tone deaf" (not *ton det*). His response was "I am not *tone* deaf; I am just beginning to learn the language."

North American visitors to Latin American countries have misunderstood why nationals stand so close to the person with whom they are conversing. After a brief campaign to Honduras, a student from Abilene Christian University remarked,

> When I was in Honduras this past summer, I was made aware that there was a difference with relationship to space in conversation. I was not aware that it was a cultural difference. I merely thought that the people were standing close to me in order to hear my broken Spanish over the roar of the passing vehicles. Naturally, I spoke a little louder, hoping that they would back away, but they did not. **Heard 1988, 1**

Physical articles are also understood differently. Two gourds hang on the wall in our kitchen—remembrances of Kenya, mere wall decorations. In Africa such gourds are used to store milk, beer, and porridge. They also have spiritual uses. Gourds are used by numerous medicine men and witch doctors. People think spirits are trapped in these gourds, and the witch doctors and medicine men call on these spiritual powers to solve villagers' problems. A Kipsigis friend told me that while he was visiting the medicine man he had "seen a gourd talk." People holding Western, naturalistic perceptions would think this man was "out of his gourd"! A vast gulf exists between the secular beliefs of America and the animistic beliefs of Africa.

A general comparison of home life in various cultures illustrates that cultures represent different perceptions of reality. First, the styles of eating are different. Americans believe that each person must have his own spoon, fork, cup, and plate. It is unhealthy for two people to eat off the same plate or with the same utensil. Kipsigis, by contrast, share food from one basket. Eating is a time of fellowship and sharing. If one is guided by the "germ theory of disease," the American way is better. If one emphasizes fellowship, the Kipsigis way is better.

Second, sleeping arrangements are different. American married couples expect to sleep together. Children have their own beds, usually in another room. Kipsigis wives and mothers, however, sleep with their children. The children feel secure because mother is near. Some Kipsigis, when first visiting our house, assumed that the room with the double bed was for the mother and children, and they were amazed that we would force our children to sleep away from their mother. The American way is better if the personal relationship between man and wife is paramount; the Kipsigis way is superior if the security of the children is emphasized.

Third, family relationship patterns are different. American families are independent and nuclear. They are *independent* because the newly married couple lives apart from both parental families and are not subject to tight parental control; they are *nuclear* because only husband, wife, and children make up a typical household. Kipsigis families, on the other hand, are patrilocal and extended. Newlyweds in *patrilocal* families take up residence on the land of the husband's parents, and families are *extended* in that a number of close relatives live in proximity on family land. The preferred eating pattern in America is for all members of the nuclear family to eat together. Within Kipsigis extended families, however, men usually eat with other men, and women and children eat later. Nuclear families emphasize a personal relationship between husband and wife; extended families emphasize personal relationships of family members of their own sex. In Kipsigis a man's wife is mate, cook, housekeeper, and mother, but he goes to a brother or cousin for advice, or when he wants a companion for a social event. American couples marry and begin "new families"; marriage in Kipsigis implies that wives become an extension of their husbands' families. The American family organization is logical to an American because the American culture stresses independence. The extended family is logical to Kipsigis, who believe that economic and emotional security is provided by families.

The sounds we ascribe to animals further illustrate cultural diversity. For example, American toddlers are taught that cows "moo" and roosters say "cock-a-doodle-doo." Kipsigis youngsters imitate a cow by saying "maw" (with the vowel sound extended) and a rooster with "kukuruku" (koo-koo-roo-koo).

Music also reflects cultural diversity. American music is based on an eight-note scale and primarily uses major keys. Many Africans traditionally have five notes in their scale and prefer their songs to repeat short rhythmic combinations. Alicia Little, an Abilene Christian University student who spent a year working with the church in Serbia, observed that "many cultures do not even have the same distance between pitches as we do. Trying to teach music that uses the Western amount of distance between pitches is like trying to teach a completely new language." Traditional Serbian music is also written in minor keys whereas Western music is almost exclusively in major keys (Little 1987, 2).

Missionaries without cultural training tend to conclude that people all over the world are exactly alike. The preceding discussion, however, has demonstrated that cultures are diverse as well as similar and that perceptions of reality are not necessarily invalid just because they are different.

> **Culture is the integrated system of learned patterns of ideas, values, behavior, products, and institutions characteristic of a society**

The definition that culture is "a people's perception of reality" is helpful in guiding beginning missions students to understand the diversity of world cultures. This definition, however, does not adequately define the concept. *Culture is the integrated system of learned patterns of ideas, values, behavior, products, and institutions characteristic of a society* (adapted from Hiebert 1983, 25). Culture is *integrated* because its components "function as an interrelated whole" (Haviland 1987, 37). Culture is *learned* when children are enculturated by family and peers to understand their environment. Culture is not a hodgepodge of miscellaneous traits without rhyme or reason but is patterned and systematic. Culture is composed of five elements: *ideas*, mental images through which people perceive reality; *values*, the worth, importance, and ethical input of ideas; *behavior*, the observable ways of doing things in culture; *products* or artifacts that make up visible, material culture; and *institutions*, the organizational structure of a culture. Culture is formulated within a specific *society*. The word "society" refers to the people who use the customs of a culture and hold to its beliefs. *Culture* is the road map followed by a *society* while traveling through life.

# Cultural Validity

Cultural validity, from a Christian perspective, is the anthropological perspective that cultures are essentially equal to one another but are ultimately judged by God. According to this concept, missionaries should never arrogantly imply that their own cultures are superior or that others are inferior. All cultures have strengths and weaknesses. Compared to tribal societies, Western peoples have strong technologies and economies. Because of their superiority in these areas, Westerners who are oblivious to their own weaknesses might be convinced that their culture is superior to other cultures. Tribal societies are characterized by strong social cohesion, emphasizing family, lineage, and clan relationships. Tribalists, critical of Westerners' intense individualism and lack of respect for elders, might perceive their own culture as superior.

All cultures demonstrate satanic brokenness on one hand and godly influences on the other. Cultures exhibit both a proclivity to sin, which alienates them from God, and attributes of goodness, reflecting divine presence. Africans who follow traditional religion seek guidance from various personal spiritual beings and impersonal forces; yet they believe in a creator God. Unfortunately, they perceive God to be distant and unconcerned about humanity. Westerners of an Enlightenment heritage believe the world is closed to spiritual influences but controlled by "laws of nature." God is excluded from the world he created. Yet these same Westerners view time as linear and have a strong sense of justice. These attributes reflect a Christian heritage. All cultures, therefore, in their own ways reflect both God and Satan.

Some missionary anthropologists have naively adopted the expression *cultural relativity* to express the perspective that cultures have various strengths and weaknesses and should not be quickly judged by outsiders (Grunlan and Mayers 1979, 26). The term implies that cultures must be "evaluated according to [their] own standards, and those alone" (Haviland 1987, 45; cf. Grunlan and Mayers 1979, 26). From a biblical perspective, however, God often brings nations under judgment, even when cultural insiders believe that things are going well. Cultural participants are never wise to judge themselves by their own standards: "When they measure themselves by themselves and compare themselves with themselves, they are not wise" (2 Cor. 10:12). God is the ultimate judge of culture. Although cultures are both valid and invalid because of divine and satanic influences, God is their ultimate judge.

# Cultural Distance

Ralph Winter has described types of evangelism according to the cultural distance between teachers and those being taught (Winter 1992, B–157–75). These designations refer to *cultural* rather than *geographical* distance.

*E–1 evangelism* occurs among people who speak the same general language as the missionary and have a similar cultural heritage. When believing Americans teach other Americans of a similar heritage or Kipsigis teach Kipsigis or Chinese teach Chinese, E–1 evangelism is taking place. These missionaries do not have to learn a new language and comprehend a new set of thought patterns. However, a significant cultural gap remains between Christians and non-Christians living within the same culture because of vastly different worldview presuppositions.

E–2 evangelism is an intermediate category between E–1 and E–3 evangelism describing Christian outreach to cultures that have some type of general similarity as that of the evangelist. Learning a new language and a somewhat different worldview, however, is necessary. This type of evangelism occurs when Anglo-American Christians teach first-generation Spanish-speaking Hispanics in the United States, Latinos in Central and South America, or Germanic-speaking people in Europe. These languages and cultures have some similarity with American language and culture and are not as culturally distant as those of Africa and Asia. E–2 evangelism also takes place when Kipsigis believers teach people of adjoining ethnic groups, such as the Kisii, Luo, and Masai. Kipsigis evangelists would have to learn other languages and new patterns of cultural thought to communicate the gospel effectively to the people of these tribes. Yet the cultural jump would not be as great as for Americans or Asians evangelizing in these contexts.

E–3 evangelism takes place when missionaries teach those of a significantly different language and culture. Examples of E–3 evangelism include Kipsigis teaching those of Asian or European heritages, Anglo-Americans teaching Hopi Indians in the Hopi language, and North Americans proclaiming the gospel in Asia and Africa. E–3 evangelism is taking place when Kipsigis Christians teach American secularists or when American Christians teach Kipsigis who hold to African traditional religion. In E–3 evangelism the cultural gap is initially wide.

E–0 evangelism (not designated by Winter) is Christian proclamation to nominal Christians who attend our churches but have not declared Christ as Lord. They may have merely accepted Christianity as a type of superior culture or as good ethical training for themselves and their family. Some nominalists have merely ascribed to the faith of their parents.

Understanding these designations enables the mission community to understand the task of world evangelism. In most situations evangelism is most effectively carried out on the E–1 level. The purpose of E–2 and E–3 evangelism is *to bridge cultural barriers to establish responsible, vigorous churches that are effectively reproducing in their contexts*. American missionaries cannot evangelize the world by themselves. They must think of themselves as soldiers going into battle to form beachheads of the gospel in hostile, Satan-controlled territories. As the newly established churches mature, national leaders are nurtured to take their nations, their tribes, and their cities for Christ.

Missionaries desiring to enter E–2 and E–3 contexts must go through a period of extensive learning before they are able to minister effectively in their new cultural contexts. They must learn the language and cultural domains of thought of their adopted people. They must learn to communicate God's message with appropriate metaphors and illustrations without losing its core essence. They must learn how to personally relate to people of their new host culture. For example, how do people give and receive gifts, express hospitality, and show respect? These focused preparations equip E–2 and E–3 evangelists to minister in cultural contexts that are foreign to them.

Some might read this section and express the popularly held belief that since these language and cultural gaps exist, it would be better to support nationals and bypass missionaries altogether. In fact, K. P. Yohannan calls Western support of nationals the "third wave" in world missions. He argues that, since Western missionaries are rarely effective in Asia, Western churches only need to provide prayers and finances for *national* evangelists (1986). His mission's agency, Gospel for Asia, based in Dallas, Texas, raises millions of dollars for the support of national evangelists.

Many dangers are involved in this approach. Too often these national evangelists are preachers for local churches rather than church planters in virgin areas. The American church begins to subsidize national leadership doing E–1 evangelism rather than supporting new movements in new ethnic areas of the world. In other cases, Americans end up giving to causes "that really are little more than private enterprises for raising money for the promoter and his family" and "whose ministry is either grossly exaggerated or even non-existent" (Hedlund 1990, 275). The greatest danger for American churches that choose to support national evangelists, however, is that this leads to the belief that it is enough for churches to simply send their money without sending their sons and daughters. Without *personal* involvement in world missions, the entire mission enterprise in Western churches will be dead within a generation (Coggins 1988, 204). Although partnerships with national churches are desirable, Western churches must never cease preparing, sending, and supporting their own missionaries.

The greatest danger for American churches that choose to support national evangelists…is that this leads to the belief that it is enough for churches to simply send their money without sending their sons and daughters.

In some cases those closest to home are the least likely to convert adjoining cultures or people within their own culture. The Christian minority of Pakistan has little contact with the 97 percent of the population who consider themselves Muslim. They are also the least likely people to be accepted by the Muslim majority (Winter 1992, B–158). Although Kipsigis are geographical neighbors of the Kisii, Luo, and Masai of Kenya, they are ill-equipped to teach them the gospel. Incessant intertribal feuds and cattle raids have created such animosities that most Kisii, Luo, and Masai would not accept a Kipsigis evangelist in their midst. American missionaries as E–3 evangelists are more effective than Kipsigis as E–2 evangelists. Also, in contexts where the culture of the sending church is idealized by the host culture, E–2 and E–3 evangelists might be allowed to communicate the gospel in ways not open to local leaders. This has been the case in certain urban contexts such as Manila, Singapore, and Nairobi, cities accommodating to Western ways. In areas where no vibrant local church exists, cross-cultural evangelists must be trained to carry God's message.

The church of Jesus Christ needs each type of evangelist. Thousands of E–1 evangelists are needed to initiate new churches. E–0 evangelists are needed to revive nominal churches and nominal Christians within vibrant churches. The church, in focusing on domestic missions, however, must not neglect God's mission to the world. E–2 and E–3 evangelists are used by God to bridge into other cultures and initiate new church movements. By so doing, they broaden the cultural and spiritual horizons of their sending churches.

## Cultural Adaptation

People who have moved from one part of the United States to another have had to make cultural adaptations. Southern culture is not the same as the culture in New England or California. Moving from New York to Texas requires an adjustment of ideas and lifestyle. After living in Texas for a long period, New Yorkers become comfortable with cowboy boots, Tex-Mex cuisine, and other aspects of life in Texas. They have become acculturated.

Acculturation is the process by which adults acquire the knowledge, skills, attitudes, values, and behaviors that enable them to become functioning participants of a new host culture (Grunlan and Mayers 1979, 85). Acculturation is for adults what enculturation is for children. Enculturation is the process by which children become functioning members of their own society (1979, 76).

In both acculturation and enculturation people are learning new cultures. Children, however, are enculturated into their first culture more completely than adults are able to acculturate into a second culture. It is comparatively easy for children to adapt because they have no previous cultural behaviors that need to be adjusted. Acculturating adults automatically compare their new culture to the one in which they have been enculturated and frequently project the ideas of the former into the new culture. This makes acculturation much more difficult than enculturation.

# Culture Shock

People moving from one cultural context to another frequently experience disorientation. They no longer know how to act appropriately in social situations. Familiar signs and symbols of social intercourse have been replaced by the patterns of the new culture. Familiar cultural props are gone, and a feeling of confusion arises. Kalvero Oberg coined the term *culture shock* to describe this feeling of disequilibrium. He writes that culture shock is

> precipitated by the anxiety that results from losing all our familiar signs and symbols of social intercourse. . . . When an individual enters a strange culture, all or most of these familiar cues are removed. . . . No matter how broadminded or full of goodwill you may be, series of props have been knocked from under you, followed by a feeling of frustration and anxiety. **1960, 177**

American missionaries are greeted with bear hugs and kisses rather than handshakes. American women are shocked by the aggressive nature of Latin men. Products have no firm price but are sold by bargaining. Eating customs, walking customs, pointing customs are all new. Americans may be uncomfortable having to eat with their fingers or with chopsticks. Language learning amplifies this pressure: Missionaries struggle to voice new sounds that represent new cultural realities. A student who spent a year overseas describes her culture shock:

> It's the little things—not being able to work this funny foreign washer, not knowing what temperature to bake cookies on, not knowing how to answer the telephone, celebrating New Year instead of Christmas, not knowing how to respond to a kiss on the cheek, and the constant confusion with the language; just confusion—not unhappiness, but just confusion. It tends to magnify emotions. It's easy to swing back and forth from excitement to depression. **Little 1988**

American missionaries are frequently preoccupied with cleanliness and health precautions. They may invest valuable time and energy making sure water is boiled for the specified time and that all vegetables are sterilized. Fear of germs or parasites may cause them to forbid their children to go barefoot or play in certain areas. The stress of trying to adapt to another culture may lead to outbursts of anger over delays or other minor frustrations. This may significantly affect a missionary's influence in areas of the world where people consider anger a chief sin. Those experiencing culture shock may feel that they are always being cheated. They may exhibit a fixation on the difficulty or the primitiveness of the language. During this time, they may also long excessively for home and feel nostalgia about everything American. It is also easy to think in terms of "us–them," comparing *our* ways to *their* ways.

> **Although Christian love is able to lead missionaries to respect and interrelate with the people, Christian love does not exempt missionaries from the effects of culture shock.**

Although Christian love is able to lead missionaries to respect and interrelate with the people, Christian love does not exempt missionaries from the effects of culture shock. Missionaries with little or no cross-cultural interaction are especially susceptible to culture shock. After hearing the material in this section, one ex-missionary said, "You must have gone with us and recorded everything we felt and said. Our performance was a classic case of not being prepared to enter another culture." Fortunately, effective training often reduces culture shock to culture stress, and it can facilitate effective adaptation to a targeted people.

## Stages of the Missionary Acculturation Process

As monocultural missionaries strive to become cross-cultural, they typically go through three stages: (1) the glamour stage, (2) the rejection stage, and (3) the identification stage.

### The Glamour Stage

During this stage (also called the honeymoon stage, or the fascination stage) missionaries glamorize the superficial elements in the new culture. The land is beautiful. The thatch-roofed mud houses are quaint. Missionaries consider eating corn mush with the fingers and drinking clabbered milk as proof that they are adapting. They tend to idealize the work among the people, making it more than it really is. Even having malaria can be an achievement of some importance! New missionaries are awed by everything they see. Statements such as "Look at that lady carry that basket on her head!", "How can she carry all that firewood?", "Isn't it great that these people have all this time to sit under trees and talk like this?" demonstrate their fascination with the new culture. Urban missionaries may idealize the bigness of their city and its historical significance. They may idealistically proclaim, "God will become Lord of this city!" without realistically perceiving the powers of Satan that stand behind the laws, rules, and government of the metropolis.

No real cross-cultural communication takes place at this stage. Since missionaries do not know the local language, they rely on English-speaking nationals, who translate concepts into Western language and thought categories. Such translations filter out indigenous concepts.

Idealizing a culture without truly understanding it is dangerous. As cultural horizons expand, missionaries begin to realize that their idealized picture of the culture is not correct. They feel cheated! Their translators or mentors have been fooling them. A psychological pendulum begins to swing from idealization to rejection. In most cases the greater the idealization or glamorization during this stage, the greater the rejection in the next stage.

### Rejection Stage

Wanting to do the Lord's work in a new language and culture, coupled with ignorance of the unknown, creates a high level of cultural stress. Under such stress the pendulum often swings from glamorizing to rejecting the culture. This stage, called the *rejection* or *fear* stage, is characterized by anxiety. Anxiety is generated by the growing realization of cultural diversity, friction between conflicting ideologies, the disappointment of learning the true motivations of some "friends," and fear of what is not yet known about the culture. Missionaries begin to experience the full sense of being in a foreign country among people who are of a different culture.

During this stage missionaries experience culture shock. They may feel that everyone is taking advantage of them and become unduly discouraged by the difficulty of language learning. Missionaries begin to talk of *us* and *them*, and nothing in the new culture is as good as things "back home." This idealization of their home culture leads them to label their host culture primitive or degenerate. Missionaries may exhibit the frustration of trying to adapt to another culture by angry outbursts.

Training in cross-cultural communication prepares a person for the struggles involved in working in another culture. If the missionary enters the field believing that all people are basically alike, that language learning is not important, and that programs from home fit anywhere in the world, the psychological pendulum swing from idealism to rejection will be intense. If, however, the missionary has learned that cultures are diverse, that language is a key to understanding culture, and that the message must be presented in a manner that will be understood locally, both the initial glamour and the resulting rejection will be less pronounced. Prefield preparation serves as "a shock absorber"—a buffer to absorb culture shocks.

Obviously, missionaries must find ways to cope with the anxieties they are experiencing. The ways of coping vary according to the psychological makeup and missiological background of the missionaries. A first reaction to cultural anxieties may impel a missionary to *go home*. Just as John Mark returned home on Paul's first evangelistic journey (Acts 13:13), a new worker, confronted with the realities of evangelistic work in a different culture, may return home. This is an acceptable solution for those who recognize their own insufficiencies and accept them. Not all have the gift of missions. Going home is not necessarily a negative reaction; it may merely be one's recognition that he or she is not yet ready for cross-cultural missions. With additional training and experience in the new culture, they will possibly mature into effective cross-cultural communicators. Even though John Mark returned home and Paul refused to take him on the second missionary journey (Acts 15:36–41), Paul later recognized him as one who was helpful to him in his ministry (2 Tim. 4:11).

A second and more typical reaction to extreme cultural anxiety is *withdrawal*. By withdrawing, missionaries reject the participation in the lives of the people that is so necessary for effective communication. They seclude themselves in mission compounds or church offices and devise impersonal programs to relate to the people. One missionary spent hours in his apartment watching Western television programs. Another one spent almost as much time traveling as he spent in his target city. Still another missionary built a high fence around his home, hired national Christians to screen visitors, and paid numerous national Christians as his evangelists. When a study was made showing that many of these "evangelists" were relatives and best friends and that very little actual church growth had occurred, the missionary humbly wrote that he was "dismayed and discouraged," admitting that he did not know what was taking place in his own area. Other missionaries built a training institute in an urban center (even before local churches were initiated), chose and paid students, and after graduation provided them with a generous salary to start churches in their home areas. Although small, scattered churches did result, no sustained growth took place in any single ethnic group. When a change of government brought anti-Christian forces to power and this particular church was banned, Christians melted into non-banned religious groups. When tested by persecution, this group lacked the strong roots it needed to continue its existence as a separate entity.

The missionaries who initiated the school did not learn local languages or immerse themselves in any one culture. Instead, they withdrew from the people into a Western-style training school. They expected the people to come to them to learn the gospel message in a Western environment using a Western language with concepts communicated from a Western perspective. Is it surprising that such an approach could not grow indigenous roots?

Withdrawal is more psychological than physical. The missionary retreats into his own "shell of culturally acquired beliefs, attitudes, and behavior; he becomes more and more unflinching in his determination to remain at all times a true blue-blooded American" (Luzbetak 1970, 99).

Withdrawal shows itself in feelings that the local culture is primitive and in nostalgia for the home culture. The missionaries judge the local language to be inadequate to convey Christian truths. Without understanding their function in society, missionaries may reject traditional rites of passage as pagan or anti-Christian. The missionaries believe that the old are beyond hope, but perhaps with education the young will be different. They become increasingly nostalgic about their home country and resentful of the local people.

*Going native*, although less typical than withdrawing, is a third method of coping with cultural anxiety. Going native is the process of abandoning the values of one's own culture and blindly accepting the values of a host culture. Luzbetak defines going native as "a neurotic longing for security and an exaggerated hunger for belonging" in a foreign culture (1970, 99). This blind acceptance of foreign values sometimes stems from a feeling of rejection and insecurity in one's own culture. Christian identification is necessary in order to teach eternal Christian values, but those who go native aim to acquire a new identity. Luzbetak compares Christian identification with going native:

> While going native is selfish, apostolic identification is selfless, altruistic. While going native is a blind and indiscriminate reaction to

cultural tensions, apostolic identification is positively willed, discriminating. . . . **1970, 99**

The missionary experiencing withdrawal rejects the host culture and glamorizes his own culture; the missionary going native rejects his own culture and glamorizes the host culture. Each shows an extreme reaction to cultural stress. Each blindly accepts one culture and rejects another, failing to see strong and weak points of each culture.

Rather than going home, withdrawing, or going native when confronted with cultural stress, the new missionary may make a conscious decision to adapt. Unlike the first three responses, *adapting* is not a blind reaction to the perceived perfection of one culture and the hopeless imperfection of another. The new missionary struggling to adapt strives to see culture as it really is—with its strengths and weakness, its divine and satanic influence.

One element of effective adaptation is *interpersonal identification*. Missionaries struggling to adapt must realize that they themselves bear the burden of identification. Rather than expecting the local people to identify with the missionaries' way of life, missionaries must learn the language and culture of the host society. In order to be effective proclaimers of Christ, they must first be learners of culture.

Several things are involved in interpersonal identification. First, missionaries must truly know themselves. Second, they must know the people and be realistic about them. Missionaries must be willing to participate as co-workers in the lives of the people. Also, missionaries should practice the principle of reciprocity; that is, just as they know the people, they must be willing to be fully known by the people. Finally, interpersonal identification involves honest love for the people.

A second element of effective adaptation is *continual self-evaluation*. Effective adaptation takes place only when new missionaries critically evaluate their reactions to the people and customs of the new culture. They must neither uncritically accept every new concept they learn, nor uncritically reject every new concept. For example, in the Republic of Georgia an important part of culture is wine. Georgians have elaborate meals at which toasts are the most important part, and these toasts may go on for several hours. In fact, the toasts are so important that they take on a religious significance. Moral issues (such as drunkenness) and theological issues (such as toasting a saint) are involved, and missionaries must sort these things out in an effort to adapt to a major part of Georgian culture (Diles 1993). Will missionaries completely reject such feasts as anti-

Christian, or will they completely accept such feasts as an indispensable part of culture? What will missionaries do when they are invited to a Georgian meal? This type of situation demands serious soul-searching from missionaries struggling to become a part of a new culture.

Because their worldview is anchored in God's revelation in the Scriptures, missionaries will relate new cultural conceptions to this eternal anchor. To be sure, they will learn great spiritual truths that they would never have grasped in their own culture. At the same time, as their understanding of national culture increases, they realize the great revolutions that must take place in order for those of the host culture to be truly Christian. Effective adaptation can take place only when the new missionary attempts to perceive culture as it really is, rather than reacting to new cultural perceptions out of past personal or cultural biases.

### Identification Stage

> When missionaries feel at home in their host culture, they have entered the *identification stage*. . . . They understand the cultural categories through which the people view reality. . . . They have friends within the culture and know how to extend and receive hospitality.

When missionaries feel at home in their host culture, they have entered the *identification stage*. In this stage missionaries have become relatively fluent in the language—able to personally teach and publicly preach in such a way that what they have to say is understandable. They understand the cultural categories through which the people view reality. Their ministries of teaching, nurturing, and training have been defined, even though they continue to change and develop. Missionary families picture their area as *home*. They have friends within the culture and know how to extend and receive hospitality.

The following diagram depicts the adaptation process. Initial glamour turns into anxiety as the new missionary realizes his inability to communicate in the new culture or to conceive new perceptions of reality. At this point he may reject culture by going home, withdrawing, or going native. On the other hand, he may consciously decide to adapt to the new culture by personally identifying with it and critically evaluating his own reactions to it.

## Conclusion

The purpose of this chapter has been to introduce the *culture concept* to future missionaries. Missionaries cannot effectively communicate the gospel across cultural boundaries without first understanding the nature of culture. When monocultural Americans understand that every culture is a *different perception of reality,* the rigidity that hampers cultural learning is

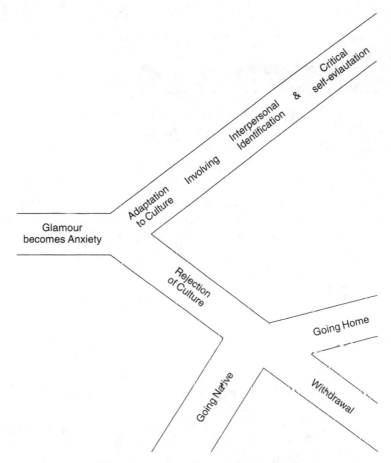

**Figure 3. The Acculturation Process**

reduced. An understanding of *cultural validity* helps the missionary realize that all cultures have strengths and weaknesses and that cultures are also ultimately judged by God. An awareness of *cultural distance* enables E–2 and E–3 missionaries to understand the need for adequate training before they cross cultural boundaries with the gospel. This awareness also causes them to realize the necessity of nurturing new Christians to become E–1 evangelists. This chapter describes how a missionary's fascination with a culture may turn into rejection. Missionaries learn that self-evaluation and personal identification will help them overcome culture shock so that they will be able to minister effectively in a cross-cultural context. The concepts of this chapter are foundations on which other concepts of missions are based.

# BUILDING ON THE CULTURAL FOUNDATIONS

## QUESTIONS:

1. On a popular level the term *culture* has been defined as "a distinct perception of reality" in order to prepare missionaries for cultural diversity. Point out at least three areas where these differences are seen and give an example of each.
2. Define *cultural validity*. Contrast the meanings of *cultural validity* and *cultural relativity*. Reflect on how understanding *cultural validity* equips future missionaries who will live and minister in other cultures.
3. Compare and contrast E–1, E–2, E–3, and E–0 evangelism and give brief yet specific examples of each.
4. How do these categories (as given in question #3) clarify the task of world evangelization? In your answer specifically describe the major goal of E–2 and E–3 evangelism.
5. Discuss inherent dangers in simply employing national evangelists of other lands rather than sending missionaries.
6. What is meant by the phrase *culture shock*? Give an example of it from your own experience, if possible, or from the book.
7. Briefly describe the three stages of the missionary acculturation process.
8. Describe the psychological *pendulum swing* that occurs between the first and second stages of the missionary acculturation process. Then discuss four possible ways to adjust to the anxieties of the second stage of this process.
9. Name and describe two elements of adaptation.

## Case Studies:

As long as we stay in Bohicon we have no time off. The work, ministry, and culture differences are constantly upon us. Living in [Zinzin] is difficult and very different from living in the States. I am more sympathetic to missionaries who retreat to their homes to avoid contact with the people and yet still feel culture stress. It is very tempting to withdraw into your private "America" at home. Although I strive to create a comfortable house where we can retreat, I also strive to be out with the people. Todd and I stay in the homes of national Christians during teaching trips once or twice a week and we frequently walk uptown (instead of driving) to greet people along the way.

1. Which stage(s) of the missionary acculturation process are described in this case study?
2. Describe the culture shock or stress that the missionary is undergoing. How well is she coping?

   In the following case studies what type of evangelism is occurring in the work of each of the major characters?

## Case Study #1

"My name is Benjamin Koske. I live and work in Nairobi, Kenya, an international city of 2 million. I once lived in the rural areas of Western Kenya but have lived in Nairobi for twenty years. When I first moved to Nairobi, I was intimidated by the big city. I felt overwhelmed by the hundreds of people who passed by without personally knowing everyone around them. In my local church I was amazed by Amos Odia who grew up in the city, knew its ways, and effectively preached there. Later Amos began teaching Sudanese refugees who have fled their country and settled in Nairobi. The founder of our congregation is a missionary from the United States who can speak to me and other first-generation people in Nairobi in Swahili."

1. Benjamin Koske:
2. Amos Odia:
3. The American missionary:

## Case Study #2

"My name is Tan Bock Hai. I am a Malaysian Christian who came to study in the United States. I was educated in a Chinese-speaking school and raised in a traditional family. In addition to Mandarin Chinese, I speak both Malay and English. While in the United States, I frequently share the gospel with Chinese from Mainland China whose first language is Mandarin Chinese. I feel more comfortable with my Chinese friends than with typical Americans."

1. Tan Bock Hai:

## Case Study #3

"My name is Miguel Gutierrez. I am a Latino Christian from Guatemala City evangelizing the Quiche Indians in the hill country of

Guatemala. My first language is Spanish, the official language of Guatemala. My co-worker is an American who has learned both Spanish and Quiche. Both the Latin and Quiche cultures have merged and min-gled cultural beliefs of both the Old and New Worlds."

1. Miguel Gutierrez:
2. The American missionary:

## Personal Application Question:

What would you say to the following statement: "It is cheaper to pay the salaries of twelve national evangelists in Zinzin than to support one American missionary family. In addition, these national evangelists already know the language and culture of their own people. Why not merely pay them to evangelize their countries?"

# MONOCULTURAL VERSUS CROSS-CULTURAL PERSPECTIVES:
## Analyzing Feelings of Superiority

## Monocultural and Ethnocentric Tendencies of Missionaries

### Meaning of Monoculturalism and Ethnocentrism

People who grow up knowing only one culture and language are *monocultural*. Having had limited cultural experience, they are ignorant of the diversity of cultures in the world. They speak only their own language and think in the conceptual categories of their own culture. Monoculturalists generally project their perception of reality on people of other cultures and into other cultural milieus. Monoculturalism, therefore, is *the assumption that all other people are like us, resulting in the tendency to judge other peoples' actions and attitudes on the basis of our own.*

New missionaries, even those who have read and studied about other cultures, are frequently monocultural. They have not learned to speak the language of their host people and communicate in their thought categories. Can long-term missionaries also be monocultural? Monoculturalism, in fact, can and frequently does continue after missionaries arrive on the mission field. This occurs because missionaries live in isolation from their host culture, communicate with local people only through translators, and think of nationals as developing Westerners. If missionaries are to identify with a new culture, they must first recognize that they are monocultural and must learn the language and culture of their host people.

Ethnocentrism is an extension of monoculturalism. When mono-culturalists are thrown into cross-cultural settings, they pridefully inter-pret reality on the basis of their monocultural assumptions. They assume that their ways are superior and thus arrogantly reject new perceptions of reality. This cultural pride may be compared with egotism. Egotism says, "My way is better than your way." Ethnocentrism says, "My culture is bet-ter than your culture." What egocentrism is on the personal level, eth-nocentrism is on the cultural level (Kraft 1976, 20). Ethnocentrism is the basis for racism, tribalism, and nationalism. It was at the root of the urban riots that inflamed our cities during the 1960s and may once again become part of the 1990s as racial tensions increase. The following news story, head-lined "Crowd Mistakes Rescue Attempt, Attacks Police," illustrates how people interpret events out of their ethnocentrism:

> Three policemen giving a heart massage and oxygen to a heart attack victim Friday were attacked by a crowd of 75 to 100 per-sons who apparently did not realize what the policemen were doing. Other policemen fended off the crowd of mostly Spanish-speaking residents until an ambulance arrived. Police said they tried to explain to the crowd what they were doing, but the crowd appar-ently thought they were beating the woman. Despite the police-men's efforts, the victim, Evangelica Echevacria, 59, died. **Min-neapolis Tribune** 1973

Monoculturalism, in and of itself, is not bad. It comes from growing up in one culture and knowing only the perspectives of that culture. The hori-zons of monoculturalists are narrow because of their limited exposure. The difference between monoculturalism and ethnocentrism is that the monoculturalist's ego is not involved; he simply does not know that the whole world does not operate according to his own rules. Since the terms "ethnocentric" and "monocultural" are very close in meaning, the terms are frequently used interchangeably.

Many missionaries come to the field with pride in the American way of life. Many are naturalistic. They believe the world operates accord-ing to natural laws and question all unseen powers. Missionaries from the United States tend to be individualistic. They assume that all individu-als have unalienable rights. Special interest groups seek their "rights" without regard to the ultimate good of society. They believe that democ-racy is the best form of government—even though the American form of democratic government is only about two hundred years old. Often they see capitalism as the only effective way to organize an economy. The purposes of this chapter, then, are threefold: (1) to help missionaries see their own monoculturalism, (2) to make them aware of their ethnocentricity, and (3) to provide them with tools and understandings to enable them to become cross-cultural.

### Illustrations of Monoculturalism and Ethnocentrism

Examples of ethnocentrism abound. During the short war with Iraq in 1991, President George Bush called for a National Day of Prayer: Today, "at this very moment, America, the finest, most loving nation on Earth, is at war. At war against the oldest enemy of the human spirit—evil that threatens world peace" (Hauerwas and Willimon 1991, 421). A professor at a Christian university claimed, "In the United States the Judeo-Christian ideals have reached their heights." The missionary periodical *Russian Good News* calls for a lecturer to go to Russia to "show the American culture as it is influenced by the Word of God" (1990, 4). The front cover of the magazine shows hands holding a Bible flanked by the American and Russian flags (1990, 1). If this symbol signifies two countries being nurtured by the Word of God, the meaning is based on the belief that brotherhood exists under God—a very fine Christian perspective. If, on the other hand, the symbol implies that the United States has Christian truths embedded in its fabric, its meaning is both ethnocentric and ill-informed.

Ethnocentrism is not limited to one culture; people of most cultures are ethnocentric. While visiting a Kipsigis home, I was examining a Kipsigis artifact and casually commented, "This looks like a Luo [another Kenyan tribe] object." Everyone looked stunned, embarrassed. Then a friend told me quietly, "That's an insult in Kipsigis. You see, Luo are like children. They are uncircumcised. To say something looks Luo is ridiculing what is Kipsigis." A Kipsigis proverb says, "One does not steal cattle from *people*" (Orchardson 1961, 41). The word *people* in the proverb refers to other Kipsigis. The proverb means that it is permissible to steal from others but never from a fellow tribesman. When an American in Czechoslovakia asked a priest if racism existed in Prague, the priest said, "No." Then the American asked, "What about the way people feel about gypsies?" The priest replied, "Oh, that's different. Gypsies are lazy and dirty" (Diles 1993).

A survey of Scripture shows that ethnocentrism has always existed. In Joseph's day Egyptians did not eat with Hebrews because such table fellowship was "detestable to Egyptians" (Gen. 43:32). Agrarian Egyptians also considered shepherds "detestable" (46:34). Jonah did not want God to show compassion on the enemies of his people but desired that calamity come upon them (Jonah 1:3; 4:1–2). Jesus asked for water from the Samaritan woman at the well even though Jews did not typically associate with Samaritans (John 4:9). Likewise, Peter acknowledged that it was "against [Jewish] law for a Jew to associate with a Gentile or visit him." God, however, had shown him that he "should not call any man impure or unclean" (Acts 10:28). Upon hearing that Peter had entered a Gentile home, Jewish believers criticized him because he "went into the house of uncircumcised men and ate with them" (11:3). The Philippians were proud of their Roman heritage and blamed the Philippian riot on the Jews, who were "throwing [the] city into an uproar by advocating customs unlawful for . . . Romans to accept or practice" (16:19–21). When the Jews put forth Alexander to speak during the Ephesian riot, the mob, recognizing that he was a Jew, yelled for two hours, "Great is Artemis of the Ephesians!" (19:33–34). The Jewish mob in Jerusalem listened to Paul *until* he described how God had sent him to the Gentiles. When they heard of Paul's commission to the Gentiles, they declared, "Rid the earth of him! He's not fit to live!" (22:21–22). Although God used Peter to open the mission to the Gentiles, Peter later "began to draw back" from fellowshiping with Gentiles because of Jewish Christians who came to Antioch from Jerusalem (Gal. 2:11–14).

### Characteristics of the Monocultural/Ethnocentric Syndrome

Because monoculturalism and ethnocentrism are closely related, *monoculturalism/ethnocentrism syndrome* is now used as an all-inclusive term. It merges the cultural pride with the narrow horizons behind it. In this discussion "monoculturalists" refers to those who exhibit the monoculturalism/ethnocentrism syndrome.

Monoculturalists *equate their own perceptions of reality with reality itself*. They make no allowances for different perceptions of reality. They believe that their views are the only true views. For example, secular Americans find it hard to accept the African view that "anger takes upon itself an impersonal force of its own and can kill. Hitting with a stick only hurts the physical body. Hitting with anger hurts both body and soul." To most North Americans, anger is merely an emotion; it has no power of its own. Their cultural myth says, "Sticks and stones break my bones, but words can never hurt me." To many Africans, witchcraft is only an extension of anger:

> **Monoculturalists equate their own perceptions of reality with reality itself. They make no allowances for different perceptions of reality.**

Anger is able to generate an awful power that can kill or maim those against whom it is directed. Anger is thus a terrible sin because of its social consequences. The African belief that illegitimate babies are usually born dead, are deformed, or die at an early age is illogical to Americans. They see few cause-effect relationships between sin and life.[1] Americans view dreams as the exercise of the unconscious mind during sleep; the mind plays as the body sleeps. Africans, on the other hand, believe that when people dream, their bodies remain behind while their spirits journey; although some are contorted in the telling, dreams are understood to be real life. Americans, who generally do not believe that spirits of the dead exist at all, have difficulty accepting the African belief that evil spirits are ancestors who have been neglected and have returned for revenge. Africans believe that James 5:15–16 shows that sickness is caused by sin, but Americans believe sickness is due to germs or some malfunction of the body. These examples show that the American naturalizes what the African spiritualizes. These views are at polar opposites on a continuum running from animism on one extreme to secularism on the other; yet each culture believes its own perceptions are valid (Van Rheenen 1991, 95–102).

Monoculturalists *assume that their beliefs were accepted because they are superior.* Their forefathers looked at all the alternatives and selected only the best. Inferior ways were all rejected. Democracy, a relatively new form of government, is best because it took the best from other governments and meshed them together. Many Americans believe that God led us to our worldview, our form of government, our economic system, and our social system. Americans, therefore, relate Christianity and free enterprise and are perturbed by the socialistic tendencies of the early Christian church. Americans do not perceive why an individualistic economic system will not work in a group-oriented society such as that of Japan. Production is the goal of Western economic systems, but among many non-Western peoples, social interaction on the job is an equally dominant feature. A monoculturalist fails to realize that there are numerous economic, political, and social alternatives from which the world's peoples might select.

*Monoculturalists have no respect for other cultures or subcultures.* This is shown by terminology they use in reference to other peoples: their culture is *heathen*, ours is *Christian*; their language is *primitive*, ours is *advanced*; their beliefs are *superstitious*, ours are *religious*; they have *myths*, we have *history*; they are *underdeveloped*, we are *developed*; they are *childlike*, we are

---

[1]With the advent of AIDS and the prevalence of child abuse, Americans are beginning to perceive a social relationship between sin and life, though the perceptions are not frequently spiritualized as in the African worldview.

*mature*. Monoculturalists look down on other languages as primitive, other customs as heathen, and other people as crude, childish, pagan.

### Justifications of American Ethnocentrism

The following are some specific devices that Americans use to justify their feelings of superiority:

*Technological Justification.* Some Americans justify their feelings of cultural superiority by alleging that, since their technology is superior, their culture is also superior. They say, "What other nation has put a man on the moon? Are there any other 'superpowers' since the demise of the Soviet Union? Look at the poverty of the *developing* world in comparison to our wealth!"

*Educational Justification.* Other Americans assert that their greatness lies in the superiority of American education. This thinking says, "Do not hundreds of international students study in the United States? Look at the percentage of Americans who complete graduate degrees. Compare the equipment and facilities of our schools to those of Russia, China, or Kenya." These first two arguments for cultural superiority critique all of culture on the basis of one aspect. If judged by one of its weak points, American culture could easily be described as inferior. For example, what if cultures were to be judged by the social cohesion within their nuclear and extended families? If family cohesion became the measuring rod of cultural superiority, tribal societies with well-developed kinship patterns would be selected as superior.

*Cultural Justification.* Still others claim that all cultures are moving to become like America because it is the most civilized nation in the world. This practice of calling one's own culture civilized and others uncivilized is not uncommon. Most early anthropologists and sociologists perceived the world from a developmental model: Cultures were developing from states of savagery to barbarism to civilization. These social scientists placed their cultures in the elevated category of civilization and the rest of the world in various categories of savagery and barbarism. This way of thinking about culture has become popular even among biblical scholars. One wrote, "An understanding of American culture is a good beginning point to help understand the emerging 'world culture'" (Getz 1978, 214). Hauerwas and Willimon describe this way of thinking in theological circles: "Because we Western, Northern European Christians have succeeded in fashioning a 'Christian' culture, we could now speak to everyone else's culture" (1991, 421.)

*Theological Justification.* American Christians frequently feel that their culture is superior because of its Christian heritage. Those promoting this justification ask, "Was not this country founded on godly principles? Have not these principles promoted justice, equality, and compassion for those in the midst of calamity?" In response, it is apparent that Christianity has significantly impacted American culture. Godly attributes—such as justice, equality, and compassion—have Christian roots. Satan, however, has also been actively working to thwart the purposes of God. American culture is not singularly blessed with divine guidance. All nations stand equal under the sovereignty of God. God is working through those of other cultural heritages as well.

Theologians subtly hold this form of ethnocentrism when they indicate that Christianity was formulated in our Western heritage. The student of theology, they say, must study the development of Christianity in this tradition in order to understand Christianity. There is much truth in this because of the long history of Christianity in the West. Christian theologians of all lands must be well-versed in Western church history. Equally valid, however, is the study of how people of other lands have viewed God. Theology is an international discipline, not merely a Western one.

> American culture is not singularly blessed with divine guidance. All nations stand equal under the sovereignty of God.

### Types of Monocultural Positions

Charles Kraft has discussed various monocultural positions typical in North American contexts (Kraft 1976, 21–22). These positions—eclectic, reactionary, and "one world" monoculturalism—will be discussed in this section.

*Eclectic Monoculturalism.* Eclectic monoculturalists believe that they have creatively selected the best customs throughout the world in order to formulate a superior culture. Although these monoculturalists acknowledge good in other cultures, they imply that they themselves are better than others in borrowing from other cultures and assimilating the good while rejecting the bad. The emphasis in this model is on effective borrowing and assimilation.

Frequently the borrowed items are only superficial—on the surface of a culture—rather than integral to its worldview. Eating various types of food borrowed from cultures throughout the world does not necessarily make one superior. It is always easier to borrow the artifacts and technologies of other cultures than their perspectives on reality.

Customs are not unplugged from one culture and neatly plugged into another. Borrowed customs are almost always reinterpreted and given new meanings within their new cultural settings. For example, the word *karma* has negative connotations within its original Indian contexts. It might be translated as "fate" or "destiny," implying that what a person does in this life will determine his future existences. The burden of *karma* prevents humans from breaking out of the cycle of deaths and rebirths and merging with cosmic consciousness. In New Age contexts, however, *karma* provides hope because humans are understood to be evolving to new levels of consciousness. In China the use of acupuncture is thought to realign the flow of energy through the body to promote healing. Many Westerners, however, look on acupuncture as a secular discipline dealing with pressure points and nerve endings. When borrowing occurs, there is almost always a reinterpretation of the meaning of the borrowed items to make them fit the overall worldview of the recipient culture.

*Reactionary Monoculturalism.* Reactionary monoculturalists ridicule their own cultures but adore their host cultures. They consider their culture to be *bad* and their new host culture *good.* This rejection of their own cultures has driven them into other cultural contexts. Levi-Strauss ascribes such reactionary sentiments to many anthropologists:

> Why does he (the anthropologist) decide to disdain (his own society), reserving for societies distant and different from his own the patience and devotion which he has deliberately withheld from his fellow-citizens? . . . At home the anthropologist may be a natural subversive, a convinced opponent of traditional usage; but no sooner has he in focus a society different from his own than he becomes respectful of even the most conservative practices. **Darrow and Palmquist 1977, 144**

The reactionary monocultural perspective is common among young people in Western educational institutions in Third World nations. These students become convinced through their studies that their own culture is inferior and seek to become part of a seemingly superior Western culture. This adaptation, however, is frequently very superficial. Western clothes, hairstyles, and music do not make a person Western. An Argentine student studying at Abilene Christian University wrote that she had become "ethnocentric about the United States. I saw America as the best country and judged attitudes and beliefs according to American culture."

After she had been in the United States several months, her emotional pendulum swung from idealization to rejection. She began to criticize the culture that she had once idealized.

*"One World" Monoculturalism.* There is an implicit ethnocentrism in the widespread feeling that all the world is headed in the same direction: accommodation to Western thoughts and ideals. This ethnocentric perspective is called *"One World" Monoculturalism.* What would the Japanese, Chinese, or French say if a public statement was read over the news media suggesting that all the world was slowly becoming American? To be sure, there is a type of coming together, but world cultures are borrowing and reshaping, not becoming Western.

# Becoming Cross-Cultural

### Definition of Cross-Culturalism

Cross-culturalism refers to *the learned skill of relating to people of other cultures within the contexts of their cultures.* Becoming cross-cultural can be compared to learning to ride a bicycle. It is impossible to learn the skill by reading a book and learning all the parts of the vehicle and how they work together to make it move. The book may even tell how to ride the bike. But learning *about* riding and learning *to* ride are very different. A child who wants to learn to ride a bicycle gets on, concentrates hard on turning the pedals and steering, loses his balance and falls, picks himself up and tries again. Each time he gets on the bike, he becomes more adept. Soon he can ride the bike without thinking about all that goes into it.

Like riding a bike, becoming cross-cultural is a learned skill. This implies that cross-cultural evangelists have entered the new culture intending to learn it. They make mistakes, and sometimes progress is slow. Learning to be cross-cultural requires performance; it is not acquired by merely reading about the culture from a book.

### Characteristics of Cross-Culturalism

The above definition implies several characteristics of cross-cultural missionaries. They *have gone through a process of culture and language learning to become cross-cultural.* Becoming cross-cultural requires many hours of listening, speaking, observing, asking, and experiencing—all within the local cultural context.

**Cross-culturalists perceive that cultures have both strengths and weaknesses and take other cultures as seriously as their own.**

Cross-culturalists *perceive that cultures have both strengths and weaknesses and take other cultures as seriously as their own.* They learn to recognize cultural strengths and weaknesses, empathizing with the people, rather than criticizing their culture.

Cross-cultural missionaries *model their cultural adaptation after that of Christ.* Their ministries reflect the incarnation of Christ. Jesus lived among the people to whom he ministered. He spoke their language, ate their food, slept in their homes, shared their joys and sorrows. Likewise, cross-cultural missionaries must participate in the lives of the people among whom they minister, speaking their language, and sharing their struggles and triumphs.

Cross-cultural missionaries *treat those of other cultures as equals, just as they would those of their own culture.* "Respond to others as you want them to respond to you" could be called the "Golden Rule" for cross-culturalists. For example, if missionaries give food and lodging to one of their own culture, should they not likewise give food and lodging to those of their host culture, yet respecting their customs about food and lodging? If missionaries give financial help to those of their culture, should they not do the same, in culturally relevant ways, to those of another culture? Just as God "does not show favoritism" (Acts 10:34), missionaries should accept those of other cultures as equals. Christ provides the power to transform monocultural myopia (nearsightedness) into cross-cultural openness. Jesus is "our peace, who has made the two one and has destroyed the barrier, the dividing wall of hostility" (Eph. 2:14). Therefore, those in Christ "are no longer foreigners and aliens, but fellow citizens . . ." (v. 19). Jesus makes it possible for people of diverse cultures to "be devoted to one another in brotherly love" and to "honor one another above [them]selves" (Rom. 12:10).

# Crossing Cultural Barriers: From Jew to Gentile (A Biblical Case Study)

### The Jewish Nature of the Early Christian Church

*The early church was clothed in the cultural garb of Judaism.* Early Christians worshiped in the temple (Acts 2:46; 3:1), circumcised their children (15:1; 21:20–21), and observed Jewish feasts (20:6). James and other elders of the Jerusalem church describes them as "zealous for the law" (21:20). The church was tied so closely to Judaism that as late as A.D. 52–

53 Gallio, the Roman Proconsul of Achaia, could not differentiate between Christians and Jews. He believed the problem between Paul and the Jews was merely a matter of Jewish law (18:12–17; note esp. vv. 14–16).

During this early period, the cultural pride of the Christian community reflected that of the Jewish community as a whole. Jews would not associate with Samaritans (John 4:9). Those traveling between Galilee and Judea would rather pass around Samaria by taking a Transjordan route than pass through an *unclean* land. The Jewish crowd in Jerusalem was "very quiet" while Paul was speaking—until he said the Lord had sent him "to the Gentiles." Then they shouted, "Rid the earth of him! He's not fit to live" (Acts 22:1–22). Christians felt this Jewish bias. Peter testified before those in Cornelius's house, saying, "It is against our law for a Jew to associate with a Gentile or visit him" (10:28). After breaking this cultural rule, Peter was accused by Jerusalem Christians of going into "the house of uncircumcised men and [eating] with them" (11:3).

With such bias, how could Jewish Christians ever teach Gentiles? From a human standpoint the barrier was insurmountable. Luke's answer in the book of Acts is that *God broke down the barrier!* God chose as his cross-cultural agent an imperfect man who had little contact with Gentiles (Acts 10:28) and was tempted at times to separate from them (Gal. 2:11–14). By intentionally acting and revealing his actions to us, God communicated his acceptance of all peoples and the conditions for their acceptance into his kingdom.

### Acts 10:1–11:18: Does God Accept All Who Come to Him?

In Acts 10 God acted decisively to affirm his acceptance of the Gentiles and to bring them into full fellowship with Jewish Christians. God worked through three mighty interventions: (1) An angel of God directed Cornelius to send for Peter (10:1–8); (2) through a vision God told Peter, "Do not call anything impure that God has made clean" (vv. 9–16); and (3) the Holy Spirit came upon those gathered to hear Peter at Cornelius' house (vv. 10:44–48; 11:15–17). When Jerusalem Christians confronted Peter for fellowshiping with Gentiles (11:1–3), he recounted God's three miracles (vv. 4–17), and the Jews concluded that "God has granted even the Gentiles repentance unto life" (v. 18). This intervention of God demonstrated once and for all that "God does not show favoritism but accepts men from every nation who fear him and do what is right" (10:34–35). Acts 10 answered the problem of *God's acceptance of the Gentiles*.

### Acts 15: Should Converted Gentiles Follow Jewish Customs?

Issues of fellowship, however, were not fully resolved with the conversion of Cornelius and his family. After Paul and Barnabas began their mission to the Gentiles in Asia Minor, questions about the nature of fellowship arose: How were Gentiles to live in the kingdom of God? Should they follow the Jewish law? Must they be circumcised in order to be saved? These questions set the stage for the Jerusalem conference in Acts 15. In essence, the meeting in Jerusalem dealt with the cultural demands a Christian community makes upon a newly emerging church in a different culture. Must new believers come to Christ in terms of the culture of the sending church?

Luke records three speeches delivered at the Jerusalem conference. Peter spoke from *history*. He declared that God had made a "choice" to accept the Gentiles. He made no distinction between Jew and Gentile but saved both by grace, not by law. Peter pointedly asked, "Now therefore why do you put God to the test by placing upon the neck of the disciples a yoke which neither our fathers nor we have been able to bear?" (Acts 15:6–11 NASB). Paul and Barnabas argued from *ministry*. God's miraculous signs and wonders that he performed among the Gentiles attested to his acceptance of them without their following the law. James spoke from *Scripture*. Amos had prophesied that "David's fallen tent" would be restored and both the remnant and "nations that bear [God's] name" would be included (Amos 9:11–12). James then proposed a judgment agreed upon by all the Christians: "Therefore it is my judgment that we do not trouble those who are turning to God from among the Gentiles" (Acts 15:19 NASB). The council decided that those from another culture should not be compelled to conform to the cultural patterns of the sending culture.

Nevertheless, in order to allow Jews and Gentiles to have fellowship within one body, the Gentiles were given certain restrictions (Acts 15:20–21). The reason for these restrictions was that in every Roman city there were Jewish synagogues where Gentile Christians would come into contact with Jews (v. 21). Paul's writings about meats offered to idols demonstrates that these restrictions were not binding in all cases (Rom. 14:13–23; 1 Cor. 8:7–13). Although eating meats offered to idols was not wrong in itself, the act became wrong when it caused a Jewish Christian to stumble. Every culture has certain nonuniversals that, when practiced, disrupt fellowship between cultures. Such practices must be eliminated if they cause a brother to stumble.

The Jerusalem conference established a precedent for the relationships between sending churches and churches established in mission areas. Those receiving the gospel cross-culturally were not required to adopt the culture of the sending church in order to be received into Christian fellowship. Specifically, Gentiles were not obligated to undergo circumcision and thus become full-fledged Jews, in order to be saved. Establishing fellowship between Christians of different cultures demanded some give-and-take on the part of nonuniversals. For example, Gentiles were not to eat meat offered to idols, because this became a stumbling block to Jewish-Gentile fellowship.

**The Jerusalem conference established a precedent for the relationships between sending churches and churches established in mission areas.**

### Acts 21:17–26: Should Dispersion Jews Continue to Keep the Law?

By the time Paul returned to Jerusalem after his third missionary journey the acceptance of Gentiles into Christian fellowship was no longer an issue. Hundreds of Gentile churches had been established and thousands of Gentiles reconciled to God by the saving grace of Jesus Christ. Jewish Christians were no longer expecting Gentiles to be circumcised and to keep Jewish customs. At this point the issue had become: *Should dispersion Jews, living among the Gentiles, continue to keep the Mosaic law?* This issue, discussed in Acts 21:17–26, illustrates how sending churches are eventually impacted by influences from the mission field.

When Paul, Luke, and others visited the Jerusalem elders, Paul related what God had done "among the Gentiles" through his ministry (Acts 21:18–19). The Jerusalem elders glorified God for this work. They then stated that thousands of Jews had also accepted Jesus Christ but were "zealous for the law" (v. 20). They informed Paul of a rumor that had spread through the Jerusalem church: Paul was teaching Jews of the dispersion to forsake Jewish customs (v. 21). To counter this rumor, the elders told Paul to purify himself, along with four others, to demonstrate that he was "living in obedience to the law" (v. 24). These Jewish leaders did not dispute Paul's teaching that Gentiles were not bound by the law. The obligation to follow the law was binding only on the Jews who had come to Christ (v. 25). Paul concurred with the suggestion of the Jerusalem elders and purified himself in the temple (v. 26).

This passage shows the Jewish concern that their churches might lose their identity because of Pauline influences in mission churches. The Jerusalem elders therefore desired to establish the principle that Jewish Christians should continue to be Jews even in mission contexts where they lived as minorities within Christian communities composed largely of Gentiles. They also wanted to confirm that even Paul, God's appointed messenger to the Gentiles, must continue to live as a Jew. Perceptions of Christianity worked out on the mission field will eventually share perceptions of the sending churches.

Two final what-if questions will help missionaries think through the implications of this biblical case study. What if Jewish leaders had refused to accept the testimony of Peter that God had intervened to bring Gentiles, such as Cornelius, into the kingdom of God (note Acts 11:1–18)? What if Jewish leaders at the Jerusalem conference had determined that Gentiles had to be circumcised and follow the Mosaic law in order to be saved? In each case the cross-cultural flow of Christianity would have been abruptly halted and the spread of Christianity would have been severely impeded. In the book of Acts Luke demonstrated how God intervened directly in the affairs of humanity to show that in his eyes people were not "circumcised or unclean," but could be remade in God's own image, regardless of their cultures.

# Conclusion

Extractionism, described in some detail in chapter 4, is largely founded on monocultural and ethnocentric feelings. When missionaries equate their own perceptions of reality with reality itself and assume that their beliefs have been accepted because they are superior, they intuitively set up programs that espouse these perceptions. Cultural pride is thus the source of many missionary mistakes. This chapter suggests that missionaries must become learners of their new host culture to overcome these feelings of superiority. God is actively working in his people to overcome earthly pride.

# BUILDING
# ON CULTURAL FOUNDATIONS

## QUESTIONS:

1. Briefly define and contrast the terms *monocultural* and *ethnocentric*. Then give one example of ethnocentrism as recorded in Scripture.
2. Using the sections entitled "*Characteristics of the Monocultural/Ethnocentric Syndrome*" (pp. 100–102) and "*Characteristics of Cross-Culturalism*" (pp. 105–106), make a chart comparing monoculturalism and cross-culturalism.
3. Which of the following terms would you consider *ethnocentric*? What inferences make them ethnocentric?
   Co-worker
   Inferior
   Evangelical
   Underdeveloped
   Superior
   Empathetic
4. Briefly define the following four ways Americans justify their superiority.
   a. Technological justification
   b. Educational justification
   c. Cultural justification
   d. Theological justification
5. Of the three *types* of monocultural positions, describe one you have struggled with.
6. Describe why becoming cross-cultural is like learning to ride a bicycle. Use this analogy to define *cross-culturalism*.
7. Why might one say that *the early church was clothed in the cultural garb of Judaism*? Describe the Jewish character of the early Christian church.
8. According to the book of Acts, how was the seemingly insurmountable cultural barrier separating Jew and Gentile breached?
9. Briefly describe God's decisive interventions in Acts 10. What missiological lessons can be learned from that chapter?

10. What was decided at the Jerusalem conference in Acts 15? What lessons of missions can be learned from Luke's account of this conference?

11. What was Paul charged with in Acts 21:17–26? What lesson(s) can current missionaries learn from this passage?

## Special Application Questions:

To what degree are you (or have you been) monocultural or ethnocentric? Explain why. Give illustrations and personally reflect.

# THE NATURE OF CROSS-CULTURAL COMMUNICATION:
## Encoding and Decoding God's Eternal Message

David Hesselgrave has contrasted the perceptions of Rudyard Kipling concerning East-West dialogue with those of Sir Rabindranath Tagore. Kipling in "The Ballad of East and West" writes:

*East is East and West is West*
*And never the twain shall meet.*
                    1924, 268–72

On the contrary, Tagore asserts that the most significant occurrence of the twenty-first century is that "the East and West *have met*" (quoted by Hesselgrave 1978, 204).

To what degree are these contrasting perspectives true? Kipling penned his words during an age of relatively little intercultural contact. Human understanding of other cultures was limited. Nevertheless, Kipling's words continue to echo whenever Easterners and Westerners attempt to understand each other's perspectives.

Tagore was commenting on the increasing interdependence of peoples of the world. International communication and transportation networks have linked the world. Global meetings are held to discuss ecological, political, technological, and religious issues. At no other time in the

**This chapter introduces the fundamentals of cross-cultural communication so that missionaries may be better equipped to speak God's eternal message in foreign cultural contexts.**

history of the world have human cultures been brought together through such interconnecting forums. The world is becoming a global village.

Perhaps the following statement by Hesselgrave more accurately captures the essence of intercultural relationships in our contemporary world: *"The East and West are ever meeting, but the East and West have never met"* (1978, 204). This "ever meeting, yet never meeting" expresses the nature of communication in the current world. In the area of missions too many missionaries merely dabble at what they do. They are like characters on *Star Trek*, who are beamed into a specific context to do their designated job and then beamed back aboard their spaceship. In their forays into other cultures, short-term missionaries are "ever meeting" new people and new situations, but they are "never meeting" the people within the framework of their culture and language. David Hesselgrave writes:

> There is a real danger that as our technology advances and enables us to cross geographical and national boundaries with ease and increasing frequency we forget that cultural barriers are real and formidable. The gap between our technological advances and our communication skills is perhaps one of the most challenging aspects of modern civilization. **1978, 615**

This chapter introduces the fundamentals of cross-cultural communication so that missionaries may be better equipped to speak God's eternal message in foreign cultural contexts.

## A Three-Cultural Model of Missionary Communication

Communicating Christ in an E–2 or E–3[1] context involves three cultures. First, missionaries must understand their own culture. If missionaries do not know themselves in their own culture, how can they sort out who they are in the context of other cultures? Second, missionaries must seek to understand biblical meanings as they were communicated within biblical contexts. Scripture was not written in a cultural vacuum. Each book was directed toward and written about people in specific situations having various cultural heritages. Third, missionaries must learn the culture in which they wish to communicate. For the Christian mes-

[1]*E-2 evangelism* is Christian outreach to cultures whose languages and worldview are similar to yet different from the missionaries'; for example, Americans evangelizing in Europe or Spanish-speaking Latin America. *E-3 evangelism* takes place when missionaries teach those of a far-distant language and culture, as Americans evangelizing among Mandarin Chinese or among Kipsigis of Kenya. See chapter 5 for an in-depth discussion.

sage to be heard, it must be communicated in the local language with impact and precision. This message must attract, impact, and revolutionize the host culture without losing its eternal essence.

### A One-Culture Model of Missionary Communication

Before cross-cultural evangelists can understand the process of communicating Christ in other cultures, they must discern the nature of communication within a one-culture context. For instance, what occurs when American evangelists communicate the gospel to other Americans? The following diagram depicts this process.[2]

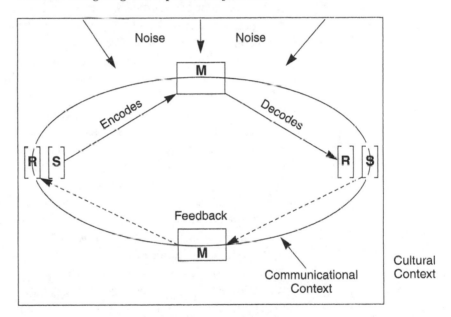

**Figure 4. A One-Culture Model of Missionary Communication**

This diagram illustrates a one-culture model of missionary communication. The evangelist is the *source* (S) who encodes the *message* (M) of the gospel. The person being taught is the *receptor* (R). The receptor never decodes the message exactly as the source intended, but precise vocabulary and appropriate illustrations can minimize misunderstandings.

[2]Eugene Nida's discussion "The Structure of Communication" in *Mission and Message* (1960, 33-61; 1990, 37–55) has been formative in this chapter. Rather than diagramming communication as a dialogical (and therefore cyclical) encounter, Nida depicts it as a linear process.

*Feedback,* either verbal or nonverbal, personal or impersonal, enables the source to know how his message has been decoded. If the receptor asks the meaning of a word or phrase, the source knows that something needs to be clarified. When giving feedback, the receptor (R) becomes the source (S), and the original source (S) becomes the receptor (R).

*Noise* is any disruption in the communication event. A blaring television, a child asking to be fed, and a receptor thinking about problems at work are all examples of noise.

The communication event takes place within a *cultural context* (designated in the diagram by the rectangle enclosing the entire communication event), which shapes the process. In this case S and R share English as their first language and think in the same general cultural categories. Increased cultural commonality within the cultural context heightens the effectiveness of communication. The use of one's cultural heritage in communicating is diagrammed by placing the outline of the culture (in this case a rectangle) on the individual. However, because individuals live in distinctive local circumstances and have various experiential backgrounds, differences within the culture must be taken into account. The message itself is even influenced by the culture. For example, the message might reflect the individualism of American culture by emphasizing what a person must do to come into relationship with God instead of focusing on the activities of God. The impact of the culture on the message is diagrammed by placing the outline of the culture (in this case a rectangle) on the message.

The immediate *context* (designated by an ellipsis in the diagram) also impacts the communication process. A Bible study may take place in the receptor's home, at a restaurant, or at a contact center downtown. A context may be biased for or against the message. In one situation a mother was so biased against Christianity that it became impossible for her son to hear the gospel over her mother's objections at home. The son, however, eagerly heard and obeyed the gospel when taught in the evangelist's home.

The communication process discussed above also occurred in biblical times. Jesus encoded the message that he was the Son of God, the King of the Jews. When Caiaphas heard Jesus claim to be the Son of God, he considered it blasphemy, a challenge to his position, and commanded that Jesus be put to death (Matt. 26:57–67). Peter, after hearing Christ speak with wisdom and seeing God's mighty acts, affirmed Jesus to be "Christ, the Son of the living God" (16:16). The same message, therefore, can be decoded in different ways. The Jewish leaders decoded it as sacrilege, and Jesus' followers as the words of life (John 6:68–69).

When Paul healed the lame man in Lystra, the people decoded the miracle to indicate that Barnabas and Paul were gods in human form. The priests of Zeus responded with visual feedback by bringing sacrifices to Paul and Barnabas. Barnabas and Paul, however, after hearing the meaning of the intended sacrifice, encoded a message proclaiming that they were not gods as the people supposed. They, too, were humans. The lame man had been healed by the power of creator God. They were to worship this God, not worthless idols (Acts 14:8–18).

Communication in a one-culture setting is a complicated process allowing much room for misunderstanding. Misconceptions occur because what is encoded by the source is not perfectly decoded by the recipient and because noise interferes with the communication process. Missionaries, therefore, must learn to communicate within their own language and culture before attempting the more complicated process of communicating cross-culturally. Knowing themselves and how to relate to others within their own culture is a prerequisite to, though not a guarantee of, effective cross-cultural communication.

## A Two-Culture Model of Missionary Communication

Each book of the Bible is an encoding of God's message for a specific people at a particular time. Paul wrote to the Galatians because new Christians were tempted to forsake the gospel of grace and return to legalistic customs of Judaizing teachers. These teachers were instructing new Christians that they had to be circumcised according to the law of Moses in order to be saved. Commentators seek to explain to people of contemporary cultures the meanings conveyed by inspiration in biblical cultures.

A cultural gap separates modern America and the ancient Near East. Concepts such as sacrifice, covenant, circumcision, and principalities and powers are all foreign to the contemporary listener. Interpreters must cross time and culture in order to uncover the intended message of the biblical text. Then they must apply it to contemporary times and issues. This twofold bridging of culture to understand biblical concepts and discern God's meanings is implied by the arrows pointing from American culture to "biblical" culture(s) in the two-culture model of missionary communication. The worldview differences are diagrammed by outlining biblical cultures as a triangle. This diagram is limited because the Bible spans many centuries and was written in the context of many cultures, not just one.

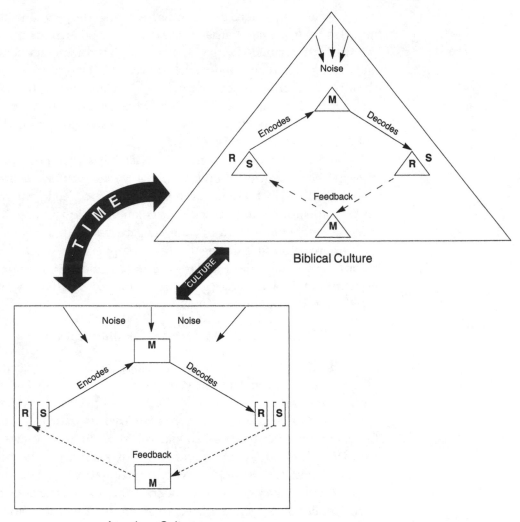

**Figure 5. A Two-Culture Model of Missionary Communication**

Two communicational issues are clarified by the two-culture model of missionary communication. First, Christian communicators must learn to interpret Scripture. Most people intuitively interpret the Bible. They assume that their worldview and that of biblical times are identical. This intuitive approach leads to misunderstandings of Scripture because people fail to study the text within its own linguistic, cultural, and historical setting. All Christians must, therefore, learn to do proper biblical exegesis.

Exegesis is the process of using the historical and cultural context of a passage to determine its original meaning. Effective biblical interpretation leads missionaries to rise above their own fallen culture and to seek an absolute, eternal, God-ordained worldview. Second, Christian communicators must apply the inspired meanings to real issues of contemporary culture. The gospel was meant to be lived and taught, not merely discussed in academic settings. A Christian worldview must practically shape the morals, ethics, and behaviors of society.

## A Three-Culture Model of Missionary Communication

When missionaries enter a host culture, the process of encoding a message that is decoded by a receptor also takes place. The host culture, of course, is different from both the sending culture and biblical cultures. While contemporary American culture is represented by a square and biblical cultures by a triangle in the illustration on the following page, a circle represents a host culture.

Two other communicational issues are clarified when considering the three-culture model. First, missionaries must learn to adapt to their new culture. When they first arrive on the field, missionaries are like square pegs in round holes. They have been enculturated to think like *squares* but come to minister where people perceive reality as *rounds*. As they learn their new language and culture, their squareness is rounded off. If basic learning does not occur, the message communicated and lifestyle modeled will not adequately reflect the Christian meanings the missionaries desire to communicate.

Second, the process of interpreting Scripture and applying it to life also occurs in the third culture. The developing Christian leaders in the host culture must learn to interpret the Bible and apply its meanings to their culture just as Christians in the missionaries' home culture do. Missionaries must become master teachers equipping the church to accomplish these functions. This perspective assumes that the missionaries believe that the people can learn to interpret the message for themselves and make divine applications of contemporary issues. As they communicate and model the Christian message, missionaries serve as *mentors of movements* rather than fathers or founders. *Mentoring* implies equality; *fathering* or *founding* denotes paternalism. Missionaries must walk alongside national leaders; they must not stand over them.

Church-planting missionaries frequently become resource people for developing Christian fellowships. They are asked how people in Christ

**Thoughtful missionaries will give the new church the freedom to innovate rites under the guiding hand of the Spirit of God.**

become adults, marry, become elders, and die. What is the role of the church and family in each of these aspects of life's cycle? Missionaries are tempted to give their own cultural answers to the new fellowship because it is easier to borrow than to innovate. Thoughtful missionaries will give the new church the freedom to innovate rites under the guiding hand of the Spirit of God so that *American* rites will not be incorporated superficially into the new culture as *Christian* rites.

Communicating the message of Christ across cultures involves asking many significant theological questions. For example, what is the biblical conception of time? A Hindu looks at time as cyclical: The dead are reincarnated into life in numerous rebirths. On the other hand, the bib-

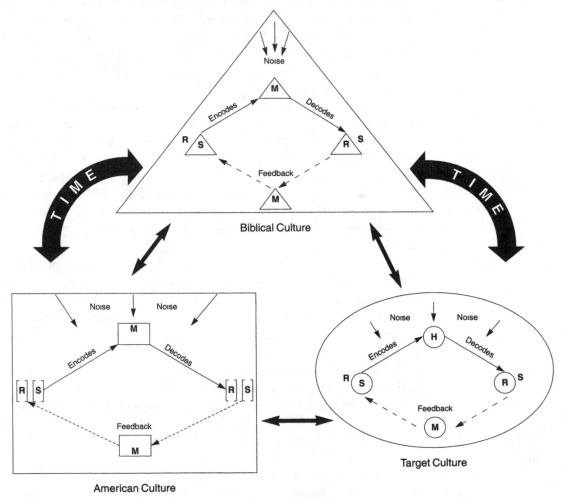

**Figure 6. A Three-Culture Model of Missionary Communication**

lical perspective is linear: At death natural bodies perish and physical bodies return to the ground, but spirits return to God who gave them (Eccl. 12:7). God, although eternal, began time with creation and will ultimately bring time to a grand finale with the second coming of Christ. Time is understood to be in the hand of God; as the great sovereign over time, he determines the length of each person's life as well as the time for Christ's return (Matt. 24:36). How do human cultures divide reality? Western culture divides reality into two large slices—the secular and the spiritual—and thereby separates God from his world. Neither Scripture nor non-Western cultures divide reality in this way. How should decisions be made? Western culture is extremely individualistic; biblical cultures are moderately group-oriented, and African cultures are extremely group-oriented. Who or what are the principalities and powers? Westerners generally believe that spiritual powers do not exist but are merely myths of primitive peoples. Scripture and most world cultures, however, recognize the presence and activity of spiritual powers and forces.

These illustrations emphasize that cultural decisions and theology cannot be separated. Missionaries must help the people with whom they work come to theologically sound conceptions of reality.

# A Practical Case Study of a Three-Culture Model of Missionary Communication

What practical problems arise when evangelists of one culture seek to Christianize those of a second culture by presenting a message that was initially proclaimed in still a third culture in another age? More specifically, how do American evangelists present Christianity to Africans living south of the Sahara? As in the matter of Jewish relations with Gentiles in the early Christian church, cultural frictions are inevitable. In a preliminary way this section presents an American cultural worldview, contrasts it with an African worldview, and then delineates the process of rethinking and theologizing that occurs as Americans attempt to communicate God's message in Africa. This case study will specifically demonstrate a three-culture transmission of the Christian message.

### American Cultural Perspectives

The American worldview is (1) naturalistic, (2) individualistic, (3) optimistic, and (4) present-oriented and linear in thinking. These cultural characteristics have permeated American Christianity to the point that they are seldom questioned. Acceptance of American values usually continues even when these values conflict with Christian truths. While Amer-

| | | |
|---|---|---|
| SUPERNATURAL REALM | Angels Demons God | Perceived by miracles and visions People act by faith |
| NATURAL REALM | Man The Church Science The World | Perceived by sight and experiemce People act by knowledge |

Adapted from Paul Hiebert, "Phenomenology and institutions of animism," classroom notes, Fuller Theological Seminary, Pasadena, Calif., 1983. Used by permission.

**Figure 7. Segmentations of Reality in American Culture**

ican culture shapes Christianity, Christianity is, in turn, a dominant force impacting American culture.

Americans are *naturalistic*. They make a distinction between the natural and the supernatural, between the physical and the spiritual.

God, angels, and demons are supernatural. People in the natural realm can perceive their activities only through miracles and visions. The tangible, physical world is considered the natural realm. This world is thought to be guided by laws of nature, studied by experimentation, and understood by scientific analysis. Everything within this world can be perceived by the five senses. People act by knowledge of the natural. Miracles are questioned, and the spiritual world is thought to have little direct contact with the physical. God is spoken of as *intervening* in his world. Some Americans go so far as to deny all spiritual powers because they cannot be perceived and so the world becomes a "closed universe" (Van Rheenen 1991, 53–57).

The American perception of disease further illustrates this point. Americans seek natural causes of disease. They do not generally believe in spiritual causation: Sin does not induce sickness, angry ancestors cannot accost their descendants, and Satan does not tempt the living by causing illness. Rather, sickness is due to germs or some malfunction of the body. No spiritual reasons stand behind these physical causes. Americans, expecting some natural explanation, ask *what* caused the illness; they do not designate personal or spiritual causes by asking *who* caused the disease or *why* one has become sick.[3]

Americans are *individualistic*. They generally believe that the individual is more important than the group. At an early age children learn

[3]The wall between the natural and supernatural is now beginning to fall among two types of people in the American population. Bible-believing Christians are challenging the secularism that denies the work of God in the world he created. The God of

to distinguish between "my things" and "your things." As adults, they differentiate "my rights" and "your rights." Nuclear families mirror the culture as a whole; each nuclear family does its own thing independent of the control of the extended family. The intense individualism of the nuclear family also erodes parental respect and leads members of the family to do their own thing. Democracy stands as the cultural ideal; each individual has an equal voice in government, regardless of his understanding of the issues involved. Praise and honor are given to the individual who achieves above his peers; certificates of achievement decorating the walls testify to a person's success. Team sports are individualized with detailed statistics kept on each player. The accomplishments of star players—the number of strikeouts, home runs, and stolen bases or field goals, free throws, assists, and rebounds—are often given more attention than the team who wins. Americans feel that people must make their own way without reliance on groups or outside help.

The intense individualism of American culture is becoming the seed of its destruction. Families are fragmenting. Culture is losing its cohesion. Special-interest groups are seeking to meet their own felt needs without consideration of others. Let us hope that the church will mobilize itself under the sovereign hand of God to become cohesive, distinct people in a fragmented, lonesome society.

Americans are *optimistic*. They are filled with confidence that they can succeed. Because the world is orderly and humans are rational, they can chart their own course to success. This optimism is rooted in the belief that opportunities are continually expanding. There are always new frontiers to conquer: undeveloped lands to the West, space beyond the stratosphere, or computer and telecommunications technology. One person's success is not necessarily at another person's expense. Even the common person can succeed. The feeling is common that only in America can one go from a log cabin to the White House.[4]

the Bible is a personal, working God (John 5:17) who desires to relate to his people (Hos. 11:1–5). Followers of the New Age movement also make no distinction between the natural and the supernatural. They believe that the physical and spiritual worlds are "interrelated, interdependent, and interpenetrating" (Groothuis 1986, 18). For example, one New Age therapist uses crystals for healing purposes because "physical problems are manifestations of spiritual problems" (Friedrich 1987, 64). As the naturalistic influences of secular American culture wane, an impending battle is emerging for the hearts of the American people between Christian and New Age ideologies.

[4]This optimism, however, has been tempered in recent years by the military defeat in Vietnam (yet amplified by victory in the Persian Gulf), the concurrent slide of the Amer-

Americans are *present-oriented and view time as linear*. A shift from a future to a present orientation is one of the most significant changes in American culture in this generation. The traditional, future-oriented attitude was expressed by religious billboards and tracts exhorting the sinner, "Prepare to meet your Maker," but now sermons are seldom heard on such topics as the second coming of Christ, heaven and hell, and the future hope of Christians. In the past the accepted philosophy was to work hard now in preparation for the future. Today, instead of saving for the future, Americans live for the present. Individuals—and the government—buy goods on credit so that they can have now and pay later. This shift in time perspective has undermined our country and humanized our churches.

The American perspective of time is also linear. Americans generally believe that life begins at birth and ends at death. Unlike people whose cultures have a cyclical orientation of time, Americans view children as being born with a clean slate, having no previous heritage. Many traditional Western psychological therapies are based on this presupposition: Early imprinting is the basis of a person's psychological makeup because a child has no previous impressions written on his personality.[5]

American secularists conclude that since people have only one life to live, they must make the most of it. They deduce that they should eat, drink, and be merry, for the future is unknown. American hedonism, under such glamorous captions as "the playboy philosophy," acclaims this perspective.

### African Cultural Perspectives

There is a significant cultural gap between the cultural presuppositions of Americans and those of Africans. Africans are spiritualistic rather than naturalistic, group-oriented rather than individualistic, fatalistic rather than optimistic, past-oriented rather than present- or future-oriented.

Africans are *spiritualistic*. All of life is pervaded by spiritual power. Africans believe in personal spiritual beings—ancestors and ghosts, gods and spirits—who guide their destinies and affect their lives. Impersonal spiritual forces—powers that have no personalities and yet impact people—are used to bless friends and family and curse enemies. Africans do

ican economy and growth of Asian-rim and European economies, and the lack of governmental consensus induced by growing individualism.

[5]This linear perspective is now being challenged by New Age perspectives proclaiming a new type of eternity. There is no such thing as physical death. Human spirits are thought to be reincarnated and live again.

not give up belief in spiritual powers when they become Christians or Muslims. Christ most frequently is accepted as the Lord who has defeated the principalities and powers. Others blend their Christianity with African Traditional Religion. They worship God yet depend on their gods and ancestors when they are sick or when catastrophes occur. Dal Congdon found that among Zulus of South Africa fully 69.9 percent of professing Christians continue to believe that ancestral spirits "protect" them and "bring them good fortune." He found that "fewer professing Christians affirmed the deity of Christ than expressed dependence on ancestral spirits for problems connected with daily living" (1985, 297). The accumulation of material goods is thought to be related to spiritual power. How could one accumulate material goods without spiritual power?

African spirituality is greatly concerned with the cause and cure of disease. To many Christian and non-Christian Africans extended illness is thought to be caused by sin. Sins are thought to come back and "eat up" those who commit them. Ancestors are also thought to cause illness. They become angry when they have been forgotten or their wishes have been violated by the living. Witchcraft and sorcery might also cause serious illness and death. Another cause of disease is spirits, usually associated with physical phenomena, which are free to roam the world. Someone who becomes seriously ill begins looking for the spiritual reason for the illness. Although most Africans will agree that germs and body malfunctions cause illness, they consider them only surface causations resulting from the activity of animistic beings and forces.

If the Western dichotomy between the physical and spiritual is accepted, the result is that the people become secular "Christians" who have little faith in the work of any spiritual power, including God. If the dichotomy is rejected, dominant African leaders are apt to split away to initiate independent movements. If the dichotomy problem remains unresolved, there is a continual tension between national Christians who believe in the spiritual causation and Western-trained leaders who deny any such cause for illness.

Africans are *group-oriented*. Their lives are tied together by intimate family relationships. They live in extended families in which the father's brothers are also called "fathers," and in many cases co-wives of one husband are all called "mothers." First-generation cousins are called "brothers" and "sisters." Disputes are solved and financial decisions are made primarily on the extended-family level. When young people move to the cities, they are considered the extension of the family in the city. Family members will attempt to find jobs for others of their family or, if they become influential, they may hire family members to work under them to provide finances for the extended family. While the practice of hiring family members for jobs in government and large corporations is considered unethical in an individualistic society, it is a way of life in areas where a person's first responsibility is to his family.

Extended families of the same totem[6] make up clans. In many ethnic groups clans live within a geographical area, such as a district or a location. In other tribes clans are dispersed over a wide geographical area and are used only in determining whom to marry and for settling disputes related to the murder of fellow clans people.

These clans make up tribes. Before the colonial era, tribes were the largest natural grouping of the people. Colonial powers artificially imposed larger boundaries on tribal areas and called them "nations." It is therefore not surprising that many African states have difficulty developing a sense of nationhood.

Local villages form another type of group. Village councils frequently serve as problem-solving forums for marriage, land, and personality problems. Disputes in families, clans, and villages are discussed at length until a consensus is achieved. Voting is thought to be divisive because it forces decision makers to take sides.

Within African society an individual seldom stands against the group. Rather, peoples' identity is formed by the group. This is indicated in Mbiti's adage "I am because we are" (1980, 11). When men of the Tiv tribe of Nigeria meet, they seek the identity of other men by asking, "U ngu uno?"—literally, "You [singular] are who [plural]?" The answer is the name of a clan (Terpstra 1996). Africans tend to come to Christ in groups rather than as individuals. Family and village groups discuss the implications of the gospel for hours and, through group interaction, come to belief or disbelief. In such contexts effective missionaries seek to teach people in their natural groups rather than individually.

Africans are *fatalistic*. They believe that people are not in control of their own destiny. They feel the control and entrapment of powerful ancestors and spirits. In certain contexts social obligations hinder the accumulation of capital so that economic advance is difficult. Wealth and position are not personal achievements but possessions of the entire family. Kipsigis farmers frequently state their inability to get ahead by saying, "*Matinye kim-*

[6]A totem is usually an animal (less frequently a plant or physical feature) that is affinely linked to the clan to empower it and give it identity.

*natet,"* literally meaning "I don't have strength." They do not have the power to plow a field for corn, the financial ability to build a house, or monetary strength to begin a business. They are bound by spiritual forces, their family, and their environment. They fatalistically believe there is no way to escape except through outside financial assistance and education.

Too often this fatalism manifests itself in churches that have had time to become self-governing and self-supporting. Instead, they declare, "We don't have strength; we need your help." Sometimes Christians who should be free in Christ continue to feel the bondage of spiritual forces. Fortunately, when people give their full allegiance to God, his mighty power can break the fetters of African fatalism.

Africans are *past-oriented and may conceive of time as either linear or cyclical.* Mbiti writes that the *tene* period—the ancient times—"is the centre of gravity in [African thought]: people's thinking and understanding of the world are orientated toward this finality—not in the future but in the past." Africans consider history to be moving "backward" rather than "forward" (Mbiti 1971, 28). The present is understood in terms of the past. Myths of the past explain the present, and proverbs, the sayings of ancient times, interpret present events. The past is projected into the present. Time is "two-dimensional" with a "long 'past,' and a dynamic 'present.'" The perspective of a distant future, however, is "virtually non-existent" in African traditional thought (1971, 24).

Some Africans conceive of time as linear and some as cyclical. In linear cultures ancestors are spiritual beings whose names are remembered and continue to be part of the family folklore. They are actively concerned about the family and intervene when forgotten or when decisions are made with which they disagree. Because of their closeness to the living, they might be considered "the living dead." Ghosts are spiritual beings whose names have been forgotten and who have faded into the realms of the spirits and gods. Because they are more distant from the living, they are called "the dead." Other African peoples are cyclical in their view of time. Man's body and spirit are distinct. When one's body dies, his spirit eventually comes back to live in other bodies. Life is considered good, death is feared and bad. Thus an ancestral spirit's primary goal is to come back into a body and live again. From an African standpoint, human spirits are fluid. Even while one lives, his spirit is able to depart for short times without his body dying. This is how dreams and visions are explained. The Kipsigis caution against waking a sleeping man quickly in case his spirit is not in his body and the shock causes death. This cyclical view of existence is illustrated in the Kipsigis *kurenet* rite. The rite takes place immediately after a child is born to ascertain which ancestral spirit has embodied the new child. An old woman will ask, "Are you Arap Tonui?" The women gathered for this rite will wait for some time for the child to sneeze, thus signifying the affirmative. If the child does not sneeze, another name is proposed until the child responds by sneezing. Orchardson writes:

> So firmly is it believed that the child really has the spirit of the *Kurenet*, and is in fact the same person, that his or her mother, when using terms of endearment, will address the child for many years by the *Kurenet's* name. **Orchardson 1961, 45**

Western and Christian influences are radically changing African conceptions of time. Western perspectives (influences), through education and media, teach people to live for the here and now. Beliefs in ancestors and ghosts are ridiculed. Conservative Christian influences teach that God, who created the world, continues to work today and will bring this world to its ultimate conclusion. At Christ's second coming God will claim his own to live eternally with him, and the church is dedicated to preparing the world for this.

## Communicating God's Eternal Message in Africa

**Effective missionaries go through a concurrent process of reevaluating their own worldview in light of Scripture, seeking God's foundational message for all humanity, and applying this message to both their own and their host culture.**

People in America and people in Africa have vastly different ways of looking at the world. Should American missionaries consider both of these worldviews equally valid within their own contexts? To what degree should they be accepted or rejected? Those who affirm Scripture to be God's particular revelation to humanity believe that the Christian community, whether in America or in Africa, should look to God's revealed message as the ultimate portrayal of reality. Although the American and African cultures are *perceptions* of reality, Scripture reveals actual reality, given in a different time period and directed to problems in specific cultures. Cross-cultural missionaries must allow God's message to shape their own worldview and seek to communicate this eternal view of reality in both their own culture and that of their host.

How then should American evangelists present biblical Christianity to people of an African culture? Effective missionaries go through a concurrent process of (1) reevaluating their own worldview in light of Scripture, (2) seeking God's foundational message for all humanity, and (3) applying this message to both their own and their host culture.

*Reevaluating Their Own Worldview*

When encountering an African culture, American missionaries will be forced to ask themselves some fundamental questions about life.

First, since Africans generally affirm spiritual powers that Americans deny, American missionaries will ask whether or not there are spiritual powers that cannot be seen. As American missionaries reevaluate their own culture, they will find, perhaps surprisingly, that Scripture actually assumes the reality of spiritual powers. The Old Testament describes them as gods; the Gospels, as demons; and the Pauline epistles, as principalities and powers. Paul's statement in Ephesians 6:12 summarizes this biblical perspective: "Our struggle is not against flesh and blood, but against the rulers, against the authorities, against the powers of this dark world and against the spiritual forces of evil in the heavenly realms."

Second, do American missionaries of an Enlightenment tradition fully understand the sovereignty of God over the world, or have they so secularized reality that they have virtually excluded God from the world he created? The theme of God working within his world is a thread running through the biblical text. Jesus describes God by saying, "My Father is always at his work to this very day, and I, too, am working" (John 5:17).

Third, if God is active, what is the role of science and scientific inquiry? Does God work on the basis of laws of nature, or does the orderliness of the world reflect the nature of the God who sustains it? The Bible shows God in Christ upholding the physical world. Paul writes that in Christ "all things hold together" (Col. 1:17). The Hebrew letter describes Christ as "sustaining all things by his powerful word" (Heb. 1:3). Scientists can never objectively study God, Christ, and other spiritual beings; they can only study what God has made. Paul writes that "God's invisible qualities—his eternal power and divine nature—have been clearly seen, being understood from what has been made" (Rom. 1:20). Therefore, Christians who scientifically study the complexity of God's world should stand in awe of its Creator.

Fourth, have we placed too much confidence in human abilities and human ingenuity? All who come to Christ do so by faith, realizing that "the foolishness of God is wiser than man's wisdom, and the weakness of God is stronger than man's strength" (1 Cor. 1:25). Salvation is ultimately based on submitting to the will of God. Humans are unable to work out their own spiritual dilemmas. Jeremiah rightly says, "A man's life is not his own; it is not for man to direct his steps" (Jer. 10:23).

Fifth, how do we perceive God? God is sovereign Lord, described by Moses after Israel's deliverance from Egyptian captivity as "majestic in holiness, awesome in glory, working wonders" (Ex. 15:11). His attributes are love and holiness. In the Old Testament God is characterized by "steadfast love" (*hesed*). He is "compassionate and gracious . . . slow to anger, abounding in love and faithfulness" (34:6–7; cf. Num. 14:18; Neh. 9:17; Pss. 86:15; 103:8; 145:8; Joel 2:13; Jonah 4:2). In the New Testament this attribute is attested by the sending of his divine Son to become flesh and die for sinful humanity (Rom. 5:8). God's eternal nature is love (1 John 4:7–8), but he is also holy. The heavenly host reflects this quality by proclaiming, "Holy, holy, holy is the Lord God Almighty" (Rev. 4:8; cf. Isa. 6:3). The sacrificial system described in Leviticus is based on a holy God who desires to unite sinful people with himself. Therefore, God identifies himself as "the LORD, who makes you holy" (Lev. 20:8).

These two attributes define both why and how God relates to humankind. God did not merely create the world and then leave it. He loves those he created and desires to live in a relationship with them. Yet he desires that human culture reflect his nature (1 Peter 1:15; cf. Lev. 11:44–45). As a holy God, he feels our sins. He is like a father who tenderly loves his disobedient son (Hos. 11:1–11), a faithful husband who devotedly loves his unfaithful wife (Hos. 1–3), a husbandman who lovingly shapes and cultivates his unproductive vineyard (Isa. 5:1–7), and a physician who compassionately cares for the sick (1:5–6; Matt. 9:12). God loves us despite our unholiness.

### Seeking God's Fundamental Message for All People

As American missionaries in Africa reevaluate their own worldview, they must also discover the fundamental message of God that must be taught, modeled, and obeyed in every context at every time. The essence of the gospel does not change with the ebb and flow of cultures but is as unchangeable as eternal God.

The essence of the gospel can be easily discerned from the great speeches of Old Testament prophets, from the teachings of Jesus, and from the sermons of early Christians. For example, Ezra's praise and confessional statement made in Jerusalem during a time of spiritual revival capsulizes significant elements of the gospel (Neh. 9:6–37). God, the righteous One, keeps his promises despite the unfaithfulness of Israel. God's desire to redeem is rooted in his great love. Jesus said, "I am the way and the truth and the life. No one comes to the Father except through me" (John 14:6). For Paul, the gospel was the death, burial, and resurrection of Christ (1 Cor. 15:1–4). This message was proclaimed in the sermons in the book of Acts whenever Paul preached to Jewish audiences. Luke's summary of this message was that "Christ had to suffer and rise from the dead," and that this Jesus was the long-awaited Messiah (Acts 17:1–3). Christ's incarnation, ministry, death, and resurrection were rooted in the love of God, who sends and saves (John 3:16). Non-Jews, who did not know the creator God, were introduced to his sovereignty and attributes (Acts 17:22–31; 14:14–18). These speeches and sermons reveal eternal themes communicated by the inspiration of God within cultural contexts.

### Communicating God's Eternal Message in the African Context

As American missionaries enter African contexts, they must learn to communicate God's message appropriately.

First, at every significant point the God of the Bible must be compared to, and contrasted with, the African view of God. Creator God, who was traditionally considered distant in African culture, must be presented as approachable, caring, and powerful. An emphasis must be placed on biblical stories and praises describing his creative power (Gen. 1–3; Pss. 8; 24), continued work (Neh. 9:5–37; Ps. 106), and divine attributes (Ex. 34:6–7; Ps. 103:8–22; Deut. 31:30–32:43). To know God, who is "majestic in holiness, awesome in glory, working wonders," is the beginning step on the path to conversion. Allegiance to him must displace allegiance to all other spiritual beings, whether they are ancestors, personal spirits, or tribal gods. The Christ of the New Testament can be understood only on the basis of the clear picture of the God revealed in the Old Testament.

Second, Christ must be proclaimed as the only way to God. In America Christ is typically presented as one who reconciles those who, because of sin, are alienated from God or as one who justifies sinners who are guilty before a pure God. Although the metaphors of *reconciliation* and *justification* are understood in Africa, they do not make a particularly strong impact. The metaphor that stirs the heart of the African is that of *liberation*: Christ has defeated the principalities and powers and rescued his people from their dominion. By his death he "disarmed the rulers and authorities" and "made a public display of them" (Col. 2:15 NASB). This liberation metaphor is the classical doctrine of the atonement that was reintroduced to Western theology by Gustaf Aulen in *Christus Victor*

Africans understand sacrifices to be human efforts to placate, propitiate, and coerce spiritual beings. . . . The Christian missionary must deal appropriately with this issue and not ignore it.

(Aulen 1931). Consistently, this message has led Africans to forsake spiritual beings and forces, which stand in opposition to God, to worship their sovereign Creator (Van Rheenen 1991, 141–42).

Third, African conceptions of sacrifice must be radically reinterpreted. Africans understand sacrifices to be human efforts to placate, propitiate, and coerce spiritual beings. They ritually offer chickens, sheep, goats, and cattle to appease angry ancestors, spirits, and gods who have brought evil upon humans and to invoke blessings upon social activities such as initiation into adulthood, marriage, and death (Van Rheenen 1991, 292). The Judeo-Christian understanding of sacrifice is based on different presuppositions. Rather than being rooted in human initiative, sacrifices are prescribed by God himself. They are not originated to manipulate or coerce but are rooted in God's love and compassion—reflecting his desire to reconcile sinners to himself. Christ's death is God's ultimate sacrifice ordained to take the place of all other sacrifices (Heb. 10:1–14). Because of the prevalence of sacrifice in African culture, the Christian missionary must deal appropriately with this issue and not ignore it.

Fourth, a Christian conception of God's sovereignty over time must radically change the African perspective of time. Christianity, like African Traditional Religion, emphasizes the past. Creating the world, electing Abraham and his descendants to be his chosen people, delivering Israel from Egyptian captivity, giving Israel the land of Canaan, and sending prophets and priests to proclaim his message are part of the history of God's mighty acts. Likewise, the past must be made to interpret the present. God expected Israel to obey and follow him because of his activities in their lives.[7] Nevertheless, the biblical accounts are not tribal myths describing human origin and initiative but God-inspired accounts of how the world came to be.

The most radical reorientation of the traditional African concept of time occurs in relation to the future. The God of the Bible has not only worked in the past but is also working in the present and will continue working until the consummation of the world. Anticipating and preparing for the end is integral to a Christian worldview.

Finally, at every critical point of culture, Christian evangelists must present relevant alternatives to traditional cultural rites. The critical areas include the blessing and naming of children, rites of transition from child-

[7]God's rationale for giving Israel the Ten Commandments was that he was Yahweh, their God, "who brought [them] out of Egypt" (Ex. 20:2).

hood to adulthood, marriage, transitions to elderhood, and death. For example, the church among the Kipsigis of Kenya has struggled with how Christians marry. Traditionally Kipsigis marriage was sealed through a ceremony called *katunisietab segutiet* ("the wedding of the grass band"). The bride and groom stood before an elder of the village dressed in traditional skins. They bound each others hands with a braided band made from crabgrass. The elder would invoke the blessings of the ancestors on the marriage by words of blessing and spitting of traditional beer. Should Christians follow such customs? The African Inland Church introduced *katunisietab petiet* ("the wedding of the ring"), a Western ceremony introduced into Kipsigis and called "Christian." Should Kipsigis Christians borrow Western customs and make them their own? The Church of Christ at various times practiced adapted forms of both of the above marriage ceremonies but has now begun to introduce an innovated form called *katunisietab kayanet* ("the wedding of faith"). This form is both Christian and Kipsigis. Marriage is not based on any physical item, like a grass band or a ring, but on faith in sovereign God. The community is called together to witness a special union of people under God.

In this section I am recounting a process I went through on the mission field. When I entered the mission field, I had to go through the process of theological reevaluation. At times I felt guilty for rethinking my presuppositions. Sometimes I was carried away by the opinions of American co-workers who wanted to reject the type of Christianity they had witnessed in their own cultures. At other times American ethnocentrism and patriotism surfaced as I encouraged Christians to accept Western options because they appeared Christian. The process of reevaluating my worldview in light of scriptural truths, seeking God's fundamental Christian message, and learning to communicate God's eternal message in appropriate, relevant, and cogent ways occurred without my being aware of it. Trust in God and in his almighty working helped me overcome the temptations to idealize the Western way as the Christian way on one extreme and to find Christian roots in all African conceptions on the other extreme.

# BUILDING ON THE COMMUNICATIONAL FOUNDATIONS

## QUESTIONS:

1. How does the phrase "ever meeting, yet never meeting" demonstrate the limitation of short-term missions?
2. Define the meaning of the words *noise*, *feedback*, *encoding*, and *decoding* in communication theory.
3. Why is it important for missionaries to communicate within their own language and culture before attempting to communicate cross-culturally?
4. Describe a two-culture model of missionary communication. In other words, discuss the cultural gap that separates modern America (or the missionaries' sending culture) from culture of the ancient Near East.
5. What specific missions lessons, summarized by the words *interpretation* and *application*, can be learned from a two-culture model of missionary communication?
6. In discussing the three-culture model of missionary communication, why might a new missionary be called *a square peg in a round hole*?
7. What do the arrows extending from the host culture to biblical culture(s) and returning to the host culture from the biblical culture(s) designate? Describe the missionary task in terms of the importance of these arrows.
8. Contrast the role of *mentoring* a movement versus *founding* a movement.
9. Discuss why cultural decisions and theology cannot be separated. In your answer give an illustration of a non-Western theological dilemma typically encountered by missionaries.
10. Make a chart contrasting American and African worldviews in the following five areas: (1) perceptions of the spiritual world, (2) orientations toward the individual and the group, (3) perspectives about optimism and fatalism, (4) understandings of time, and (5) causes of illness.
11. Describe a three-fold, concurrent process that missionaries must go through in order to communicate God's eternal message to those of other cultures. In your answer discuss the value of understanding this

three-fold process. (Use the last paragraph of the chapter as a resource to answer the second part of this question.)

12. Apply the three-fold, concurrent process that missionaries must go through to communicate God's eternal message to some world culture. Use the African illustration used in the text if you are new to the study of missions.

## Special Application Questions:

Have Christians in your home congregation been able to proclaim the gospel across cultural barriers? What has hindered them or aided them in communicating across cultural barriers? Have you taught someone of another cultural background? What has hindered or aided you in communicating across cultural barriers?

# THE ROLE OF STRATEGY IN THE STUDY OF MISSIONS:
## Developing a Philosophy of Strategy

Missiology is made up of three interdependent disciplines: theology, the social sciences, and strategy. To facilitate understanding, these disciplines are described separately, even though they are closely related in the actual practice of missions. Picturing the disciplines in tiers implies that some disciplines are foundational to others.

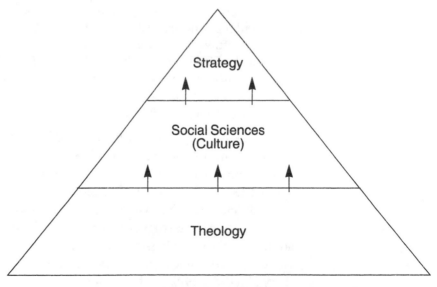

**Figure 8. The Three Disciplines of Missiology**

# Theology: The Foundation of Missiology

All missiological decisions must be rooted, either implicitly or explicitly, in theology in order to mirror the purposes and mind of God. Theology provides the purpose, the focus, and the life of missiology and is therefore the very foundation of the discipline. It produces the message proclaimed in missions—a message not of human origin but revealed by God. Theology also furnishes the motivation of mission, which is rooted in the attributes of God, who sends and saves. It gives "the work of ministry its heart and fire" (Wells 1992, 186). Finally, theology provides the ethical lenses through which missionaries evaluate human cultures and determine practical strategies of ministry. The study of theology thus enables Christian missionaries to perceive the social contexts through the eyes of God and develop strategies shaped by the touch of the divine. This understanding of theology as the foundation of missions is reflected in the organization of this book: chapters 1 and 2 examine significant theological issues, and theology is integral to every subsequent chapter.

Too often, however, we take the theological foundation of missions for granted. Paul Hiebert writes:

> Too often we choose a few themes and from there build a simplistic theology rather than look at the profound theological motifs that flow throughout the whole of Scripture. Equally disturbing to the foundations of mission is the dangerous potential of shifting from God and his work to the emphasis of what we can do for God by our own knowledge and efforts. We become captive to a modern secular worldview in which human control and technique replace divine leading and human obedience as the basis of mission. **1993, 4**

Hesselgrave confirmed the absence of theological foundations in contemporary missiology when he made a thematic content analysis of book reviews and articles published in major mission journals (*Missiology, International Review of Missions,* and *Evangelical Missions Quarterly*) between 1973 and 1986. He concluded that the social sciences and history have been given more attention in the study of missiology than has theology (1988, 139–44) and asks, "Of what lasting significance is the evangelical commitment to the authority of the Bible if biblical teachings do not explicitly inform our missiology?" (1988, 142). Without a theological foundation missions quickly becomes merely another human endeavor.

Christian strategists who prioritize God's role in missions do not begin with the pragmatic question "Does it work?" They rather begin by asking fundamental theological questions: "How does God desire that we minister within this cultural context? Do these plans enact the rule of God and challenge ungodly allegiances? Do these strategies reflect the nature of God?" A Christian leader thus makes plans based on Christian presuppositions. Missions reduced to methodology is as empty as spiritual gifts without love—like "a resounding gong or a clanging cymbal" (1 Cor. 13:1). Strategy must be a servant, never a master, to the mission of God.

## Culture: The Arena of Missions

The *social sciences*—anthropology, sociology, and psychology—form the second layer of missiology. These social sciences inform missionaries of the cultural context in which they are living and the nature of the human psyche. Cultural similarities and differences and the difficulty of communicating across cultural barriers become apparent. Specific studies of marriage customs, kinship patterns, cultural roles, and patterns of organizing thought greatly impact how the gospel is communicated. Effective strategies take into consideration the cultural context. Chapters 5 to 7 of this book consider the importance of the cultural understandings without disconnecting these understandings from the theology.

## Strategy: The Implementation of God's Mission

*Strategies* form the final tier of missiology. The arrows in figure 8 reflect how the formulation of Christian strategy begins with the desires and perspectives of God, then considers the reality of the social situation, and finally constructs strategies compatible with these understandings and commitments. This bottom-up methodology guides missionaries to construct strategies that are both godly and relevant. Strategies, therefore, must not be rooted in mere pragmatism but developed on the basis of theological insights and cultural understandings. Strategies without a firm theology and realistic cultural understandings are like sloughed-off snakeskins—empty and useless. There is no life in pure methodology. Effective strategy grows out of theological and social science considerations.

Strategy is indispensable to the doing of any task. For example, students cannot do research without many strategy decisions. Students must first determine the exact focus of their topic. They will ask, "How do I determine my topic? How do I uncover the significant resources on my topic? How should research for the paper be categorized and filed—on note cards, under headings on one continuous sheet of paper, or on various files on a computer disk? What style of writing do I choose—narrative, deductive, inductive? When do I do my research—in early morning, afternoon, or evening?" Without making such methodological decisions, the student would be unable to write a research paper. Although the ultimate purpose of the paper may be to seek some eternal truth, significant strategy decisions must be made along the way.

Some theologians deal with the bottom two layers of missiology but seem to have no need for the third layer. They may feel that the message of the gospel can speak for itself, and they are so concerned for the content of Christianity that they exclude its practice. Some missionaries, on the other hand, disengage strategical considerations from their theological undergirding. They become mere pragmatists desiring success as measured by the number of people converted and churches started. The following definition of strategy guides missionaries to eliminate these two extremes.

# Definition of Strategy

**Strategy in missions is . . . the practical working out of the will of God within a cultural context.**

Because missions must begin with the wishes of the sovereign God yet function within the context of a social situation, strategy is defined as *the practical working out of the will of God within a cultural context*. Missionaries ask, "How does God desire that we minister within this context?" Seeking God's will for the culture, they work with national leaders to develop creative, God-centered, biblically critiqued strategies with well-defined goals.

Paul's letter to Titus illustrates the development of strategy for a specific cultural context. Titus was ministering among people of a demoralized culture where no central government existed, the economy had disintegrated, and insolence and arrogance reigned. A prophet, quoted by Paul, characterized his own people as "liars, evil brutes, lazy gluttons" (Titus 1:12). Even the Christians on Crete were described as "rebellious people, mere talkers and deceivers" who were "teaching things they ought not to teach" (vv. 10–11). Paul suggested to Titus an appropriate strategy for working in this demoralized culture. He directed Titus not to handle all the problems of the Cretan church by himself and to avoid petty arguments because they were "unprofitable and useless" (3:9). Rather, he was to appoint elders in every town, who would then determine God-ordained solutions to Cretan dilemmas. Throughout the process Titus was to remember that conversion is of God and that all believers were once foolish and disobedient, enslaved by passions and desires, but had been saved by God's mercy (vv. 3–7). Titus was to "stress these things, so that those who have trusted in God may be careful to devote themselves to doing what is good" (v. 8). Because of the demands of the gospel and the demoralization of the cultural milieu, Paul calls Titus to a focused ministry of mentoring, training, and ordaining Cretan leaders.

Old Testament leaders were also concerned about strategy. Moses' father-in-law, Jethro, saw that Moses was being worn out by the impossible task of judging all the disputes of Israel and that the people were also growing tired because of the lengthy proceedings. He, therefore, proposed a strategy for dealing with the situation. Moses was to appoint trustworthy, godly officials over thousands, hundreds, fifties, and tens, and these were to judge the people. Only difficult cases would be brought to Moses (Ex. 18:13–26). With such a strategic organizational model, the people of Israel could be more effectively judged.

The book of Proverbs provides numerous reflections and pieces of advice from godly people concerning effective planning:

> The mind of man plans his way,
>     but the LORD directs his steps. **16:9** NASB
> Every prudent man acts out of knowledge,
>     but a fool exposes his folly. **13:16**
> Plans fail for lack of counsel,
>     but with many advisers they succeed. **15:22**
> Commit to the LORD whatever you do,
>     and your plans will succeed. **16:3**
> Make plans by seeking advice;
>     if you wage war, obtain guidance. **20:18**

These verses express what Dayton and Fraser call "the tension of a paradox. God is in control and is sovereign; yet humans are free and responsible" (Dayton and Fraser 1990, 11). Making plans while praying and searching for God's will is not a denial of divine sovereignty but an acceptance of the fact that God works through faithful servants.

Christian strategies must leave room for the sovereignty of God. Humans are not self-sufficient nor able to predict all eventualities. Who could have predicted the fall of the Berlin Wall and the opening of Eastern Europe to the gospel? In 1985 Mikhail Gorbachev vowed that he would accomplish what his predecessors had failed to achieve: "the elimination of religious belief in the Soviet Union" (Johnstone 1986, 60). As recently as January 1989, the East German official who had been in charge of the actual building of the Berlin Wall in 1961 said that he could visualize the wall remaining for another hundred years. From a human perspective the wall was impenetrable. But as God used Nebuchadnezzar to deport an unfaithful Jewish nation from Israel and Cyrus to return these people from captivity, so God has used Gorbachev to open parts of the world that had been closed to the gospel. Should we not, likewise, expect God to shake the Muslim world and to continue to open China to the gospel?

Few churches question the urgency for the gospel to be proclaimed to the entire world, yet most Christians do not evangelize. This occurs because Christians have not been motivated by the message of God to make specific goals or strategies to evangelize. Having no goals is comfortable; without goals, there is no failure. If the gospel is ever to be proclaimed in all the world, Christians must feel God's compassion for the lost, understand the cultures of people among whom they live, and make specific plans for reaching them with the gospel, for nurturing them to maturity, and for training them in Christian leadership.

It is naive for missionaries to assume that all they need to do is exegete Scripture, learn the local language, and empathetically communicate with people. Although biblical, linguistic, and communicative skills are imperative to the missionary task, they do not displace the need for missiological strategy. Many movements stagnate because Christian leaders have not developed the creative capacities for strategic planning.

> **Many movements stagnate because Christian leaders have not developed the creative capacities for strategic planning.**

# Types of Strategies

For the sake of clarity strategies may be grouped under four general headings: (1) standard-solution strategies, (2) being-in-the-way strategies, (3) planning-so-far strategies, and (4) unique-solution strategies (adapted from Dayton and Fraser 1990, D36–39). Each of these four types of strategies has its own strengths and weaknesses and a degree of validity. However, unique solutions are needed if the goal of missions is to nurture initial believers to maturity in cohesive, reproducing churches with trained leaders and not merely to baptize individuals.

### Standard-Solution Strategies

Those who advocate standard-solution strategies assume that one approach can be used in every context of the world; it is the one-size-fits-all mentality. Evangelists develop methods that effectively work in particular contexts and then apply them to every situation. One example is the World Literature Crusade. This organization attempts to put a piece of Christian literature into the hands of every person in every city in the world. The assumption is that all people can read and make a decision for Christ if they are exposed to the right kind of literature. This approach also takes for granted that all people have the same problems and think in exactly the same ways. Churches of Christ developed a program called *One Nation Under God*. In this program an advertisement in *Reader's Digest* announced a nationwide mailing of 100 million booklets entitled *One Nation Under God*. Campaigns and campaign meetings were scheduled in every major center to reap a harvest of souls touched by the message of the booklet. The printed material has now been translated into various other languages, and the program exported to other areas of the world. While this standard-solution approach encouraged many local churches to cooperate, little long-term response was generated because of the lack of particularized application and training and the lack of impact of such a generalized approach.

The strength of the standard-solution approaches is that they reach many people in a short period of time. Awareness of the gospel or the church is enhanced, and doors are usually opened to a few new people.

These approaches, however, do not take into consideration the fact that cultures vary and that different approaches are needed in different contexts. They fail to account for people's cultural and social differences. Social contexts vary just as electricity varies in voltage and in the apparatuses used to harness it: Machines of 240 voltage cannot be powered by 110-volt systems, and two-pronged strategies will not be able to access power in three-pronged contexts. The voltage and prongs must be adapted to the context.

Thus standard-solution approaches typically reach many people but do not make a significant impact on them except where there is a spiritual vacuum. Standard-solution strategies must be coupled with other types of strategies.

### Being-in-the-Way Strategies

Being-in-the-way strategies emphasize the role of God in missions and evangelism and assume that human planning negates the divine role. Christians are not to worry about the future but simply allow themselves to be used by God. Long-range planning is not important; it is God's business.

There is much truth in this approach. God does lead in powerful and unexpected ways. God put Philip in the way of the Ethiopian, and the Ethiopian became a Christian (Acts 8:26–40). God directed Peter to teach Cornelius and his household (10:1–48).

Unfortunately, this strategy eliminates the possibility of failure and negates personal responsibility. If things go wrong, it is because God has other plans. When a summer campaign in Central Europe had low attendance, one missionary remarked that God sent only as many people as the missionaries could effectively handle. In reality, the missionaries had done very little to organize and publicize the campaign.

The strength of this philosophy is confidence in the working of God; its weakness is the negation of the need for long-range planning and training.

### Plan-So-Far Strategies

*Plan-so-far strategies* focus on beginnings rather than outcomes. Those who use this approach believe that if they plan to begin a work, God will do the rest. Plans are made to "hold a campaign" or have a "Bring Your Friend" day. During the early 1990s North American campaigners went into receptive areas of Eastern Europe. They attempted to plant a church through public lectures, distribution of tracts, teaching English as a second language, and personal Bible studies conducted through translators. Almost invariably the short-term workers left soon after the campaign, and little organized follow-up occurred. The focus was on converting the lost without a concurrent plan to nurture the lost to come under the kingship of God. The most significant long-term problem of missions is reversion, not conversion. Much more thought and effort must be put into nurturing new converts to fully come into the kingdom of God rather than merely converting people and leaving them.

Plan-so-far strategies, however, have one strength. They sometimes make beachheads into areas where the gospel would not otherwise go. Long-term missionaries, using unique solution strategies can then follow. For example, Partners in Progress, a medical missions organization overseen by the Sixth and Izard Church of Christ in Little Rock, Arkansas, has opened countries as diverse as Guyana, Romania, and Laos to missionaries of Churches of Christ. In each case the compassion of God expressed through medical missions teams opened the nations to long-term Christian missions.

## Unique-Solution Strategies

**Because people are unique, strategies must also be unique.**

Unique-solution strategies are based on the assumption that cultures and situations are different and each one requires its own special strategy. Dayton and Fraser write:

> People and culture are not like standardized machines that have interchangeable parts. We cannot simply use an evangelism approach that has worked in one context in another and expect the same results. Strategies must be as unique as the peoples to whom they apply. **1990, D38**

Ideally, Christian missionaries who use unique-solution strategies examine strategies that others have used in various contexts but do not copy them as such. These experiences, rather, become the reservoir out of which they are led by God to form unique strategy models appropriate for their own context. Some ideas are prayerfully borrowed and reshaped to fit the new context; other ideas are innovated as the community of believers determines how they should practically work out the ramifications of the kingdom of God for their context. Unique-solution strategies tend to be holistic in the sense that they emphasize both conversion and nurturing, and because of this, they lead to germinal churches. Because people are unique, strategies must also be unique.

In many ways strategizing for the mission of God is like preparing to preach a sermon. The preacher must prayerfully consider the biblical themes that his congregation needs, properly exegete Scriptures that speak to these themes, ardently look for metaphors and illustrations that make these themes live, and fervently pray for God's empowerment in delivering the sermon. Planning the sermon is a testimony of faithfulness to God. A well-developed strategy, reflecting the same interaction between the will of God and the condition of the culture, is an acknowledgment of the sovereignty of God, not a negation of it.

# BUILDING ON THE STRATEGICAL FOUNDATIONS

1. What discipline is described as the foundation of missiology? Give three specific reasons why this discipline is the foundational tier of missiology.
2. Describe the secondary tier of missiology. Why is the study of this area crucial to missiology?
3. Describe why strategy must be developed on the foundations of the lower two tiers of missiology.
4. Define *strategy*. Use Paul's letter to Titus to describe the importance of strategy to missions.
5. Why is it better to ask, "How does God desire for us to minister within this cultural context?" than to ask, "Does it work?" What is the difference between these two questions?
6. Briefly compare four types of strategies. Which type are you in basic agreement with? Why?

# CREATIVE STRATEGIES FOR PLANTING, NURTURING, AND TRAINING:
## Practical Ways of Implementing God's Purposes

Developing a strong movement of God in a new city or ethnic area requires the accomplishment of three essential tasks. First, initial evangelism must lead to planting new churches. Second, Christians must be nurtured to maturity within these churches. Third, leaders must be trained to evangelize and plant other churches, pastor and shepherd the community of believers, and train still other leaders. This chapter briefly surveys various strategies for accomplishing these primary mission tasks. While other mission tasks may amplify these three central tasks, a strong movement of God cannot come into being without their accomplishment.

## Planting New Churches

The theological and strategical foundations on which churches are planted greatly affect their ability to grow and mature. Paul encourages the church planter to "be careful how he builds." Sooner or later the builder's work will be tested with fire. Those who build with incombustible materials (gold, silver, and costly stones) will receive a reward, but those who build with combustible materials (wood, hay, and straw) will experience loss (1 Cor. 3:10–15).

## Definition of Church Planting

Church planting may be defined as *initiating reproductive fellowships that reflect the kingdom of God in the world*. A number of characteristics of church planting are reflected in this definition.

First, church planting is aimed at the creation of *fellowships*. The church is the *family* of God, the *body* of Christ (Eph. 1:23), a *people* "belonging to God" (1 Peter 2:9). These biblical metaphors indicate that the church must become a cohesive body reflecting the qualities of God in an alien world (vv. 11–12). Evangelistic methodologies should not scatter contacts who cannot be molded into bodies of believers; they must focus evangelism in one area for the purpose of creating a community of God. Converts must not be treated merely as individuals but must be incorporated into the body of Christ. Matayo Lang'at, a Kipsigis evangelist of Kenya, used a farming metaphor to explain why new Christians must work together to become part of a functioning fellowship:

> Here in Africa one person cannot cultivate with oxen by himself. There must be people in the field to guide the oxen on each side as well as one who holds the plow. Likewise, one cannot be the church by himself. He must call others who are in Christ to work together with him. **Translation from Kipsigis Sermon, 1976**

McGavran concurs: "Would-be disciples must be joyfully built into his body—they must not wander alone in the wilderness" (1990, 7). Too frequently a few new Christians are left to fend for themselves after a short campaign. New converts are led to the Lord and then left before a fellowship of believers has come into existence. These few Christians will likely fall away from God because they have not been incorporated into a fellowship that can mold and guide them in their spiritual journey.

Second, effective church planting focuses on cultivating *reproductive* fellowships. Many times churches are established without expecting the new converts to teach others. They are like seedless grapes, delightful to taste but without reproductive power, or they are like the fig tree that Jesus caused to wither because it did not bear fruit (Matt. 21:18–19).

Professor Wendell Broom has graphically described such churches as *terminal* (Broom 1976, 88–89). Terminal churches may have spiritual vitality but can reproduce only arithmetically (2, 4, 6, 8, 10, 12, etc.). Missionaries are teaching others but not training their converts to become reproductive; they are initiating churches but not preparing leaders of these churches to plant other churches.

Ten missionaries can each plant one church each year. If the churches they plant have *terminal* life, after ten years their field will have 100 churches. If the missionaries die or return home, the number of churches remains static, for they do not plant other churches. The same ten missionaries, by planting churches that have *germinal* life, will in ten years have 5,110 churches in their field. If the missionaries die or return home, the churches will continue to multiply, because they have germinal life. **Broom 1976, 88**

The author of Hebrews described terminal churches when he wrote, "Though by this time you ought to be teachers, you need someone to teach you the elementary truths of God's word all over again. You need milk, not solid food!" (5:12).

**Geometric church growth can be illustrated by strawberry plants or Bermuda grass, which sends out runners in every direction; these runners develop their own root systems and send out still new runners until the field is covered.**

Germinal churches grow geometrically (2, 4, 8, 16, 32, 64, 128, 256, 512, etc.). They reproduce like rabbits in Australia, bananas in Bermuda, and papayas in fertile areas of tropical Africa. They are like starfish, which multiply when cut into pieces. It is within the nature of each part to reproduce. Geometric church growth can be illustrated by strawberry plants or Bermuda grass, which sends out runners in every direction; these runners develop their own root systems and send out still new runners until the field is covered. The roots each represent a new church or cell group planted in a new village or new area of the city. Once the Christian community develops sufficient roots it is able to plant still other fellowships. Paul urged Timothy to encourage his converts to become germinal: "The things you have heard me say in the presence of many witnesses [germination 1] entrust to reliable men [germination 2] who will also be qualified to teach others [germination 3]" (2 Tim. 2:2).

Greg Newton describes such germinal growth among the Sukuma of Tanzania. The first churches established among the Sukuma were *missionary plants*. The missionaries planned where they would preach and did all the teaching. The next six churches were *co-plants*. Sukuma Christians worked with missionaries in selecting the locations for establishing new churches, went with them each week to the meetings, and did some of the teaching, depending on their level of maturity. In March 1994, after three years of work among the Sukuma, two *independent plantings* occurred. The location of the plantings, plans for the evangelistic meetings, and the teaching in the area were all done without missionary participation (Newton 1994a, 1). Germinal church growth had begun!

Certain Christian beliefs provide special impetus to germinal growth. Anticipation of and preparation for the second coming of Christ is one such belief. When Christians perceive of themselves as standing between the first and second comings of Christ, they are motivated to teach those around them to prepare for his return. The reality that this world is temporary—that the Christians' real identity is in heaven—helps disciples of Christ to understand their place in the world and propels them to speak of eternal realities. The understanding that God is active and is convicting the world of sin through the Holy Spirit (John 16:7–11) is another germinal belief. Christians who believe in God's mighty acts will be ready when the Holy Spirit touches them to teach a Cornelius or an Ethiopian. Their lives are tuned in to God's reality rather than secular "realities" that deny the active working of God. Greg Newton reflects on the great church growth among the Sukuma with this comment: "We praise God for the Spirit which is moving to inspire Christians to evangelize" (1994b, 1). Belief in the temporary nature of this world and the working of the Holy Spirit are thus two beliefs foundational to germinal growth.

Third, church planting is more than the mere creation of fellowships. These fellowships must have accepted God as their sovereign and struggle to reflect his nature. Thus church planting is the *developing of reproductive fellowships that reflect the kingdom of God in the world*. The term *fellowship* expresses the horizontal relationships among Christians within the body; the phrase *that reflect the kingdom of God in the world* expresses the vertical relationship between God and the fellowship over which he reigns. This distinction is vital because a church fellowship can divorce itself from the divine and become largely a social fraternity, much like the local Kiwanis or Rotary club. This type of fellowship has no divine impetus to germinate.

Fourth, this definition assumes that nurturing must follow the initial planting of the church. Bodies of believers are not superficially planted and then left but are cared for until they "reflect the kingdom of God in the world." The term *initiating* implies that something must follow the planting of the church.

### Guidelines for Effective Planting of New Churches

Specifics of church planting vary from context to context. However, four general guidelines are fundamental in every context:

First, church planters must look at their work as a spiritual activity. They must pray and fast both for the city or ethnic group in which God has placed them and for God's empowerment for the task of evangelizing. They must realize that the people of this particular area have not previously become followers of God, because they are still under the dominion of Satan. Christ, however, has come "to destroy the devil's work" (1 John 3:8). Church planters, therefore, must pray for wisdom and empowerment from God, realizing that evangelization is ultimately the taking of territory that once belonged to Satan and claiming it for the kingdom of God. Prayer is a recognition of God's role, an acknowledgment that only God in Jesus Christ can deliver the people from the grip of sin and the clutches of the Evil One. Evangelizing unbelievers and nurturing them to grow in Christ is not primarily a human endeavor but God's working through his people.

Second, church planters must visualize what God's church should look like within their target culture and seek to implement this vision. In every culture the church must reflect the presence of God because it is *the distinctive people of God called by him through his mission and set aside for his mission*.[1] However, the forms of church vary from culture to culture. These forms include such items as language, worship, and decision making. Should a Russian church speak English in worship services and rely on American models of the church? Should the songs reflect the rhythms and harmonies of Western music? Are decisions made by foreigners or by nationals, are they reached by voting or by consensus? Christian meanings must be communicated in indigenous forms. The people of the land should not perceive the church as a foreign religion but as a part of the indigenous society. This does not mean that Christianity will be compromised or that syncretism with non-Christian religious elements will take place. It means that Christian beliefs will be communicated in terms acceptable and meaningful to the culture in which the church is planted. Like a banana plant in the Bahamas,[2] the church thrives within the culture because it allows God to use the resources of the culture rather than superficially borrowing cultural forms from a foreign source.

Third, church planters must learn to communicate God's eternal message within the plausibility structures of the people in the culture.

---

[1]Chapter 1 offers a fuller theology of the church.

[2]One day while traveling in Canada I noticed banana plants set out before a house. I inquired how banana plants could grow in Canada and learned that they must have special care. During cold periods, the plants were uprooted and taken indoors to be replanted during warm summer periods. The plants had also never produced fruit! Like transplanted banana plants, American churches planted in foreign lands need special care just to survive and are not able to reproduce.

The thought that Christ has defeated the principalities and powers (Col. 1:15) has little impact on secular Americans who have little understanding of spiritual powers. This concept of Christ, the triumphal One who has defeated the spirits is, however, the metaphor that stirs the heart of the animist and brings him to the foot of the cross (Van Rheenen 1991, 141–42). Only in Christ is there deliverance from the fear and control of the satanic realm. Church-planting missionaries thus enter a new culture as *learners* seeking to glean understandings concerning how to communicate God's message and to initiate a church that reflects the kingdom of God within this cultural context.

Fourth, church planters must learn what web relationships[3] tie people of the culture together. Kinship, although more dominant in rural societies than in urban cultures, is the dominant web relationship. In Africa, Asia, and Latin America,

> the web counts tremendously. Every man has, knows and is intimate with not merely brothers, sisters, and grandparents, but also with cousins, uncles, aunts, great-uncles, sisters-in-law, mothers-in-law ... and many others.... Members of other clans or families can become Christian and he remains unmoved; but let "one of us" become Christian and he is deeply stirred. **McGavran 1970, 321**

The Kipsigis of Kenya live in patriarchal extended families. According to the research of Fielden Allison, 87 percent of all churches in Kipsigis were initiated through kinship contacts, and the strongest churches were those with many interwoven kinship relationships. The most effective teaching relationship was that of an older brother teaching a younger brother or sister (1983, 56–67).

Relationships in urban contexts become increasingly complex. Occupational and associational ties vie with kinship relationships for the time and allegiance of the people. Mr. Chun is a Christian banker who leads a cell group of financial leaders in Seoul, Korea. This group meets each week in the nonthreatening atmosphere of a restaurant. Their goal is to bring two monetary consultants to Christ each year and nurture them to maturity within their small group. Evangelization in this context is following occupational networkings.

[3]Web relationships are the kinship and associational ties that connect people of a culture together.

The church-planting missionary must map out the web relationships that serve to connect people to people. The gospel travels down these relational pathways.

# Nurturing New Christians

The second major task of missions is nurturing new Christians to maturity. The Kipsigis say, "We cannot give birth to children and then leave them" (*"Magisiche lagok si kebagach."*). In this age of international travel it is relatively easy for Western Christians to travel to another land, preach the gospel through translators for a few days, convert a few souls hungry to know God (and sometimes to know Americans), and leave them without basic understandings of the Christian faith and without the ability to work out this faith in their everyday lives. It will become obvious in this section that the major problem of missions is not *conversion* of unbelievers to Christ but *reversion* from Christ.

### Definition of Nurturing

Nurturing stems from the very heart of God. God is a vinedresser who devotedly tends his vineyard (Isa. 5:1–7), a physician who tenderly nurses his patients (Jer. 8:22), and a parent who lovingly teaches his child to walk (Hos. 11:1, 3). These prophetic metaphors reflect God's desire to relate personally to Israel, his chosen people. God is portrayed in Scripture as the ever-present, compassionate Lord who sends his messengers to nurture his people to come into relationship with him.

Paul had much to say about nurturing in his letter to the Ephesians. The church is described as the body that, although living on the earth, dwells in the heavenlies with the resurrected Christ. This body has been transformed from death to life by the extension of God's grace in Jesus Christ (1:18–2:10). Those of Christ's body—both Jews and Gentiles—must grow together to become one. They should no longer be "foreigners and aliens" but "fellow citizens with God's people and members of God's household" (2:11–22, esp. v. 19). This unity is based on God's four-dimensional love. Paul writes,

> I pray that you, being rooted and established in love, may have power, together with all the saints, to grasp how wide and long and high and deep is the love of Christ, and to know this love that surpasses knowledge—that you may be filled to the measure of all the fullness of God. **Eph. 3:17–19**

The gifts of the body are to be joined together so that each part does its function. When this occurs, the body "becomes mature" in Christ, no longer like "infants, tossed back and forth by the waves, and blown here and there by every wind of teaching" (Eph. 4:14; see vv. 7–16).

Nurturing, then, is building up the body of Christ so that each part of the body supplies its gift or gifts to the whole. It is the process of bringing individual Christians and the Christian community as a whole to maturity. It implies that new believers must be taught how a Christian worldview shapes and influences all facets of life. Nurturing is the preparation to withstand the fire of Satan's persecution. It is relationally mentoring new believers to live out Christian principles in their life.

### Guidelines for Effective Nurturing

Methodologies of nurturing, like those of church planting, vary greatly, depending on the philosophy of missionaries and church leaders and the context in which they are working. However, there are certain general guidelines that apply to all situations.

First, nurturing is most effectively done in the context of a loving, caring community of believers. Roberta Hestenes writes, "The Christian life is not a solitary journey. It is a pilgrimage made in the company of the committed" (1983, 11). A recurrent theme of early Christian writings is that spiritual nurturing took place within the context of Christian fellowship. It was not an individual endeavor:

> They devoted themselves to the apostles' teaching and to the fellowship, to the breaking of bread and to prayer. . . . Every day they continued to meet together in the temple courts. They broke bread in their homes and ate together with glad and sincere hearts, praising God and enjoying the favor of all the people.
> **Acts 2:42, 46–47**

Nurturing, therefore, is not an individual endeavor but must become part of the structure of the Christian community. Christians are guided to know God and find their gifts and ministries within the context of intimate fellowship within the body of Christ.

Second, nurturing leads new Christians to visualize specifically what God desires them to become. Because they only feebly understand the transforming grace of God, undiscipled Christians are frequently overwhelmed by their own sins and inadequacies. They must grow to know the radical nature of conversion and how to live distinctively as pure people in the kingdom of God. Conversion is a radical *turning of self to God*

(Wells 1989, 30–36). The lost must turn from darkness to light, from death to life, from the dominion of Satan to the kingdom of God (Acts 26:18). They become new creatures who have spiritually been elevated into the heavenlies to dwell with Christ (Eph. 2:6). Through such understandings new Christians begin to perceive that they can become holy as God is holy (1 Peter 1:15). They can imagine themselves standing with the heavenly host proclaiming, "Holy, holy, holy is the Lord God Almighty" (Rev. 4:8; cf. Isa. 6:3). They are so consumed by the love of God that they love their enemies in the midst of suffering, forgiving as Christ forgave those who crucified him.

Third, nurturing involves modeling the Christian disciplines. Christians must be discipled to turn their hearts and wills to God in *prayer*, humble themselves before God in *fasting*, acknowledge through *worship* that God is God, seek God's truth through *Bible study*, and reflect on God's work in their lives through *meditation*. Without specific mentoring, "Christians" may embrace the forms of Christianity but not grow spiritually through the Christian disciplines.

Fourth, nurturing must be an ongoing process; otherwise, the church grows stale and dies. One generation teaches the next generation, which in turn teaches the third:

> *He commanded our forefathers to teach their children, so the next generation would know them, even the children yet to be born, and they in turn would tell their children.* **Ps. 78:5–6**

Nurturing is passing the baton of faith from generation to generation. Without effective nurturing the baton is seldom passed to the next generation.

### Rural Models of Nurturing

Effective mission workers in rural areas almost always target a specific ethnic group, one homogeneous unit. The people typically live in large extended families and know everyone in their village. Contacts for evangelism and church planting flow principally along kinship lines. Numerous congregations are initiated because of the distance people live from one another and the expense of travel. The model of church nurturing used in the Kipsigis work in western Kenya has been adopted and revised by the works of numerous African missions (Van Rheenen 1983a, 79–86). It will be presented in this section in revised form.

From the beginning of the work in Kipsigis, church-planting missionaries were concerned with church nurturing. A methodology of maturing churches was developed after an in-depth study of the concept of the church as the body of Christ in the book of Ephesians (Van Rheenen 1983a, 73–79). A mature church was understood as a congregation organized with its own elders, deacons, and evangelists who had matured to the point that it could "build itself up in love, as each part does its work" (Eph. 4:16). The people within the church had grown to become "fellow citizens with God's people and members of God's household." They were no longer "aliens and strangers" (1 Peter 2:11).

Building on this foundation, Kipsigis church planters developed four stages through which all churches were to be matured. The role of the initial church planter, whether missionary or national evangelist, changed according to the degree of maturity of a local church (Van Rheenen 1983a, 79–88).

The *Initial Church Stage* is the introductory evangelism phase of the church, when the first converts are brought to Christ. At this point the new converts are hardly a group. They will likely not yet know the names of the books of the Bible, how to pray, or how to teach the central themes of the Christian faith. They are like newborn children, not yet knowing how to walk. As "foreigners and aliens" to one another, they must be incorporated into the body of Christ. During this stage the church planter serves primarily as an *evangelist* who proclaims the foundational message of the gospel: God has acted to save his people despite their sins; God has accomplished this mighty act of reconciliation in Jesus Christ; humankind, however, must respond to him in faith and obedience. The objective of this stage is to gain enough converts to form a vibrant group. This stage may take from three weeks to three months, depending on the receptivity of the people within the village. It is important to begin the second stage as soon as possible in order to incorporate the young Christians into a body. The joy of this stage is seeing a congregation born through public and private proclamation of the gospel.

The incorporation or "body building" period is called the *Developing Church Stage*. During this stage initial Christians are mentored to become a germinally reproducing, cohesive body through both cognitive and experiential teaching. The church planter serves as a *church maturer*, nurturing each member of the body to serve the function that God has given him or her within the body. The church planter assumes the role of mentor, spending one or two days each week visiting from house to house and holding evangelistic and nurturing meetings throughout the village. This relationship with the new Christians is like that of Paul during the early days of the Thessalonian church:

> *We were gentle among you, like a mother caring for her little children. We loved you so much that we were delighted to share with you not only the gospel of God but our lives as well, because you had become so dear to us.* **1 Thess. 2:7–8**

**New Christians should never be elevated to leadership roles by outsiders in developing mission churches. Leaders should be called by God in the midst of active church life rather than artificially selected before nurturing.**

During the Developing Church Stage, the church planting evangelist seeks to nurture all Christians within the fellowship. Out of this in-depth congregational training, leaders emerge as God works within the body. *New Christians should never be elevated to leadership roles by outsiders in developing mission churches.* Leaders should be called by God in the midst of active church life rather than artificially selected before nurturing.

The church planter asks two significant questions during this incorporation stage. The first question is, "Do Christians understand the central truths of the Christian faith?" The concepts taught during this stage are the basic building blocks of the Christian faith. Although I published a list of concepts that should be taught during this stage (Van Rheenen 1983a, 81–82), I now think it wiser for each church planting team to develop its own curriculum for teaching and nurturing during each stage. The second question the church planter must ask during this stage is, "Is the Christian worldview, defined by biblical truths, being practically lived out?" The church planter must so intimately relate to the new Christians that he not only teaches the concepts of the Christian faith but also guides the new Christians in living out the concepts. The joy of this stage is seeing new Christians grow into a cohesive body able to stand on their own.

Two extremes must be avoided during the Developing Church Stage. If the church planter concentrates on a particular church for too long, the church may look foreign and become dominated. If, on the other hand, there is not enough concentrated teaching, the church may not internalize basic Christian concepts. This can result in its eventual disintegration or syncretism with non-Christian beliefs and forms.

This stage takes from six to fifteen months, depending on how quickly the church matures as a body. Frequently stronger churches mature quickly and weaker ones more slowly.

The third period of maturation, the **Independent Church Stage**, begins when the founding church planter is able to allow local leaders to assume all major leadership roles. The church is able to stand on its own feet, independent of the founding evangelist. Frequently a rite of separation—a time of commissioning, of laying on of hands to commend the

> As a guest, the church planter may come periodically to exhort and strengthen the body, but his presence is not needed for the ongoing life of the body.

new church to the Lord—occurs as a church enters this stage. The church has now developed enough leadership to function as a cohesive body without the continual presence of the initial church-planting missionary.

A church in the independent stage is ready to begin leadership training. God has raised up those qualified to become the leaders of a mature church. The church planter thus becomes a *periodic catalyst to train leaders*. The objective is to train leaders to the point that local Christians are able to "build themselves up in love" (Eph. 4:16). The joy of this stage is seeing leaders develop.

If leadership training precedes the congregational training of the Developing Church Stage, a sharp distinction between clergy and laity develops, one that can rarely be overcome merely by concentrated teaching on the subject. Also, if leaders are selected by outsiders and trained before a fellowship is incorporated, those trained leaders often are not respected by local village leaders and therefore are seldom able to initiate a fellowship. It is better for church leaders to be selected from fellowships that are maturing. The nature of leadership training will be more fully described in the next section.

The **Mature Church Stage** is the final period of church maturation. At the beginning of this stage and after intense leadership training during the Independent Church Stage ordained church leaders are selected. Elders are selected to pastor the flock; deacons are chosen to serve in various ministries; evangelists are set aside to lead the congregation to proclaim God's redemptive message both in the local village and in adjoining areas. Sunday school teachers and other ministry leaders are also selected. The founding church planter can now look at the church and see with joy how God has worked to bring this body to maturity. The ordination of these trained leaders thus implies that the founding church planter now assumes the role of occasional guest. As a guest, the church planter may come periodically to exhort and strengthen the body, but his presence is not needed for the ongoing life of the body. He must overcome the temptation to maintain control over the mature church, thus preventing the church from continuing on its own.

Churches in Kipsigis were classified according to their stage of maturity. For example, of the one hundred Kipsigis churches in 1987, twelve were in the Initial Stage, thirteen in the Developing Stage, sixty-eight in the Independent Stage, and seven in the Mature Stage. Specific goals were set each year in terms of church maturation. For example, in 1982 my personal goals were to (1) plant two new churches during the year (one during the first six months of the year and one during the next six months), (2) nurture one initial and one developing church all the way to the Independent Church Stage, and (3) teach ten leadership courses to leaders of Independent churches on how to use the themes of prophetic literature to strengthen local churches in Kipsigis.

The following time line depicts the spiritual maturation of a Kipsigis church from its inception to its becoming mature.

| Stage of Church Maturation | Initial | Developing | Independent | Mature |
|---|---|---|---|---|
| Role of the Church Planter | Evangelist | Church Maturer | Trainer of Leaders/ Periodic Catalyst | Guest |

**Figure 9. Time Line Designating the Kipsigis Nurturing Model**

Our schedule in Kipsigis reflected in a practical way our goals to plant initial churches, nurture Christians to maturity in developing churches, and train leaders in independent churches. I reserved Monday as family day. From Tuesday through Thursday I worked one day with other Kipsigis evangelists to initiate a new church and two days to nurture two developing churches to become independent. On two weekends each month (Friday to Sunday) I taught areawide training courses for leaders of independent churches. Kipsigis was divided into ten areas with training courses conducted in all ten areas. During alternate weeks when I was not conducting a leadership course, I gave additional attention to the village where a church was being planted, to the two congregations who were being nurtured to maturity, to lesson preparation, or to special family activities. I also worked to prepare lessons every morning before leaving for the day's activities. An effective teacher is always a prepared one. This schedule provided diversity of ministry and contact with numerous types of people: In one week I worked with initial, developing, and independent churches.

### Urban Models of Nurturing

*Contrast Between Rural and Urban Contexts.* Because of differing social contexts, strategies for urban church planting are significantly different from those for rural models. Rural areas are largely homogeneous whereas urban centers are heterogeneous and pluralistic. In rural localities people tend to live in extended families and know everyone within the immediate village; in urban contexts people live in close proximity to thousands of other people but paradoxically are neighbors with few of them (Smalley 1978, 708–10). In rural communities kinship is the dominant relationship connecting people; in urban societies associational and occupational webs overlay kinship relationships and frequently are considered more important. In the urban environment people become more job oriented and less family oriented. In rural areas education originally consisted of the informal learning of subsistence skills; urban contexts, however, required the formal learning of technological and informational skills. People grew to believe that they could control and manipulate their universe rather than live in submission to it.

*Urban Mentalities.* Four characteristics delineate the mentality of the world's urban people:

First, a passion for commodities consumes the urban consciousness. People are overwhelmed by culturally induced "needs" for material things. Advertisements bombard the senses, declaring that people cannot live without certain items.

Second, communities are disintegrating. Many people are so focused on the demands of their jobs and the social responsibilities inherent in them that family time and involvement are minimized. The cohesion traditionally present in world cultures is disintegrating as a result of the breakup of extended and nuclear families. Jerrold Footlick in a special edition of *Newsweek* on "the 21st-century family" writes:

> Marriage is a fragile institution—not something anyone can count on. . . . The divorce rate has doubled since 1965, and demographers project that half of all first marriages made today will end in divorce. Six out of 10 second marriages will probably collapse. One-third of all children born in the past decade will probably live in a stepfamily before they are 18. One out of every four children today is being raised by a single parent. About 22 percent of children today were born out of wedlock; of those, about a third were born to a teenage mother. One out of every five children lives in poverty; the rate is twice as high among blacks and Hispanics. . . . Parents feel torn between work and family obligations. Marriage is a fragile institution—not something anyone can count on.
> **1990, 16**

This disintegration of the social fabric results in intense loneliness! People, as social beings, yearn to live in community but are forced by culture to live privatized lives.

Third, culture is becoming exceedingly complex. Humans, therefore, are forced to make innumerable decisions. The increasing options of the material marketplace—models of cars, brands of food, and types of housing—are reflected in the ideological marketplace. Many people believe that they can choose to be homosexual or bisexual; monogamous, polygamous, or promiscuous; married or single. They can ascribe to Buddhism, Hinduism, Islam, New Age, or Christianity, or any form of these religions. People can seek to relate to the god *within* through meditation (pantheism), or believe that God is uninvolved in the world he created (deism), or seek to relate to a personal creator God through prayer (theism). In this pluralistic culture the innumerable options available create disequilibrium.

Fourth, cultural relativism, spawned by Western individualism, is a typical urban response to culture's complexity. Cultural relativism is the perception that there is no absolute truth in the world. Relativists believe that diversity should be tolerated, that each person is entitled to his own beliefs, and that all perceptions of truth are valid.

In order to survive and to reflect the nature of God, the church must encounter each of these urban mentalities. The church must seek release from the bondage of materialism by teaching and modeling sacrifice for the cause of Christ. In the midst of the disintegrating community, the church must be the community of God—an intimate fellowship ministering to the lonely who live among the urban masses. In complex, urban contexts Christian leaders must become "meaning-makers," clearly articulating the central tenets of the Christian faith eternally rooted in the nature of God. Posterski writes:

> Meaning-makers are people who make sense of life, people who make sense of God, people whose lives ring with clarity in the midst of contemporary ambiguity, people who have integrity, people who reside in today's world revealing with their living and their lips that Jesus' death is the source of vital life. **1989, 15**

These urban mentalities demonstrate the need for radically different models of strategy. These urban strategy models must provide community in an impersonal urban environment and stand against the materialism and relativism of urban life. Urban churches that lack organized structures for providing nurturing on an intimate, personal level are nominal and stagnant, unable to reach out.

*Small-Group Methodologies in Urban Contexts.* Many urban missiologists are suggesting various types of small-group ministries. Roberta Hestenes describes using small-group evangelism in the context of more traditional program-based churches (1983). *Program-based churches* organize the church around specialized ministries (Sunday schools, 12-step programs, "Friends Day," etc.) and seek to attract unbelievers through these programs. Ralph Neighbour (1990) and Carl George (1991), suggest creating cell-based churches. *Cell-based churches* organize the spiritual life of the church around small groups. These cells serve as beacons for reaching the lost, assimilating new Christians into Christian fellowship, and providing spiritual nurture for all Christians. George's *metachurch model* suggests a highly organized church that worships together on Sunday in a large celebration meeting but uses small cell groups of fifteen or fewer people to nurture believers and incorporate unbelievers.

Ralph Neighbour's *cell-group church* considers the cell a fundamental unit of the church. Neighbour suggests that cell-group churches are more appropriate for world-class cities because (1) they involve many more than the traditional 10 to 15 percent of the membership in the activities of the church; (2) Christians become part of a community of believers in which they feel a sense of belonging; (3) Christians in small groups focus on prayer; (4) the church personally and deeply penetrates the structures of the city; (5) their structures are "flexible, able to adapt to their environment"; (6) they are not "circumscribed by the size of a building"; and (7) the gospel is communicated in terms of the life of the community rather than through cognitive, impersonal propositions. These cell groups effectively reach non-Christian urban cultures because (1) they provide numerous points of light within neighborhoods, (2) they focus on the needs to make contacts with unbelievers, (3) the group holds members accountable to God and equips them to break the strongholds of Satan, and (4) the laity are trained to testify and proclaim the message of Jesus Christ within the context of intimate community (Neighbour 1990, 21–23).[4]

Yonggi Cho of Seoul, Korea, was one of the first to form a cell-based church. This congregation grew from 5 people meeting in a tent in 1958

---

[4]Perhaps the most significant text on developing a cell-based church is William A. Beckham, *The Second Reformation: Reshaping the Church for the 21st Century* (Houston: Touch Publications, 1995).

to a church of over 700,000 people today. In 1964, when this congregation had grown to 3,800 members, Cho fainted from mental exhaustion because he was trying to do all the work of the church himself. During this time, he read Jethro's advice to Moses: "The work is too heavy for you; you cannot handle it alone. . . . But select capable men from all the people . . . and appoint them as officials over thousands, hundreds, fifties and tens" (Ex. 18:17, 21). Soon afterward he instituted cell groups to be channels of growth and to provide pastoral care for the church. By so doing, he began to equip hundreds of lay people to carry on the work of the church.

These cells were developed around the homogeneous (people group) principle, namely, that Christian groups most effectively evangelize if they minister to similar types of people. McGavran expressed the principle by saying, "Men and women like to become Christians without crossing barriers" (1979, 227). Housewives find more in common with other housewives than with female teachers; factory workers have more in common with other factory workers than with medical practitioners. Financial administrators sense more commonality with other money managers than they feel with doctors or college professors. Cell groups based on geography are consumed with trying to develop a feeling of oneness; groups based on homogeneity more easily develop a sense of unity. All other programs of the church, including the Sunday assembly, make no distinction between types of people within the church. Cho writes that

> the homogeneous unit principle is used in developing our cell system, not in developing our entire church. We do not differentiate between rich and poor, high and low, or well-educated and uneducated; we are all one in the body of Christ. **1984, 51–54**

McGavran said that this church may be the most organized in the world (see Towns 1982, 66). Members are intimately related to the members of the cell group that they attend and are nurtured within this context. All cell group leaders go through a prescribed training program to prepare them to nurture the group. Cell group leaders are trained both in special training courses and by working as assistants to trained leaders. When a group grows to become two, an assistant is prepared to lead one of the groups. A treasurer is chosen to handle the finances of each group. A *licensed* minister shepherds participants of every thirty cells. The cells are divided into twelve districts, each overseen by an *ordained* minister. Each level of leaders has a specific type of experiential training (Cho 1984, 54). Cho expects these leaders to surface naturally. His job is then "to direct that leadership quality toward useful service to the whole church" (1984, 59).

Cho, in collaboration with church leaders, prayerfully sets goals for growth. Upon entering their new facility in 1973, the congregation set a five-year goal of 50,000 members by the end of 1978. That goal was attained in only four years. A goal to grow to 100,000 members by 1981 was achieved two years ahead of schedule. Each cell group set specific goals for outreach, and each family was asked to reach another family during the year. Expectation of growth was, therefore, built into the life of the church.

Although nurturing in small groups is neither exclusively urban nor the only model of effective urban modeling, it does (1) provide the community that is so necessary for urban missions, (2) multiply the number of trained lay leaders, and (3) can personally nurture disciples to live distinctive lives in the midst of the complexity and relativity of urban cultures.

# Training Leaders

The third major task of missions is training leaders. As I stated earlier, in rapidly maturing Christian movements leaders are seldom *selected*; they are *found*. They are raised up by God while the whole church is being nurtured to perform various ministries within the body. Congregational nurturing, therefore, must always precede or be coupled with leadership training. In the midst of this congregational nurturing God raises up leaders and places them in the body "just as he [wants] them to be" (1 Cor. 12:18). Once these leaders rise to the surface, they should be specifically trained.

### Definition of Leadership Training

Christian leadership training is *the equipping of "God's people for works of service, so that the body of Christ may be built up"* (Eph. 4:12). Christ is the prime mover of leadership development because he has provided, by his grace, specific gifts to the body (vv. 7–8,10; cf. 3:7) and thus prepares various leaders (apostles, prophets, evangelists, and pastors and teachers) to nurture the body (4:11). *Equipping* implies a process of growing to maturity: The separated become unified; infants grow to maturity; the empty attain to the "fullness of Christ"; those blown about by worldly winds or "tossed back and forth" by non-Christian cultural currents become anchored in Christ (vv. 13–14). The *works of service* of these leaders can thus be summarized by the phrase *spiritual formation*. The leaders, performing their diverse tasks, guide the entire body to "grow up into . . .

Christ" by "speaking the truth in love" (v. 15). These ministries of spiritual formation lead to building up the body of Christ to become a mature church. A mature church is one in which all parts are related to Christ and joined to each other, while the body continues to grow and "builds itself up in love, as each part does its work" (v. 16).

In the social sciences, leadership is frequently defined as *the process of influence*. Leaders are those who exert influence over followers within the immediate situation and in the overall community in which they live. Leaders shape the goals, values, and worldviews of the people within these contexts (Elliston 1992, 21). Clinton defines a Christian leader as one who brings the Christian influence into his particular group or situation. He writes that a leader is "a person with God-given capacity and with a God-given responsibility to *influence* a specific group of God's people toward God's purposes for the group" (1988, 245). Although it contains truth, the influence metaphor has its dangers. Too frequently influence is understood as power to manipulate the material and social order. When influence is defined as power, it stands in contrast to biblical metaphors.

Elliston suggests three dominant metaphors that define leadership in Scripture (1992, 23–24). First, Christian leaders are *servants* who voluntarily submit themselves to the lordship of Christ and the sovereignty of God. This meaning of the term is frequently inverted: the mighty become servants of the weak. Christ "did not come to be served, but to serve, and to give his life as a ransom for many" (Mark 10:45). Just as divinity serves humanity, those "great" in this world must become servants (v. 43). Second, Christian leaders are *shepherds* who tenderly care for their flock. This analogy implies that the shepherds feed, protect, and guide their flock. They know the names of their sheep and will even lay down their lives for them. The true shepherd "gathers the lambs in his arms and carries them close to his heart" (Isa. 40:11). Third, leaders are *stewards* who "are entrusted with the message of the gospel, gifts for ministry, and [God's mission] to perform" (Elliston 1992, 24). Stewards are "trustees" guarding "what has been entrusted to [their] care" (1 Tim. 6:20). Blending the metaphors of servant, shepherd, and steward produces the distinctive hue of leadership intended by God.

### Types of Leaders

Vibrant Christian movements require different kinds of leaders. Five types will be described in this section.[5]

[5]The writings of Elliston (1992, 26–35) and Clinton (1988, 246) have been formative in this discussion. They have built on the initial classification of Donald McGavran,

**Blending the metaphors of servant, shepherd, and steward produces the distinctive hue of leadership intended by God.**

*Type A* leaders are lay servants who provide massive grassroots leadership in local churches. Within the church they may serve as cell-group leaders, Bible class teachers, youth organizers, and committee participants and leaders. Within the community they serve as beacons of light for the gospel—the frontline soldiers of the kingdom of God. Unbelievers have most contact with this type of leader, and new believers are typically nurtured by Type A leaders in vibrant, growing churches.

*Type B* are also lay leaders, but they have more authority and broader influence than Type A leaders. They serve as elders and deacons of local churches, supervisors of Sunday school programs, mentors of cell-group leaders, and lay counselors. In various mission contexts, especially in the Two-thirds World, Type B leaders are unpaid evangelists who preach in local churches or work to initiate other churches. Like Type A leaders, their ministries are direct or face-to-face but, unlike Type A leaders, their influence extends beyond their immediate group.

*Type C* leaders in Western contexts are full-time ministers in local congregational settings; they are involved in face-to-face ministry but are likely to be bivocational in the Two-thirds World. Their sphere of influence is the local church and the community in which it exists. They usually have some form of theological education that has equipped them to preach, teach, and evangelize. Their influence is generally deep but not broad—significant among those to whom they minister but not extensive beyond their local area.

*Type D* leaders have a regional influence much wider than in the church or agency in which they work. They serve as full-time ministers of multistaff or multicell churches, as administrators of small agencies, or as missionaries planting churches, nurturing new Christians to maturity, and training leaders in a domestic or foreign context. These leaders have completed a formal system of training, and their influence reaches beyond the people with whom they personally relate (adapted from Elliston 1992, 31).

*Type E* leaders are those Christians who have national or international influence. These are highly competent professional leaders who, because of their writing, teaching, and speaking, greatly influence the nature of ministry. They provide the philosophical models out of which ministry occurs. Although much of their ministry is indirect, they influ-

who in 1969 in a lectureship at Columbia Bible College first described five types of leaders for growing churches, and Lois McKinney's article, "Training Leaders," in *Discipline Through Theological Education by Extension*, edited by Virgil Gerber (1980).

ence many people. Type D and E leaders, to some degree, must remain Type A and B leaders in order to continue to be connected to real life.

Understanding these different types of leaders enables local and national church leaders to make plans for appropriate leadership training. As we consider these types of leaders, it becomes apparent that mature churches need hundreds of Type A and B leaders but, in many contexts, no program for training them exists. For effective evangelism to occur, all people in a community must be influenced personally, face-to-face. Elliston says, "The number of people one may . . . directly influence at a worldview level may range between ten and twenty." If there are 100,000 people in a community and if leaders relate to an optimum of ten people personally within the community, 10,000 Type A leaders are needed, 1,000 Type B, 100 Type C, ten Type D, and one Type E (1992, 31). Since Types C, D, and E leaders usually have a broad theological education, they tend to understand leadership training only in formal terms: Leadership training is interpreted as formal training. Specifically, what types of training do Types A and B need? Broadly, what modes of training are effective for different types of leaders?

## Modes of Leadership Training

A study of curriculum theory is significant in planning the training of leaders. Elliston writes:

> Curriculum theory suggests that the broad outlines of the results can be predicted from the kinds of educational structures and processes which are employed. One can look at the goals and then work backward to design or modify the structures and processes to match the goals. Or, we can begin with a structure and predict the kind of results we are likely to achieve. **1988, 211**

Curriculum theory differentiates among three modes of training—formal, nonformal, and informal. Effective leadership training blends these modes of training into different combinations in order to train various types of leaders.

*Formal Training.* Formal training refers to classroom instruction within an organized school setting. This mode is extremely beneficial in conveying paradigms of thinking and information. Applying knowledge and developing communication skills are secondary. Formal education is hierarchically organized: teachers guide the learning process of students through syllabi and tests; teachers, in turn, are supervised by administrators, etc. Students are trained outside the arena in which they hope to minister and, upon completion of their training, they receive diplomas or certificates that attest to their level of training.

Formal modes of training have long been used by those of the Judeo-Christian heritage. Ezra established synagogues for the purpose of teaching the law. Because of this firm teaching, many Jews retained their identity in Babylon and continued to believe God's promises to restore his people. Jewish rabbis, especially the Pharisees, embraced this form of training. Hillel wrote, "The more teaching of the law, the more life; the more school, the more wisdom; the more counsel, the more reasonable action. He who gains a knowledge of the law gains life in the world to come" (*Aboth* 2.14). Paul was taught in this manner by the rabbi Gamaliel (Acts 22:3). Origen of Alexandria established a school in Egypt "for elementary instruction in the faith," but this school also became an evangelistic agency when unbelievers began to attend (Green 1970, 204). Centers of formal education have been in the forefront of the mission movement of North America.

*Nonformal Training.* This mode of training is based on the premise that students most effectively learn through designed experiences in a deliberately organized program. The training, however, is both "non-programmatic" and "non-institutional" (Clinton 1988, 251). Edgar Elliston writes that nonformal education is "planned, staffed, and organized, but structured outside the normal school system" (1988, 212).

Currently the Department of Missions of Abilene Christian University is initiating a program to combine formal and nonformal training. It is felt that formal education alone is not adequate to prepare candidates for the mission field. All students are mentored in four significant areas of development: (1) *character* (C) that reflects the mind of Christ in areas of values, ethics, emotional stability, and self-discipline; (2) *ability* (A) that is demonstrated by competence in the use of Scripture, mission principles, interpersonal skill, and public communication; (3) *relationship with God* (R) as evidenced by consistent, meaningful communion with the Lord through the Christian disciplines; and (4) *experience* (E) as an active follower of Christ in a local community of believers, including evangelism, nurturing, and cross-cultural practicums. At a *Foundations Retreat* during the first month of school, initial assessments are made in each of these four areas, described by the acronym CARE, and students are prayerfully joined to a mentor and a small group. Within a week after the retreat, students meet with their mentors to review the results of their assessments and set objectives for the coming semester. Between two and four objectives are mutually agreed upon by student and mentor for focused attention during each semester. These objectives are clearly written and signed by both student and mentor. Mentors meet with students as a group on a weekly basis to deepen personal relationships and they meet individually with trainees at least twice a year to assess progress made on their objectives and plan for the coming semester. Each year a weeklong assessment period occurs for all students who will graduate within the year. Results of this assessment are used by students and mentors to clarify the most significant objectives to be addressed during their remaining months in training. At the close of academic work, a board of review within the department considers students' overall development and readiness for the mission field. Based on this review, students receive a recommendation concerning their ministry for the next twenty-four months. This recommendation takes one of three forms: (1) recommended for mission work; (2) recommended with qualification, with specific remediation suggested; (3) not recommended for the following twenty-four months, with specific remediation suggested. It is understood that most of those in the third category are channeled into other disciplines by the mentoring process before reaching the end of their program of study. Students commended for mission work (#1 and #2 above) receive a certificate of commendation signed by their mentor and the department chairperson. This program, although coupled to a formal educational institution, is an example of nonformal education.

*Informal Training.* Informal training "uses life-activities as the basis for purposeful training" (Clinton 1988, 244). This type of training is highly relational yet is "unstructured in the sense of being controlled and deliberately planned" (Elliston 1988, 212). This mode is participatory: Teachers and students participate together in accomplishing the mission of God. Teachers model effective behavior in ministry while students learn how to minister. The following account relates how I informally trained two Kipsigis evangelists:

> Each Wednesday I am presently working with two Christians, Michael Chepkwony and Johanna Lang'at, from the Kapsinendet church in Kipsigis to initiate a new church in a nearby village. Michael works as a night watchman at a nearby tea estate, and Johanna is the overseer of the local cattle dip. I chose these two men because they both have the God-given gifts to plant churches and nurture new Christians to maturity. They also desire to teach relatives and friends in an adjoining village.

Michael, Johanna, and I meet at the village about 12:00 each Wednesday. We first go from house to house visiting those we think might be interested. Later in the day we have a large meeting in one of the homes of our first contact people. In these home visits and evangelistic meetings Michael and Johanna learn the fundamental gospel message and how to teach this message to different types of people as they hear me teach. I also gently guide and encourage them as they teach. When the first converts were baptized, I began to teach them how to nurture new Christians to maturity. We then worked to equip our new brothers and sisters in Christ to teach the first principles of the kingdom of God and the gospel of Christ to their relatives and nurture them in the Christian lifestyle.

I remember that day when the first five people were baptized in Mombwo. I told Michael, "These are your friends who now believe in Christ. It is your responsibility to baptize them." On the way to the river, Michael pulled me off to the side and said, "I have never baptized anyone. Would you show me how?" I then demonstrated to Michael how to baptize.

This training is informal. It is based on the perspective that Christian ministry must not only be taught but also modeled. We have grown to believe that formal and nonformal training without concurrent informal training is inadequate. **Van Rheenen 1983b, 40–41**

Peter Wagner writes that informal training is one of the great reasons for the growth of Pentecostals in urban contexts of Latin America (1973, 89–100). Evangelists conducted "seminaries in the streets" to train developing Christians for effective ministry. In fact, before Christian leaders could be ordained, they had to start a self-supporting church. Jonathan Chao comments that the training of itinerant evangelists in "seminaries of the field" is the cause of the great growth of the church in China (Chao 1989, 58). Jesus took twelve men, as diverse as a tax collector and a Zealot, revamped their conception of reality, and molded them into a cohesive group. He appointed these twelve "that they might be with him and that he might send them out to preach and to have authority to drive out demons" (Mark 3:14–15).

### Guidelines for Effective Leadership Training

So far, five types of leaders and three modes of training them have been discussed. This section seeks to specifically apply these understandings: What modes of training best equip different types of leaders? How do training patterns change as a movement matures? Although the need for training Christian leaders exists in every developing and mature church, modes and methodologies of training vary within each congregation and from context to context. The following four general guidelines are, however, fundamental in every context.

First, leaders need training appropriate for their ministries and time schedules. Type A and B leaders almost always need informal training to carry out their ministries within the body effectively. Small-group leaders learn to facilitate a group while serving as interns under small-group leaders; Bible class teachers learn to teach while studying in Bible classes; lay youth ministers learn to organize activities by participating in youth programs; committee leaders learn the functions of their committees while serving as members of them; new Christians learn to evangelize by seeing older Christians model evangelism. Formal and nonformal training, however, greatly enhance what these lay leaders learn by experience. Week-long or weekend formal seminars effectively provide lay leaders with the theologies and philosophies that undergird their ministries. Models of nonformal learning provide task-oriented experiences and exercises that greatly enhance what has been learned informally. Type C, D, and E leaders generally require some level of formal training because the informational undergirding required is broad. How can one preach the message if he has not studied it thoroughly? How can one organize the curriculum of a large church if he does not know the resources available? However, years of formal training without corresponding informal and nonformal training create informational nerds, who are able to relate ideas conceptually without personally ministering. Many of the disciplines required of Type D leaders are best learned through nonformal learning and many of the specialties of Type E leaders through informal learning.

Second, effective training integrates various modes of training. In the following case study I am working with leaders from Independent churches in Kipsigis to train them to initiate a new church. Elements of formal, nonformal, and informal education are all present:

> Presently I am working each Thursday for seven weeks with twelve vocational evangelists of the Kamaget and Kipsuter churches in Kipsigis. My purpose in these weeks is to spiritually, theologically, and practically equip these evangelists to initiate and mature a new church in an adjoining rural village. To accomplish this goal, I combine aspects of formal, nonformal, and informal training.

**Although the need for training Christian leaders exists in every developing and mature church, modes and methodologies of training vary within each congregation and from context to context**

Each Thursday I arrive at a designated home in Kamaget about 12:00, after an hour and a half trip from my home in Sotik. After a fellowship meal the evangelists and I discuss and apply the content of a home-study course that they have been studying during the week. The topics covered during the seven weeks are: God—The Source of Mission; Christ—The Message of Mission; The Holy Spirit—The Power of Mission; The Church—God's People in the World; The Church—The Embodiment of God's Mission; Paul—The Preacher; and Nurturing—Preparing New Christians to Live Within the Kingdom of God.

An initial planning session was used to help organize the course. During this session, I taught a lesson outlining fundamental Christian motivations for evangelism. These motivations were then discussed at length and compared to earthly, pride-directed motivations. We then prayed as a group for God to spiritually work in our hearts to prepare us as his messengers and help us select a nearby village to initiate a new congregation. After prayer, we selected Chepng'ung'ul as the focus of our seven-week evangelistic effort because there was no organized church there and many people in Chepng'ung'ul have kinship relationships with Christians in Kamaget. Because of the prayers and mutual consent of the Christians, we feel that God guided us in the selection of Chepng'ung'ul.

After the village had been selected, we began discussing key people in Chepng'ung'ul who would not only be receptive to the message of Jesus but also could become leaders in a newly forming church. Five names were then written on the blackboard and prayer made to God for each of these people. We then selected one older man and his family unit to initially teach and prayed that they might become the host family for the initial evangelism meetings in the village. Evangelists from Kamaget were chosen to go and make plans for the meeting for the following week. Finally, I gave each developing evangelist the first lesson to study before our meeting the following week.

On subsequent Thursdays we continued to meet at Kamaget for our evangelists' meeting at 12:00. This was our period of interaction about the lesson of the week. About 2:30 p.m. we began our trip to Chepng'ung'ul for our "practicum". As the weeks progressed, new evangelists from Kamaget were learning what spiritual resources God had given them and how to organize a plan of evangelism to initiate and mature a new church. Timothys were trained in action to become Pauls. Disciples were trained to become apostles.

As I write this, we are in the fourth week of training at Kamaget. In our third week thirty seekers attended a vibrant meeting at Chepng'ung'ul. One evangelist, Edwin Rono, daily teaches people house to house in this village. He also has started a Sunday school for children there. Kamaget evangelists are saying, "We know that God is working through us to start the church at Chepng'ung'ul." **Van Rheenen 1983, 38–40**

The effectiveness of this methodology is attested by the fact that the church at Chepng'ung'ul has grown to become one of the strongest churches in this area of Kipsigis. In this example the material studied by the evangelists in their homes each week was formal, most of the activities in the weekly training session were nonformal with a small portion of the formal, and the late-afternoon trips to evangelize Chepng'ung'ul were informal.

A third guideline for effective leadership training is that modes and methods of training should vary, depending on the maturity of the Christian movement. When churches are newly established and Christians know little of the Christian lifestyle, almost all training must be done informally. New Christians are trained to lead prayers, read the Bible, share their faith, and live a Christian life within the arena of life. They learn through effective modeling, which must continue even when churches grow to maturity with their own Type C, D, and E leaders. When early Christians grow toward maturity and a sufficient number of Christian leaders develop, short intensive courses are of significant value. They provide leaders with a knowledge of Scripture and an understanding of practical ministry in a short period of time. When developing leaders study together, motivation is also greatly enhanced. Leadership training by extension, as illustrated above, becomes an alternative.[6] As the movement matures, nationals and missionaries working together must make plans for the more structured training required for Type C, D, and E leaders. This will give the movement both cohesion and the necessary formal training for developing Christian leaders.

[6]*Leadership training by extension* (LTE) is the model of instruction in which the teacher goes to the students to teach and mentor them where they live rather than have the students come to the teacher. LTE is highly adaptable. Instruction occurs where and when the students are able to study, adapts to their economic and academic levels, and takes cultural differences into consideration. Mathews suggests that teachers consider

**Frequently, whenever missionaries fail to prioritize the essential tasks of missions, little is left after they depart.**

Fourth, churches must be initiated with a comprehensive strategy for phasing out missionary personnel once local leaders have been trained. Steffen writes that too often strategies develop piecemeal: New missionaries "focus more on 'phase-in' activities (e.g., evangelism and discipleship) than on 'phase-out' activities (e.g., activities that would empower nationals to develop leadership among themselves with an eye toward ministry that reproduces)" (1993, 3). He suggests a phase-out model consisting of five distinct stages: preentry, preevangelism, evangelism, postevangelism, and phase-out. Missionaries' roles change during each phase. During the preentry stage, missionaries are primarily learners. During ensuing stages, phase-out oriented missionaries develop the overlapping roles of evangelists, teachers, resident advisors, itinerant advisors, and absent advisors while continuing to be learners (1993, 24). Church movements are initiated with the understanding that missionaries will eventually phase out when their tasks have been completed. Let us hope that they will also phase *into* new areas when they phase *out of* old ones. One of the saddest events in missions is seeing mature missionaries leaving the mission field when they are still in their prime.

## Conclusion

The purpose of missions is frequently nebulous to untrained missionaries. They go to the mission field to do whatever they are sent to do. *It is sad that frequently, whenever missionaries fail to prioritize the essential tasks of missions, little is left after they depart.* Teaching English or literacy, digging water wells or treating physical bodies, instructing students in schools or camps, while expressing the compassion of God and opening doors for gospel proclamation, do not in themselves lead to the development of churches. The emphasis of this chapter is that the church must prioritize and intentionally do the major tasks of missions: planting churches through evangelism, nurturing new Christians to maturity, and training leaders to continue the process of planting churches, nurturing new Christians, and training still other leaders as the church matures and reproduces. These churches will then holistically glorify God in all that they do. It is always better for compassionate activities to flow from local churches than through foreign parachurch organizations.

themselves *catalysts* creatively employing nonformal models of instruction rather than merely formal models (1976, 123–39).

One basic guideline applies to formulating plans for each of these three significant missionary tasks. Church leaders must visualize what God desires in each of these three areas, set specific goals in each category, and then work backward to the type of plans required to fulfill these goals.

# BUILDING ON THE UNDERSTANDINGS OF PLANTING CHURCHES, NURTURING NEW CHRISTIANS, AND TRAINING LEADERS

## QUESTIONS:

1. Briefly describe three primary tasks of missions.
2. After reading the section defining *church planting*, write the definition of the term and briefly describe the meaning of each significant word of the definition.
3. Contrast a verse from the Bible describing germinal growth to a verse depicting terminal growth.
4. What theologies give special impetus to germinal growth? Why?
5. What four guidelines for effectively planting new churches are given in the chapter? What other guideline(s) might you add to these?
6. What application does the Kipsigis proverb "We cannot give birth to children and then leave them" (*"Magisiche lagok si kebagach"*) have to missions?
7. What four guidelines of effectively nurturing new Christians are given in this chapter? What additional guideline(s) might you suggest?
8. Describe (1) the four stages of church maturation developed by missionaries among the Kipsigis of Kenya, (2) the changing role of the church planter during each stage, and (3) what is taught to the maturing church during the first three stages.
9. After reading the section of the chapter on *urban mentalities*, make a chart contrasting rural and urban perspectives. How do these mentalities influence the strategies for nurturing new Christians in urban contexts.

10. After reading the section defining *leadership training*, write the definition of the term and briefly describe the meaning of each significant word of the definition.

11. Contrast leadership as *the process of influence* with biblical metaphors of leadership. Why is this distinction significant?

12. Describe five types of leaders present in all vibrant Christian religious movements.

13. Briefly describe three modes of training.

14. Discuss the mode(s) of training that best trains each of the five types of leaders.

15. What four guidelines of effectively training leaders are given in this chapter? What other guideline(s) might you add to these?

## Special Application Question:

Reflect on the following quotation from chapter 8: "Many movements stagnate because Christian leaders have not developed the creative capacities for strategic planning." From understandings derived from chapter 9, how do Christian movements stagnate because strategies are inadequate or ill-conceived?

## Creative Exercises:

1. Picture an area of the world (domestic or foreign) where God might use you to plant a new church within the next ten years. Creatively imagine how you might devise a strategy to plant and mature a church (or churches) in this area and what type of strategy this church would come to have as a mature church.

2. Describe the strategy model of your local church and how God will use you for his glory within this body to nurture fellow members and to train leaders.

## Case Study

You have just been hired as the education minister of a major church in Big City, America. The Big City church will soon complete a major building program and would like to use the finances that once went toward their building program for world evangelization. Their total missions budget will likely go from $75,000 this year to $325,000 in five years. Because you have been overseas, graduated with a Bible degree, and have an interest in missions, the elders have asked you to become an adviser to their missions committee. The missions committee has tentatively decided to focus on the nation of Zinzin because other churches in their area have targeted adjoining countries. During December, a committee member joined others on a survey trip to different cities in Zinzin and placed ads for English Bible correspondence courses in Zinzini newspapers. This summer they desire to conduct two-week campaigns to begin the church in Zinzin. At the present they know little of the country they hope to target.

The missions committee desires to move quickly to evangelize Zinzin before a change of government closes the door. The elders are more cautious because, as executives of large companies, they know how easily business mistakes occur in international contexts. The pulpit preacher is interested in missions and is willing to help you. As the new residential *authority* in missions, you have been asked to give guidance to the committee and help them make decisions. How will you advise them? Describe the (1) content and (2) process of advising them.

# CHAPTER 10

# CHURCH MATURATION:
## Building Responsible Churches

Why do some church movements flourish, grow, and mature while others stagnate, wither, and die? Why do some churches brilliantly reflect the love and holiness of God while others mirror the jealousies and divisions of the world? In some instances the difference may be due merely to the motivations and commitments of those who have come to Christ. Frequently, however, the attitudes, methods, and organizations introduced by missionaries create stagnation and promote division.

Suppose, for example, that a certain American missionary desires to establish a preacher training school in a foreign country in order to train leaders for an entire continent. During the initial stages of his work, he shares his vision with national leaders. These leaders become excited! They envision training that will equip their young people to become more effective in Christian ministry and anticipate dreaming and planning for the future with the missionary. It soon becomes evident, however, that the missionary works autonomously. He stridently condemns those who suggest that national leaders should be included on a board overseeing the school and claims that these suggestions come from divisive elements that aim to take over his school. He considers their advice an intrusion. As years pass, the school attracts mostly nationals from other countries, who receive support from the missionary while they study and return to their home nations as evangelists supported by the missionary. The Christianity exported by this school is narrow and dogmatic and is controlled and empowered by foreign finances. Frequently meetings between the missionary and the national

179

leaders end in conflict. And national leaders themselves are divided: Some desire to ask immigration authorities to deport the missionary; others desire merely to separate and allow the missionary to do his own thing; a minority desire to join the missionary to reap the benefits of American finances. Paradoxically, what was meant to help the church actually divides it.

Alex Araujo uses the Amazon *pororoca* to illustrate this missionary-national relationship. The *pororoca* is a loud popping noise heard when the massive waters of the Amazon meet the rising tide of the Atlantic Ocean. Like the violent collision of two gigantic bodies of waters, missionaries and developing national leaders frequently clash, creating havoc for anyone caught in the maelstrom (1993, 362–63).

The missionary-national leader relationship, however, need not be tragic. An American missionary team enters another area with few Christians of their religious fellowship. As newcomers to the culture, the missionaries know that they have much to learn; they focus on learning the language and culture of the people. They first develop a reciprocal relationship with the few Christians in the area. These Christians help them find language tutors and become intimately involved in their lives. Although the church in this country is weak, the team of missionaries find three or four visionary thinkers among church leaders. They meet with them for prayer, planning, and preparation for establishing spiritually vibrant and germinally reproductive churches. While cultural and even religious perspectives differ, over a period of time the missionaries and early Christians grow together in their thinking. The focus of missionaries and national leaders during the first ten years is on developing cohesive churches that, in turn, plant other churches. The aim, therefore, is to initiate new churches in this culture, nurture new Christians to maturity, and train leaders in established churches. During the early years, much training is done informally as the missionary and mature local Christians model the doing of Christianity in their non-Christian context. The concepts of the Christian faith are intentionally taught, first through congregationally based Bible courses and later in small, yet appropriate Christian institutions overseen by national leaders. Over a period of years the missionaries make a transition from training evangelists and equipping young Christians to becoming trainers of leaders. Finally they begin to phase out their involvement in order to initiate another Christian movement. While the beginnings are slow (because missionaries begin as learners), the Christian movement gains momentum because people were intentionally taught, Christians were nurtured, and leaders were trained in ways suitable to their culture.

This missionary-national relationship can be illustrated by two of the large rivers that merge near Manaus, Brazil. The Negro River appears dark and clear, like Coca-Cola seen through a glass. The Solimoes River, however, is full of sediment and appears grayish white. For miles downstream they appear as two rivers sharing the same river bed, but gradually the waters intermingle to become one mighty river. Likewise, in missionary-national relationships two leadership movements, one foreign and one local, begin as distinct entities flowing together but gradually become one (Araujo 1993, 362–63).

These illustrations reflect the missiological concern of this chapter—that missionaries must develop models of working with local churches and equipping national leaders rather than establishing paternalistic structures that can be supervised and supported only by Western personnel and finances. This concern presupposes that missionaries must pass the leadership baton to nationals who can more effectively lead their own local churches and church movements. It also assumes that missionaries must overcome the tendency of paternalism, i.e., the dominance of the sending culture over the mission process.

In this chapter we will first consider past models of building responsible churches and then discuss proposed guidelines for the use of these models.

> **This concern presupposes that missionaries must pass the leadership baton to nationals who can more effectively lead their own local churches and church movements.**

## Paternalism

The modern mission movement, beginning with William Carey in the nineteenth century, grew out of deep piety, which accounted for both its initial strength and weakness. The strength of the movement lay in its sincere devotion to God, expressed through acts of service and zeal for winning the lost. But the search for spirituality negated discussions about the structure and organization of the church. This neglect, coupled with the paternalism of the day, resulted in the establishing of churches that were spiritually and materially dependent on the European and American missionary movement (Beyerhaus 1979, 15).

Paternalistic attitudes were very common. Hiebert writes:

> Paternalistic missionary attitudes . . . were stifling the maturation and growth of the young churches. Leadership remained in the hands of the missionaries. National leaders were suppressed and

frustrated. In many cases they broke away and established churches independent from the missionary agencies, but that did not solve the problem for those who wanted to keep ties with the churches that had brought the gospel to them. **1986, 193–94**

The dangers inherent in this paternalistic system soon became evident to responsible missionary leaders because "it doomed the work to complete stagnation as soon as the sending bodies . . . exhausted their . . . personnel and funds" (Beyerhaus 1979, 15).

## The Three-Self Formula: Focus on Independence

During the nineteenth century two prominent leaders of major missionary agencies developed the three-self formula. According to this theory, young churches on the mission field would gain their independence on the basis of three principles: self-propagation, self-support, and self-government.

Rufus Anderson, an American congregationalist who served as secretary of the American Board of Commissioners for Foreign Missions, coined the terminology. On his trips to visit field missionaries Anderson perceived that most mission efforts focused on social activities and failed to propagate the gospel. He discerned that the apostle Paul established local churches, each with its own independent presbytery, and that from their inception these new churches were not dependent on Paul but immediately began to propagate the gospel in their areas. He concluded that "missions are instituted for the spread of a Scriptural, self-propagating Christianity" (Anderson 1856, 3). Four activities would accomplish this goal: the conversion of the lost, organizing new believers into local churches, training a competent native leadership, and guiding the church to become independent and self-propagating. He believed that schools should be established only to train "native teachers and preachers" (Verkuyl 1978, 65, 186–87). While maintaining that Pauline churches were self-propagating, self-supporting, and self-governing, he was chiefly concerned with self-propagation (Beyerhaus 1979, 16).

The role played by Anderson in American missiology is similar to that of Henry Venn in the English arena. Venn exerted great influence as the secretary of the Church Missionary Society of the Church of England.

He perceived the stagnation of the mission churches established by his society and believed that "spoon-feeding" by missionaries created "rice Christians." He emphasized the need for true conversion, and this was reflected by the willingness of local Christians to support the work of the church. He believed that the mission was like the scaffolding used by carpenters in the erection of a building. Once the building was constructed, the scaffolding was to be removed. But many mission works were like buildings that could not stand without the support of the scaffolding.

After 1861 Venn began to employ Anderson's three-self terminology to describe his perspectives. Their perspectives, however, differed. Venn, as an Anglican, perceived the three "selfs" not only in terms of establishing independent local churches but also as an entire diocese under a national leadership with a native bishop. While Anderson felt that churches should quickly achieve the three selfs, Venn understood this development as a longer process of organizing small companies, congregations, pastorates, and finally churches (Beyerhaus 1979, 16–17).

During the last half of the nineteenth century and the first half of the twentieth century, almost all perspectives of church maturation were judged by the standards of the three-self formula. Although this formula was accepted as normative, viewpoints of missiologists varied. Some, like Gustav Warneck, a German missiologist, argued that although the formula was an ideal for which to aim, the actualization of the goal should be gradual, implemented through a process of education. Others, like the Anglican missiologist Roland Allen, argued for a radical implementation of the three selfs. He believed that, being universal, the Holy Spirit would compensate for any insufficiencies (1962).

The independence movement of the twentieth century amplified this drive toward church autonomy. Once the countries of Asia and Africa became independent, missionaries could no longer overtly ascribe to any type of nineteenth-century paternalism. It was assumed by missionaries and national leaders alike that in newly independent countries the churches should make their own decisions and have their own leaders.

Perceptions about components of the three-self theory also varied between mission and national leaders. The aspect of self-propagation generally raised little controversy. Mission churches were usually as deeply concerned about evangelism as were the sending churches and missionaries. Unfortunately, in some cases missionaries had planted churches but failed to instill in them a vision for evangelizing. In these terminal churches self-propagation was more of an ideal than a reality. This demonstrates that "churches do not automatically become evangelically minded. That vision must be as consciously taught and modeled as the rest of the Christian life" (Hiebert 1986, 194).

Controversy became most heated over the issue of self-support. Missionaries frequently pushed hard for self-support, and nationals only reluctantly took charge of the institutions that the missionaries had built with foreign money. Many missionaries and a few national leaders argued that young churches should learn to support themselves because continued reliance on outside support creates a dependency that hinders their maturation and growth; churches could achieve maturity only if they were self-supporting. Many national leaders, however, argued that the economy of their churches could not support the schools, hospitals, and high-level support of national workers established by the mission movement.

Self-government was even more controversial than self-support, but this time the roles were reversed. National leaders wanted the power to make their own decisions. They argued that they would never mature until they could choose their own preachers and appoint their own teachers. Missionaries, however, were reluctant to give up their authority within developing churches for fear that inexperience and local politics would ruin the church (Hiebert 1986, 194–95).

Results of the implementation of the three-self formula varied, depending on when and how three-self principles were introduced. Generally a tradition of self-initiative is created if the principles are implemented at the inception of a movement. For example, John Nevius, a Presbyterian missionary in China, was a younger contemporary of Anderson and Venn. His Nevius Plan, which incorporated systematic Bible study with the economic independence of the three-self perspective, influenced the beginning of the church in Korea and became "one of the most important factors in the dynamic development of the Korean Church" (Sundkler 1965, 293). If the three-self principle is introduced to existing movements that have depended on Western aid and oversight for decades, the results will frequently be disastrous. Richter contends that Venn's reforms in India precipitated "decades of stagnation in Anglican churches." The church in Sierra Leone became paralyzed in 1960 when missionaries were withdrawn and a "Native Pastorate" set up. Stephen Neill alleged that "Venn's dictum proved almost wholly disastrous" (Kasdorf 1979, 80).

The three-self formula contains many essential truths important to the missionary endeavor. It challenged missionary paternalism and acknowledged the responsibility of all Christians regardless of social and economic heritage. It promoted a freedom that allowed local Christian leaders to develop programs and institutions that reflected the purposes of God yet were different from those of mission-sending cultures. It called people to Pauline principles of planting churches. Paul expected churches to quickly mature, yet he was always ready to reenter churches through personal visits, visits of intern evangelists, and letters to correct and exhort. He ordained leaders soon after establishing churches and expected the churches to be self-supporting from their inception.

It is easier to reflect critically on the three-self formula today than during the days in which there were no alternative proposals. The most fundamental criticism of the three-self formula is on its emphasis on *self*. Positively the word is an "affirmation of identity." Churches are able to operate autonomously, independent of their founders. Negatively, the term implies "isolation, ceasing to be influenced and supported by others" (Beyerhaus 1979, 25).

From a theological perspective, however, no affirmations about *self* can fully describe a mature church. A church is never self-propagating but empowered and equipped by God to seek the lost. It is never self-governing but is ruled by the sovereign God and the Lord Jesus Christ. It is never self-supporting but provided for by God, the giver of all things. In a real sense Christianity is a denial rather than an affirmation of self. As Beyerhaus comments, "It is possible for a church to manage its own affairs, maintain its own economy and win quite a number of new members, without any of these activities meeting God's approval" (1979, 26). The affirmation of self has meaning only when applied socially rather than theologically.

The application of the three-self formula was given special impetus during the era when many countries were seeking their independence, and to a certain degree the formula reflects nationalistic thinking. This perspective claims that "every group of people united by a common language, geographic region and cultural and historical heritage is entitled to determine its own way of life and its own destiny" (Beyerhaus 1979, 28). Just as nation-states must seek independence from their colonial masters so must mission churches achieve "ecclesiastical independence" from founding missionaries or mission agencies (1979, 27). In the contemporary interconnected world, however, in which nation-states increasingly hold less significance than international consortiums, interdependence frequently becomes more of a goal than independence.

# The Indigenous Church: Focus on Cultural Appropriateness

The term *indigenous* soon began to be used to describe Anderson and Venn's three-self formula. William Smalley, editor of *Practical Anthropology*, wrote that it had "become axiomatic in much missionary thinking that a church which is 'self-governing, self-supporting, and self-propagating' is by definition an 'indigenous church'" (1958, 51). Smalley challenged this connection by suggesting that the three-self perspective is not "necessarily diagnostic of an indigenous movement. The definition of such a movement has to be sought elsewhere" (1958, 51). A church may be self-propagating, self-supporting, and self-governing and yet not be indigenous. A church may be self-governing, but methodologies used to make decisions are foreign. The result might be a self-governing church organized "in a slavishly foreign manner." Local leaders have merely adopted the democratic decision-making methodologies of Western churches. Neither is self-support descriptive of an indigenous church. For example, receiving aid from other churches during a famine did not infringe on the independence of the Jerusalem church. Although Smalley claims that self-propagation is most descriptive of an indigenous church, in some areas of the world (especially in areas that are rapidly Westernizing) the very foreignness of the church provides its attraction. Foreigners, in such contexts, may be more effective propagators of the gospel. True indigeneity, according to Smalley, is more than the three "selfs" (1958, 51–65).

Smalley was following the heritage of Pentecostal missiologist Melvin Hodges, who, in *On the Mission Field: The Indigenous Church*, defined an indigenous church as "a native church . . . which shares the life of the country in which it is planted and finds itself ready to govern itself, support itself, and reproduce itself" (Hodges 1953, 7). This formative definition expands the old three-self formula. Not only must indigenous churches be self-propagating, self-supporting, and self-governing, they must also reflect God's will in culturally appropriate ways so that church patterns fit indigenous contexts. This perspective is based on the presupposition that "God has always, everywhere, dealt with men in terms of their culture" (Smalley 1958, 56). A. R. Tippett gave a slightly different twist:

> When the indigenous people of a community think of the Lord as their own, not a foreign Christ; when they do things as unto the Lord meeting the cultural needs around them, worshipping in patterns they understand; when their congregations function in participation in a body, which is structurally indigenous; then you have an indigenous church. **1969, 136**

The church, according to Hodges, must be like a banana plant in Central America. The plant is so indigenous to its environment that it requires no special attention to thrive and is found growing wild wherever

**The goal of missions is not social work or evangelism but the establishment of indigenous churches. Only indigenous churches, rooted in their cultures, will be able to accomplish effective social and evangelistic ministries.**

there is adequate water. A banana plant, however, cannot naturally survive in Canada without special care. In the winter it must be dug up and transported indoors and seldom, if ever, is able to bear fruit (1953, 7–8).

Hodges perceived that the goal of missions is not social work or evangelism but the establishment of indigenous churches. Only indigenous churches, rooted in their cultures, will be able to accomplish effective social and evangelistic ministries (1953, 8–9).

The fruit of Western paternalism, according to Hodges, is anemic mission churches that are not allowed to grow naturally in the soils in which they were planted. Early missionaries seldom understood their "transitory" role but rather became indispensable to the running of the mission. Authority of the movement was centered in mission compounds where missionaries lived rather than in local churches. Hodges adamantly claimed, "God did not send missionaries out to build mission stations, but to build the church" (1953, 13). A disproportionate number of missionaries in one area frequently stifled ministry rather than empowered it. Hodges' axiom was that "a missionary should never hold a position which a national is able to fill" (1953, 13). The emergence of indigenous churches was hindered both by the missionaries' excessive fondness for the "American way" and by "failure to adapt to native psychology and methods." National Christians depended on foreign aid and did not seek to develop of their own faith (Hodges 1953, 14).

Smalley, reflecting the heritages of Roland Allen and Melvin Hodges, believes that the Holy Spirit empowers local churches to become indigenous. An indigenous church, according to Smalley, is

> a group of believers who live out their life, including their socialized Christian activity, in the patterns of the local society, and for whom any transformation of that society comes out of their felt needs under the guidance of the Holy Spirit and the Scriptures. **1958, 55**

Smalley perceived that an indigenous church is a society that develops patterns of interaction common to those who live within that culture. A church that follows patterns superimposed on it by missionaries is not indigenous. The Holy Spirit within indigenous churches, however, transforms the lives of individual people and of the society as a whole. From this perspective an indigenous church is "one in which the changes which take place under the guidance of the Holy Spirit meet the needs and fulfill the meanings of the society and not of any outside group" (1958, 55).

Understandings of the indigenous church have broadened the three-self theory to include both cultural sensitivity and amplified dialogue about appropriate communication of the Christian message. The original three-self principle placed too much emphasis on external forms (self-propagation, self-support, and self-government) as signs of church maturity. Indigenous church concepts moved beyond these forms to suggest that mission churches must appropriately reflect their culture—like banana plants, which thrive in Central America, or rattlesnakes, which flourish in West Texas. This perspective has heightened awareness of the role of culture in the mission enterprise. It has amplified the church's effectiveness in welcoming people into their community of faith and allowing God to work through their cultural context to reach people. Eventually the indigenous church began to be defined not only by forms of worship and church life but also by the gospel's being made intelligible and meaningful to the recipient culture. Paul Hiebert proposed the fourth self: self-theologizing (Hiebert 1986, 195–98); William Dyrness has written about local or vernacular theologies (1990, 1992); and many missiologists have written about how to contextualize the gospel appropriately.[1]

The perspective of the indigenous church contains at least one significant weakness. "Indigenous" implies that the church must become part of the culture. The term literally means that which is "born from within"—what is local, innate, or native to a culture as contrasted to what is foreign, alien, or exotic (Kasdorf 1979, 72). Cultures, because of their fallen nature, seldom uphold the values of God. Although created by God, culture at the Fall rejected God. The world became primarily sinful, alienated from God, the arena of Satan. John testified that "the whole world is under the control of the evil one" (1 John 5:19). Christians, like Christ, live *in* the world but are not *of* the world (John 17:16). Christians dwell in this world as "aliens and strangers" who struggle to live exemplary lives among the pagans (1 Peter 2:11–12). While acknowledging that the church must speak the language of culture and be sensitive to peoples' understanding of reality, the indigenous perspective fails to prepare disciples of Christ for countercultural living in pagan culture. If Christianity becomes totally indigenous, it loses its divine distinctiveness.

A better phrase for the indigenous concept is "building *responsible* churches." The term *responsible* implies many of the intended meanings

---

[1] Two formative texts discussing contextualization are *Contextualization: Meanings, Methods, and Models* (Hesselgrave and Rommen 1989) and *The Word Among Us: Contextualizing Theology for Mission Today* (Gilliland 1989).

of *indigenous*, without much of its baggage. *Responsible* implies that the church has grown to maturity in Christ and can now walk alongside those who founded her. An equality has been established, and mutual relationships that glorify God take place. The church is able to propagate itself, support itself, govern itself, and demonstrate the attributes of God in the midst of pagan society. *Responsible churches are those that have grown to maturity and are fully able to reflect the attributes of God in appropriate ways within their cultural contexts.*

# Partnership: Focus on International Cooperation and Networking

### Rationale for Partnerships

Because of the changes in the world, mission leaders are moving toward consensus regarding partnerships; they realize that partnerships are essential for the mission of the church and especially vital in international, multicultural, urban contexts. Luis Bush, International Director of the AD 2000 Movement and co-author of *Partnering in Ministry* (1990), is a formative leader in this dialogue. He identifies four new realities of the world—realities that create the need for partnering.

First, our world is shrinking. As the world is rapidly reduced to a global village by advances in communications and technology, greater dialogue and interdependency can be expected among different parts of the universal body of Christ. This shrinkage of the world is reflected by the internationalization of university education. Presently my oldest daughter, who studies at Abilene Christian University, lives with housemates from Japan, Panama, and South Africa. Her Panamanian housemate is Chinese. The mother of her South African housemate lives in England, and this housemate is dating, via e-mail and international visits, a graduate of Abilene Christian who is of Chinese descent and resides in Singapore. My daughter is an American citizen born in Kenya. She spent last Christmas in Panama and this June in England. Over three hundred international students attend our small school—a microcosm of internationalization. The nature of mission changes when people of the nations meet together for study, business, and diplomacy and easily communicate by telephone and e-mail.

Second, Two-thirds World churches, which now comprise the majority of Christians, have grown to maturity. Samuel Escobar writes:

> Internationalization of Christian mission means acknowledging that God has now raised large and thriving churches in nations

where sometimes the Bible was not even translated a hundred years ago. In these churches of the Southern Hemisphere, churches of the poor, churches of the Third World, God is raising up a new missionary force. Internationalization has become necessary because it is in partnership with these young churches that mission will take place in years to come. **1992, 7**

Third, the number of missionaries from the Two-thirds World is rapidly growing and "is projected to surpass the number of their Western colleagues" by the year A.D. 2000 (Pate 1991, 59). Larry Pate and Lawrence Keyes write:

> If present trends continue to the year 2000, there will be 6.135 billion people on this planet, 81.4 percent of them living in the non-Western countries. Fifty percent of the total will live in an urban environment, but 75 percent of the world's sixty largest cities (over 5 million) will be in the non-Western countries. Some of the largest classes of missionary candidates will be trained in Korea, Nigeria, India, and Brazil. There will likely be well over 1,000 non-Western mission agencies, and one of every two Protestant missionaries will be from the emerging missions of non-Western countries. **1986, 160**

Urbanization and technology have greatly added to the complexity of this world. No one church or agency is able to understand the interworkings of urban contexts and provide all the resources required to mobilize a Christian movement.

Fourth, Western and non-Western missions have much to learn from each other and will frequently target the same areas. Therefore, partnering with emerging missions will be essential to the advancement of the gospel in the coming decade.

## Definition of Partnership

Luis Bush defines *partnership* as "an association of two or more Christian autonomous bodies who have formed a trusting relationship, and fulfill agreed-upon expectations by sharing complementary strengths and resources, to reach their mutual goal" (Bush and Lutz 1990, 46). These autonomous bodies may be mature churches, mission agencies, or a mixture of the two that partner with one another to evangelize an unreached people or accomplish some other agreed-upon Christian ministry. For example, OC International helped to initiate a mission society in North-eastern India, where the Christian movement is strong, in order to send missionaries to Uttar Pradesh, an unreached area of India having a population of 138 million with only 0.15 percent of the people following the way of Christ (Keyes 1994, 229–35). At that time residential missionaries could not enter India. Mission agencies, however, could develop strategies with vital Christian movements within India to initiate missions among unreached peoples of that country.

This definition implies *synergy*, the perspective that the combined understandings and actions of two or more people or groups are able to make and implement mutual decisions that are better than those made individually. For example, one draft horse can pull four tons. If two draft horses are harnessed together, they are able to pull twenty-two tons (Taylor 1994, 6). William Taylor writes, "The church of Christ already has the resources for total world evangelism. But if we go our individualistic ways, we will only fragment our resources, our spirit, and the desires of the Spirit of God" (1994, 240).

After the fall of the wall dividing East and West Germany in 1989 and the subsequent opening of Eastern Europe, over one thousand Christian movements from the West invaded the former Soviet Union. The same translators were frequently employed to preach to the same people during the same week but with different messages and methods. Taylor suggests that we should learn from this experience:

> Too many Western groups blitzed Russia with high-cost programs, with limited or non-existent regard for Russian culture or the existing churches already there, and with no concern for learning the heart-language of the people. We are learning some hard lessons from this experience, and while we glory in the advance of the gospel, not always was this done properly or with good motives. **1994, 240–41**

What would the results have been if Christians had joined together in partnership, planning well-thought through approaches to each context?

### Five Qualities of Christian Partnership

Bush's definition implies five qualities of partnership.

First, *trust* is foundational to partnership. A partnership is "an association of two or more Christian autonomous bodies *who have formed a trusting relationship.*" Samuel Escobar writes:

To accept national leaders as co-workers in international teams demands a measure of confidence in the process by which these leaders have been selected by their respective churches and mission organizations in their own communities. It is difficult to move ahead as a team with insecure leaders who have to check every one of their movements for fear of censorship and control of national or foreign leaders above them. . . . *Lack of trust breeds paternalism.* **1992, 9, italics mine**

"True fellowship, friendship, and trust" form a "spiritual infrastructure that makes international partnerships possible" (1992, 12).

Second, partnerships require the development of *interpersonal relationships*. Those of Two-thirds World cultures develop these relationships much more readily than do Westerners. Many Two-thirds World cultures make decisions based on personal relationships. Business is conducted face-to-face with those they know. In many cases, "good interpersonal relationships take precedence over competence and efficiency" (Sookhdeo 1994, 59). Western cultures, on the other hand, value efficiency and prefer a more structured, institutional mode of decision making. Sookhdeo comments:

In the West, procedure determines practice and takes precedence over relationships. The emphasis is on institutions and on standardization through filling in endless forms and feeding endless computers. **1994, 59**

Paul McKaughan, Executive Director of the Evangelical Fellowship of Mission Agencies, describes why task-oriented Americans have difficulty forming international partnerships:

I find that the demands of time are exhausting. If real, honest, and open communications are to be carried on, to a large degree they must be done face-to-face and at great length. . . .

Partnerships take immense time, and the question is still open as to whether we can afford the amount of time necessary to form meaningful partnerships internationally on a deep and personal level, or whether our partnerships will be structured on a merely utilitarian, businesslike basis. **1994, 68, 77**

During June 1992, the World Evangelism Fellowship convened an international consultation on partnership in Manila. Throughout the conference interpersonal relationships were described, especially by non-

Western participants, as a significant core value of partnerships. William Taylor writes:

> Essentially they focused on relationships that grow after extended time for developing trust and mutual understanding. The terms "personal relationship," "time," and "trust" came up repeatedly. Some Western groups are perceived as tending to focus on functional, tangible, measurable, task-oriented, cooperative agreements. These come across as management programs, lacking the personal dimension of gracious mutuality in the body of Christ. **1994, 4**

Developing personal relationships is innately tied to practicing the spiritual disciplines. Those within the partnership, because they are Christians working together for God's purposes, pray together, spend time in periodic fasting, and reflect together on God's direction in their lives.

A third quality of partnership is *accountability*: A partnership must "fulfill agreed-upon expectations . . . to reach their mutual goal." In this area it is necessary to overcome the widely held misconception that accountability is a Western concept. All institutions, whether national or international, are able to function effectively only if they have developed processes of accountability. Likewise, Christian churches and institutions cannot grow and mature in any place in the world without accountability. Accountability in Christian partnerships goes beyond general accountability. It is based on Christian values and rooted in "good faith and mutual trust." Accountability, therefore, must be "welcomed as a blessing rather than being viewed as a restrictive imposition" (Araujo 1993, 121).

*Mutual complementation* is the fourth quality of Christian partnership. Partners share "complementary strengths and resources, to reach their mutual goal." Members of a partnership are like organs within the body: The heart cooperates with the lungs, which in turn cooperate with the brain. Each provides vital functions within the whole. Like organs of a body complementing each other, missionary agencies and churches must work together to finish the task of world evangelization. The following illustration demonstrates the fruits of mutual complementation:

> High in the Atlas mountains of North Africa, in a small village, lived a young Muslim by the name of Aziz. This young man provided for his widowed mother and siblings, sustaining them with the earnings of a small shop he managed.
>
> Aziz became increasingly disillusioned with Islam, with the impossibility of continuing his education, and with other factors

in his life. So, late at night he began to listen to Christian radio programs and became fascinated by this person called Jesus Christ. After listening for a number of months he wrote a letter to the producers. They wrote back. And then began a flow of letters that continued for months.

Eventually, the producers suggested that Aziz might like to get involved in Bible correspondence courses. They did not offer Bible correspondence courses, but (and this is a key point) they knew a group that did.

So Aziz enrolled. He found it tough work, running the shop all day making income for his family, completing the courses, and listening to radio programs at night, but he persevered. After a couple of years of working through two or three courses, he finally penned these words to the people with whom he corresponded: "I would really like to meet someone who is a believer in Jesus."

That trigger kicked off contact by a Moroccan national evangelist associated with yet another organization known to the correspondence course people. The evangelist had tea with Aziz. In fact, they continued to have contact over a considerable period of time. And eventually this young man opened his heart to the Lord Jesus Christ.

Subsequently he was passed on to a so-called tentmaker, an expatriate who lived in the town, and this person began a process of discipleship with Aziz.

Now the moral of this story is quite clear: the individual parts of Christ's Body had combined to do something that none of them could do separately. What we have here is an integration of four or five different ministries linking hands in succession, accomplishing different parts of a process; the process of sowing, watering, reaping, and eventually discipling. This was a conscious, intentional integration of the body of Christ for a specific objective. **Butler 1991, 27–28**

*Focusing on a well-defined goal* is the fifth quality of partnerships found in Bush's definition. Mission agencies and churches partner together in order "to reach their mutual goal." This statement, however, fails to designate what the purpose of missions is. Too frequently that purpose is nebulous and ill-defined. While profit is the bottom-line arbiter of international business, confusion exists over the purpose of Christian mission. As expressed in chapter 9, the church must prioritize and intentionally engage in three major tasks of missions: planting churches through evangelism, nurturing new Christians to maturity, and training leaders to continue the process of planting churches, nurturing new Christians, and training still other leaders as the church matures and reproduces. These churches will then holistically glorify God in all that they do. Compassionate activities should flow from local churches rather than through foreign parachurch organizations.

### Principles of Partnerships

In a paper originally prepared for the regional meeting of the Evangelical Missiological Society, Samuel Chiang discusses important working principles of partnerships: First, partners must agree on doctrine and ethical behavior. This does not mean they must totally agree on every detail, but there should be enough agreement to prevent differences from becoming issues. Second, partners must share common goals. These common goals enable them to overcome individual agendas and "foster a sense of co-laboring for the kingdom" (Chiang 1992, 288). Third, partners must develop an attitude of equality. Churches and agencies in the Two-thirds World have much to offer. Chinese Christians are able to speak out of a heritage of suffering and martyrdom. Korean Christians can teach about the power of prayer. Fourth, partners must avoid dominance of one over the other. Partners should mutually determine policies, make decisions, and control resources. Fifth, partners must communicate openly. The saying goes, "Misinformation thrives in a vacuum." They should also recognize differences in communication styles. Westerners are direct and confrontational; the Chinese tend to be respectful and try to save face concerning differences; Africans communicate circuitously. Thus partners must develop an effective cross-cultural model of communication. Sixth, partners must demonstrate trust and accountability. Seventh, partners must pray together. According to Chiang, praying together is the "fundamental activity in working together to build the kingdom" (1992, 288–89). Thus developing partnerships is fully living out the Christian life while making plans for global evangelism partners.

### Types of Partnerships

Tokunboh Adeyemo presents eight types of partnership models and states his preference for the eighth. (1) The *Mother/Daughter* model occurs when mission agencies and churches plant new churches and maintain ongoing relationships with them. The Western church or agency typically remains dominant, since the "umbilical cord" has not been com-

Partners must pray together. According to Chiang, praying together is the "fundamental activity in working together to build the kingdom."

pletely severed. (2) Under the *Parachurch Establishment* model the parachurch relief or evangelism agency establishes its own structure and hires nationals to carry out its objectives. Such "renting of the nationals" frequently leads to discontent, since nationals are employees rather than mutual co-workers. (3) In the *National Support* model Western agencies and churches arrange for the support of nationals and their projects. It soon becomes apparent, however, that Western finances support national churches rather than missions to new areas. (4) The *Nationals-on-the-Team* model integrates nationals and Westerners working together on the same team. These missionaries, both nationals and Westerners, are expected to raise their own support to be part of the team. In actual working relationships the paternalism of some Western workers hinders such globalization. (5) In the *Paternal Network* model local mission agencies or churches ask for assistance from Western agencies and churches. (6) Under the *Secondment* model Western missionaries are loaned to national churches for a period of time. (7) In the *Empowerment* model Western agencies and churches equip national churches by supplying money, personnel, and technical assistance. They work through national churches rather than setting up their own structure. This model is more frequently used for relief and development than for evangelism and church planting. (8) The *Multinational Church Network (Enablement)* model also assumes the validity of the local church in missions. "Mission and vision are church-rooted." Churches from different parts of the world enable each other to do God's work. Christian leaders from both churches pray together, envision together, plan together, and work together to do God's work. While control of property belongs to the nationals, decisions are mutually agreed upon (1994, 245–46).

These types of partnerships fit into at least three major classifications: bilateral, vertically integrated, and global partnerships. The simplest and most prevalent form of partnership is bilateral. In bilateral partnerships "one mission entity links up with another, be it church/church, church/mission, mission/mission, east/west or north/south" (Butler 1994, 13). Sometimes more than two agencies or churches partner to accomplish a specific task. For example, Churches of Christ in Fresno, California, and Stillwater, Oklahoma, partner with the Great Commission School and the Rainbow Church of Christ in Nairobi, Kenya, which in turn partners with an emerging church in Mbulu in northern Tanzania.

Since 1986, vertically integrated partnerships have begun to appear as major churches and missions have begun to pray, plan, and work together to evangelize unreached peoples. Vertically integrated partnerships "represent a conscious effort to get all the key elements needed to reach a particular people group together—from Scripture translation to mass media, development work to personal witness—each playing its own unique role but all linked in a conscious commitment to a common objective" (Butler 1994, 13). For example:

> Achmed, a man in a "closed" country, came to Christ after having had contact with five different ministries. Radio, literature, Bible correspondence courses, visiting national evangelists, and local "tentmakers" all had a part. The key was their knowledge of each other and the conscious coordination of their efforts as Achmed was passed from one ministry to another in an active, working partnership. **Butler 1994, 10**

Global partnerships are also now beginning to appear. Globalization is "the process by which organizations move beyond merely operating on the field from a single or dominant national base to operating transnationally, not tied to any particular country" (Hicks 1993, 7). The organization of the mission agency transcends any one culture so that neither the country from which the agency originated nor the location of headquarters is significant. Operation Mobilization (OM), which began as a student-initiated, student-led movement, is an example of a developing global mission. Fully 60 percent of OM's funding comes from outside North America. Thirty-four percent of OMers come from Asia, 36 percent from Europe, and only 24 percent from North and South America (Hicks 1993, 18–19). Transcultural teams minister on the field. Hicks writes:

> As our witness goes out from a team with a south Indian leader from a Hindu background, an Italian driver with a Catholic upbringing, a north Indian Pentecostal as team treasurer, a British Baptist leading the study program, a Muslim convert in charge of literature supplies and a few others from different language areas in India, *the concept of Christianity as a Western religion forever united with colonialism melts away before we even open our mouths. People devoted to Christ from all nations are going to all nations for Christ.* **1993, ii**

The development of globalized missions reflects what is happening in international business. Management specialist Kenichi Ohmae describes five stages by which businesses gradually move toward internationalization (Ohmae 1990, 89–97). In the first stage a national business exports products that are marketed through local distributors. The second stage, called the multinational phase, begins when the company assumes the marketing of its product in a foreign country. A company in stage three manufactures and markets in foreign nations. In stage four the company duplicates in foreign contexts the research, development, and engineering capabilities that exist in the home company and thereby attains a full insider position in the foreign market. The business becomes fully internationalized during this stage. Stage five is the globalized phase. The company transcends "national boundaries, not only in reaching the goals of [their] mandate, but also in the processes of planning, organizing, and implementing the mandate" (Hamm 1991, 47). Personnel who lead and supervise the company come from many cultures and countries.

It is important for churches and mission agencies to develop appropriate partnerships. Most partnerships are and should be bilateral. They tend to be specifically focused toward accomplishing specific tasks for the glory of God. It is extremely important for churches and agencies to enter into bilateral partnerships before they attempt to develop vertically integrated partnerships. No agency should naively attempt to become artificially globalized without first developing extensive roots in numerous international contexts.

Larry Pate and Lawrence Keyes encourage churches and agencies to enter into task-oriented partnerships. The tasks include partnering to evangelize unreached people, researching fields for receptivity, building support structures to assist emerging mission churches and agencies, and training Two-thirds World missionaries. While globalized agencies have the advantage of enhanced credibility because they reflect the "supracultural character of the gospel," they also carry a number of disadvantages: Globalized agencies distract from the development of indigenous, home-grown, national mission structures, and non-Westerners of globalized agencies may be perceived as paid agents of the West. Pate and Keyes reflect that peoples of the world continue to think nationally even as an international era begins to break in. They believe that global agencies are most effective in areas of relief and development and least effective when engaged in church planting (1986, 159).

## Problems With Partnerships

Today there is a tendency for mission leaders to idealize partnerships without considering some very significant problems. Maurice Sinclair's statement "There is nothing more interesting, exasperating, and exciting than partnership" (Davies 1994, 46) seems appropriate. As Paul McKaughan aptly states, the expected results have not always been forthcoming:

> For all of the personal benefit that I have gained (and some of these partnerships have been extremely productive), over the years there has grown within me a series of reservations flowing from the tremendous costs, both personal and financial, of maintaining both monocultural and multicultural partnerships. At times I have been dismayed by the paucity of results in light of the investment by all of the members of the group. **1994, 68**

This section on partnership, therefore, concludes with a discussion of the problems of partnerships. These will be divided into the cultural, economic, and leadership problems (Hicks 1993, 13).

Cultural misunderstandings, amplified by the tendency toward cultural paternalism, is the first major problem of partnerships. Paternalism continues to raise its ugly head because Westerners are pridefully aware that their culture carries significant influence in both the church and the world. Hicks writes:

> Western culture predominates the church and the world. Not only does Western culture pervade mission methods, strategies and structures, but it is glorified and promoted throughout the world as *civilized* culture. Most elements of what is sometimes called *world culture, are Western*. Non-Western people, Christian and non-Christian, often covet Western culture and lifestyle. **1993, 13**

It is easy for Westerners to dominate partnership relationships, because they know the cultural and linguistic landscape. Most partnerships use Western decision-making patterns and Western languages, especially English, in meetings and retreats. Those from the Two-thirds World frequently have to learn the layout of the landscape and do not feel as comfortable with the environment. This tendency toward paternalism is amplified when Western missionaries and agencies initiate a partnership and feel responsible for its success and continuance. As puppeteers control marionettes, Westerners frequently pull the strings that guide decision-making processes. One mission executive wrote, "The least complicated model of partnership that I have been able to observe is the one where there is a dominant partner, the partner who sets the cultural agenda or styles of the partnership" (McKaughan 1994, 76). In reality, paternalism frequently continues under the guise of partnership. Such paternalism is likely the reason that Westerners tend to idealize partnerships and non-Westerners feel a higher degree of dissatisfaction (Butler 1994, 11–12).

Philip Butler makes three suggestions aimed at reducing cultural problems and enhancing effective communication. First, partnerships must begin by acknowledging that cultural differences do exist and will have significant influence on the success of the partnership. Second, participants must take seriously their colleagues involved in the partnership deliberations. Third, they must take time to talk through their "*mutual* understanding of key elements" of the partnership. It is of great importance that prayer and reflection on the will of God permeate the entire deliberation (1994, 12).

Samuel Escobar, while critically reflecting upon the "discovery" of emerging missions in the Two-thirds World, wisely counsels that Western armor may not adequately equip Christ's soldiers being raised up in the Two-thirds World:

> Around the world David is accomplishing his mission for God with his staff, five smooth stones, and a sling. Suddenly his movements are detected by Saul's computer and officialdom discovers that David exists, because you exist only when your presence is registered by Saul's computer. And Saul now rejoices that David exists and wants to offer David his coat of armor, his bronze helmet, and his sword, so that David may accomplish the mission that Saul has devised for him. I hope for the sake of God's mission that David will be able to accomplish his mission God's way [and not Saul's]. **1986, 162**

The second major problem with international partnerships is the economic disparity between some non-Western cultures and Western cultures. Hicks writes:

> The West economically predominates the world. No matter how much a servant mentality is lived out by mission agents, the majority of funding influences the structures and direction of ministry. Even when Western missions refuse to control, government requirements and donor expectations create pressures. **1993, 13**

Perhaps the greatest danger of the partnership philosophy is that a Western subsidy system is introduced under the guise of partnership. Mission finances go into church maintenance rather than into initiating new works and creating responsible churches. Tebbe and Thomson comment that "sometimes the question, 'How can we cooperate?' is only a way of saying, 'How can you help us do our thing which we have already decided?'" (1994, 141). Some national leaders challenge paternalism on the one hand yet desire parental attention on the other:

> Many times the nationals look to the parents (the Western world) to supply and to provide funds and materials for these projects, even for staff salaries. The money and materials may continue to come, but they may be accompanied by a parental directive on how to use the funds and materials. This system has been going on for many years, and the Westerners never learned from the previous occurrences. The paternalism in different forms is conducted in the style of 'He who pays the piper calls for the tune!' **Kure 1994, 90**

In this case one wonders whether what is considered paternalism is in reality a rejection of accountability by national leaders who desire the benefits of partnership without true mutual complementation. Such confrontational attitudes make partnership both frustrating and disillusioning. Samuel Escobar wisely comments, "Internationalization of mission demands a disposition to deal with authentic leaders incarnate among the people rather than with obsequious mercenaries" (1992, 11).

Third, leadership issues pose significant challenges to partnership. Core to leadership is the expression and definition of vision. According to Samuel Escobar, people of various cultures define leadership differently:

> Most Latin Americans and Europeans, and to some degree Africans, will articulate a vision on the basis of a clear, consistent theory and historical background. North Americans and some Asians will articulate a vision more in terms of a task-oriented sequence of steps to be followed in order to achieve a goal. . . .

> The predominant missiological trend in North America is what I call "managerial missiology," an approach to mission as "a manageable task" for which technology and the social sciences can provide the necessary methodology. This trend represents the epitome of the task-oriented type of a vision. . . . It finds resistance and criticism among many evangelicals in different parts of the world who would like more a missionary vision that includes clear, theologically grounded, and historically aware concepts. **1992, 13–14**

Effective partnerships will take into account these different vantage points. It is vitally imperative that Western missiologists develop the theological and philosophical undergirdings necessary to understand missions. Fundamental mistakes are made whenever decisions are based merely on achieving a goal or accomplishing a task. This, however, does not negate the need for the right sort of pragmatism—practical approaches to mission and evangelism undergirded by biblical theology and an understanding of culture and context.

# Final Guidelines for Use of Missiological Models for Developing Responsible Churches

Problems in the areas of culture, economics, and leadership do not negate the need for partnership but give missiologists understandings to overcome them.

The three perspectives of this chapter (the Three-Self Formula, Indigeneity, and Partnership) are human models developed to guide missionaries and church leaders. As such, none is infallible, and some are more appropriate to certain contexts than others. Generally, indigenous perspectives appropriately apply to rural, face-to-face cultures, which do not have a high degree of specialization and do not relate extensively to the international arena. Urban situations are frequently quite international, and models of partnership are more likely to empower the church rather than to create dependency and control from the outside. In most urban settings developing church movements have an extremely difficult time beginning without some type of partnership with churches and agencies of other countries. Building standards are stringent, and partnering is necessary to provide the urban space necessary where rents are high and hotels inaccessible.

Mission history indicates that operating without any model of church maturation tends to predestine a work for paternalism. These models equip missionaries, agency and church leaders, and national church leaders (1) to begin mission works in line with the patterns and realities of local economies rather than planned on the basis of Western economy, (2) to be sensitive to differing cultural realities, and (3) to learn to partner cross-culturally in an increasingly internationalized, interconnected world.

Finally, it must be said that developing responsible churches is not merely a human endeavor. Effective Christian leaders are primarily spiritual leaders. The Word of God is "a lamp to [their] feet and a light for [their] path" (Ps. 119:105). Christian leaders are prayer warriors who turn to God continually for guidance. They are churchmen—seeking to amplify the community of believers of which they are a part. They continually reflect on spiritual things and allow this spirituality to permeate their lives. The church of Christ does not need mere practitioners and strategists but people with lives transformed into the image of Christ (2 Cor. 3:18). Unregenerate humanity tends to contort every model for selfish purposes.

> The church of Christ does not need mere practitioners and strategists but people with lives transformed into the image of Christ.

# BUILDING ON UNDERSTANDINGS OF CHURCH MATURATION

1. Contrast the case studies at the beginning of this chapter: Contrast the *pororoca* to the Negro/Solimoes model of national/missionary relationships. How do the attitudes of missionaries in these case studies vary?

2. What is meant by the term *paternalism*? Why was paternalism a significant problem during the colonial era? To what degree do you feel it continues to be a problem?

3. Describe the three-self formula promoted by Rufus Anderson and Henry Venn. Describe the importance of this formula in missions during the last half of the nineteenth century and the first half of the twentieth century. What are strengths and weaknesses of this formula?

4. Contrast the attitudes of missionaries and national leaders towards each of the *selfs* in the three-self formula.

5. In what ways did the *Indigenous Model* of church maturation go beyond the thinking of the original three-self formula? Briefly describe the role of William Smalley and Melvin Hodges in this expansion of missiological thinking.

6. What are some strengths and weaknesses of the Indigenous Model of church maturation? Why does the author prefer the word *responsible* to *indigenous*?

7. List four new realities of the world that create the need for partnering.

8. Define the terms *partnership* and *synergy* and describe the relationship of the two terms.

9. Describe five qualities of Christian partnership. Why is each principle important for effective partnering?

10. Many international partnerships will crumble because they are naively constructed and implemented. Discuss problems with partnerships in the areas of culture, economics, and leadership. Propose guidelines to overcome each problem.

11. After reading the final section of the chapter, discuss the appropriateness of the various models of church maturation to various world contexts.

12. Describe the meaning of the following statement from the concluding section of the chapter: "Mission history indicates that operating without any model of church maturation tends to predestine a work for paternalism."

# Case Studies:

### Case Study #1

Discuss the wisdom and limitations of the approaches employed by missionaries of this case study based on the perspectives of this chapter.

We are making plans for the time that missionaries will leave Zinzin by equipping Zinzini leaders to take over our leadership roles. About ten representatives of the churches are being selected to work with us missionaries in setting goals for the year. During this time, they will have equal input into what we missionaries teach and where we plant churches with them during the next year. We will meet again in June for mid-year evaluation. Just as I report to you regularly, our team will report our progress in the areas where the Zinzini church leaders have commissioned us to work.

### Case Study #2

Those who have been working toward the establishment of a preacher training school in northern Zinzin met in Big City, Texas, at the Mainstreet Church of Christ to organize the Zinzini Christian Foundation. A charter and by-laws are currently being written by the board. New members added to the board since our last newsletter are John Doe from Abilene, Texas, and Jim Someone from Nashville, Tennessee. An active search is still underway for an eldership that will assume spiritual leadership for the organization. . . . Members of the board visited Zinzin this summer. After lengthy discussion with Zinzini preachers about the teaching concept espoused by the Zinzin Christian Foundation, there was a universal agreement that it is the correct one. . . . You may send contributions to help them with the purchase of the land and buildings for the school to Big City Church of Christ, Big City, America.

1. Does this case study illustrate healthy or deficient partnering? Discuss the reasons for your answer.
2. Who are making the decisions about the work in Zinzin? Why do you think they have assumed this right of decision-making?

3. When should a preacher school be established in Zinzin—when the church is young or after a number of churches have been established and nationals are mature enough to partner with foreign missionaries to organize the school? Why is this question important?

4. Who should oversee the school—nationals, missionaries, or both working together? Should there be a board in America? If so, what should be the role of the American board? Should there be national leaders of the school? If so, how should they relate to missionaries and international leaders?

5. What should be the role of Western finances and expertise in the development and operation of the school?

# 11

# SELECTING AREAS
# FOR MISSION SERVICE:
## Critiquing the Criteria

What criteria should be used to select areas for planting new churches and nurturing them to maturity? Should mission personnel and resources be evenly distributed throughout the world, or should certain areas be prioritized while others are held lightly? If some are prioritized, what rationale should determine priorities? What is the role of God and his Spirit in the selection? These questions will be examined in this chapter by evaluating two primary perspectives toward field selection—unreached peoples and receptivity—and two secondary considerations—personal preference and urban expansion.

## Unreached Peoples

According to researchers of unreached peoples, such as David Williard (1993) and David Barrett (1990, 26), the world can be divided into three major slices. People who have never heard of the saving power of the blood of Jesus and have no access to the gospel comprise *World A*. Those of World A are called *unreached* or *unevangelized*. World B is made up of those who have heard the message of the gospel but have rejected it. These people are called *evangelized non-Christians*. World C is composed of those who have accepted the gospel and claim to be *Christians*. The unreached people perspective urges missionaries and mission agencies to focus on the unreached portion of humanity, who make up World A because unreached people "will perish, not because [they have] rejected

Christ, but because [they have] no understanding of what Christ has offered" (Williard 1993).

According to this perspective, mission resources should be directed toward reaching the unreached but such commitments are not being made. Christians in World C spend approximately 99.9 percent of all financial resources on themselves, 0.09 percent on World B, but only 0.01 percent on reaching the unreached in World A (Williard 1993). Bryant Myers writes:

> Too much mission money is spent in that part of the world which already identifies itself as Christian. Far too few human and financial resources are directed at the many people who live in places where it is likely they will never hear the Good News of Jesus Christ unless someone goes to tell them. Too many Christians give where the fields are ready unto harvest, while being unwilling to support taking the gospel where the going is tough. This must change. **1993, 45**

Mission personnel are also committed to fields other than World A. Although World A comprises 23 percent of the world's population, it receives only one percent of the world's Christian missionaries. While 33 percent of the world's population live in World C, fully 91 percent of all missionaries minister there, mostly in newly evangelized parts (Williard 1993).

### Defining Unreached Peoples

The Lausanne Committee for World Evangelization defines an unreached people as "a people group among which there is no indigenous community of believing Christians with adequate numbers and resources to evangelize this people group without requiring outside [cross-cultural] assistance" (Efta 1994, 28). Some mission agencies call peoples unreached if "one percent or less of the group are born-again Christians" (1994, 29). Unreached peoples have been variously described as social groupings who have never heard the gospel, have not responded to the gospel, do not have a community of believers within their midst, or do not have a Bible in their mother tongue or readily available for people to read (Efta 1994, 29).

The words *unevangelized* and *unreached* are given special significance by unreached peoples' advocates. The unevangelized must be given an opportunity to respond to the gospel. The unreached, despite cultural, linguistic, and political barriers, must be reached with the Good News of the kingdom. Luis Bush specifically defines these terms:

The *unevangelized* are people who have a minimal knowledge of the gospel, but have had no valid opportunity to respond to it. The *unreached* are the two billion people who have never heard of Jesus as Savior, and are not within reach of Christians of their own people. There are, in fact, some 2000 people or nationalities in which there is not yet a vital, indigenous church movement. **n.d., 2**

The terms *unreached* and *unevangelized* are used to define the extent to which people groups are in contact with (or have heard) the gospel, instead of their traditional meaning to describe the unsaved wherever they live.

Unreached peoples' proponent Ralph Winter recounts three phases of modern missions. The focus two hundred years ago was on the coastlands of the world. One hundred years ago the focus shifted to the interiors of the continents and has switched within the last century to the unreached peoples in all areas of the world. Thus, according to Winter's journal *Mission Frontiers*, "the purpose of missionaries is to go where the church is not present rather than expand the church where it already exists" (1994, 11).

### The 10/40 Window

At the 1989 Lausanne II Conference in Manila, Luis Bush proposed that if the goal of missions is to reach the unreached, mission finances and personnel must focus on what he called the 10/40 Window. This "window" extends from ten to forty degrees north of the equator and stretches from North Africa through the Middle East to China and Japan. Because this area is largely unreached by Christian missions, it constitutes the "core of the challenge" for world evangelization. Almost all of the fifty-five most unevangelized countries in the world are in this sector of the world. Although the three billion people living in these fifty-five countries constitute 57 percent of the world's population, only 18 percent of all missionaries minister there (Bush n.d., 2–3).

Besides being unreached, peoples living in the 10/40 Window exhibit a number of other characteristics (Bush n.d., 3–8). All three major non-Christian religions—Islam, Hinduism, and Buddhism—originated in the 10/40 Window and have their greatest strength there. The poorest of the poor live in this part of the world. More than eight out of ten of the poorest people of the world, those whose yearly income is less than $500, live in the 10/40 Window. The majority of the unreached people live in

All three major non-Christian religions—Islam, Hinduism, and Buddhism—originated in the 10/40 Window and have their greatest strength there.

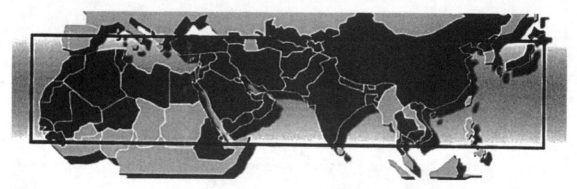

**FIGURE 10. THE 10/40 WINDOW**

the poorest countries of the world, demonstrating a correlation between poverty and lostness (Myers 1989, 94–95). The gospel, however, has always been "good news to the poor" (Luke 4:18). Finally, Satan has a significant stranglehold on this area of the world. Bush writes:

> The people living in the 10/40 window have suffered not only hunger and a lower quality of life compared with the rest of humanity, but have also been kept from the transforming, life giving, community changing power of the gospel. **n.d., 7**

In this part of the world the "gospel is veiled" because "the god of this age has blinded the minds of unbelievers, so that they cannot see the light of the gospel of the glory of Christ, who is the image of God" (2 Cor. 4:3–4). God's people must seek to break these strongholds of Satan. They must reflect the ministry of Christ by proclaiming "good news to the poor" and "release [to] the oppressed" (Luke 4:18).

North India, described by many as "the most spiritually dark place on earth," is an example of an area of unreached peoples. While most missionaries to India work among tribal and outcast groups, the Hindu core of the nation (65 percent of the population) and the Muslim minority (15 percent) are notably neglected. Beyond the typical cross-cultural barriers of language and culture, antagonistic religious, political, and caste barriers hinder Christianity's entry into and evangelization of North Indian cultures. For example, the northern state of Himachal Pradesh, the center of Hindu pilgrimages in the Himalayas, has no sustained Christian presence. In the adjoining state of Haryana pioneering mission work is occurring among large castes though the church is less than one percent of the population. Generally the growth of the church among Hindi people of northern India is "disturbingly slow." People from tribal groups and lower castes are more receptive than those of middle and upper castes (Winter 1994, 10–14).

### Strengths and Limitations of Prioritizing Unreached Peoples

Prioritizing unreached people has many strengths, among them the following three:

First, this perspective has helped the mission movement focus on those areas of the world where Satan's stranglehold is strongest. By the power of God these fortresses of Satan must be breached and Satan's strongholds claimed for the kingdom of God.

Second, the vision of reaching the unreached has attracted many to become long-term missionaries. Efta writes:

> The logic that led my wife and me to become missionaries went something like this: "We have so many opportunities to hear the gospel on television and radio, in books and magazines, and at many evangelical churches, but because so many other people have little or no exposure to the gospel, we should focus our efforts on those who may never hear it. Work in our country is certainly legitimate and pleasing to God, but we should put more emphasis on those in unreached areas." This logic also influenced our decision about what country we wanted to serve in. We wanted to go to people who had never heard the gospel. **1994, 28**

The frontier mentality—to go where the gospel has not penetrated and to challenge the powers of Satan where he reigns—has drawn adventuresome, dedicated servants into ministry among unreached people.

Third, the desire to reach the unreached has led to the development of special types of missions necessary to break into resistant areas. Vocational missionaries are entering countries where full-time, church-planting missionaries cannot go.[1] Nonresidential missionaries are mobilizing resources

---

[1] J. Christy Wilson has been in the forefront of the vocational missionary movement. His book *Today's Tentmakers* (1979) discusses this alternative model of missions and has been formative to subsequent thinking and dialogue. In 1994, seventy strategists from seventeen countries met in Thailand to form the Tentmakers International Exchange (TIE), a gathering of mission thinkers planned since the Lausanne II conference in 1989. *Intent*, formally the United States Association of Tentmakers (USAT), seeks to network and train evangelical tentmakers or, in their own words, to "network professionals for global impact" (P.O. Box 35, Cascade, Colorado 80809). The Glorietta consultations (Glorietta, New Mexico, in 1991 and Charlotte, North Carolina, in 1994) brought together missionaries and tent-

and training personnel for areas traditionally closed to the gospel.[2] Special movements, societies, and consultations creatively mobilize and strategize for reaching the unreached.[3] Prioritizing unreached people has thus made a significant contribution to missions.

Prioritizing field selection on the basis of the unreached, however, has a number of limitations:

First, unreached peoples are generally resistant to the gospel. Bush himself calls the 10/40 Window "the resistant belt" of the world (n.d., 1). In many countries becoming a Christian is a crime punishable by death, and Christians suffer intense persecution. They are frequently beaten and harassed, face financial discrimination and job loss, and are repudiated and disowned by their families. Planting churches, nurturing new Christians to maturity, and training leaders is difficult and frequently impossible.

The lack of receptivity among many unreached peoples makes it necessary for missiologists to ask several significant questions: How is God working to make unreached peoples receptive to the gospel? When should sending churches, missionaries, and mission agencies wait for God in his Holy Spirit to break down the political and social barriers that make the unreached resistant to the gospel? When should they proceed with confi-

---

maker leaders "to multiply the momentum and the effectiveness of the missionary-tentmaker movement" (USAT description of the 1994 conference). The recent interest in 10/40 Window has heightened the need for tentmaking, but the fact remains that up to this point, the effectiveness of tentmakers has been marginal and many idealistic tentmakers return home broken because of inadequate preparation. There are many "skeletons lying out there in the desert of people who have gone out there and didn't know what they were doing and weren't connected with anybody" (Dave Brown in Guthrie 1995, 81). A beginning guide to effective vocational missions is *Working Your Way to the Nations: A Guide to Effective Tentmaking* (1993), published by the World Evangelism Fellowship.

[2]V. David Garrison's book *The Nonresidential Missionary* (MARC 1990) provides a model of opening areas that are either closed or resistant to the gospel. The nonresidential missionary is a career missionary who is matched up with a single unevangelized population segment, but who lives somewhere other than in their midst, because legal residence for a missionary is prohibited or highly restricted. He or she surveys the situation of the population group, becomes fluent in the population's main language, and mobilizes every form of Christian ministry to the group. The nonresidential missionary concentrates on the priority of initial evangelization and on eliminating gaps or duplications with other mission agencies (Garrison 1990).

[3]The A.D. 2000 and Beyond movement and the International Society for Frontier Missiology plan strategies for the evangelization of unreached peoples. The purpose of the Global Consultation on World Evangelization in 1995 in Seoul, Korea, was to "encourage continued momentum building toward the fulfillment of the goal of a church for every people and the gospel for every person by the year 2000" (Bush 1994, 1).

dence that God is using them to bridge political and social barriers? What is the role of God's timing? How can the whole gospel be presented during times of social and political oppression so that the unreached are able to fully understand the grace of God? When, on the other hand, are missionaries to unreached peoples merely giving pieces of the gospel that can easily be rejected and thus intensify opposition to the gospel? When do small doses of the gospel inoculate unreached people so that when the culture is ready to change, the gospel is not an option? God's missionaries among unreached people must, therefore, have the patience to wait for God—to know how to plow the field and plant the seed as well as reap the harvest.

Second, some proponents of the unreached peoples' perspective focus too narrowly on one area of the world. One mission strategist told the European director of an evangelical mission, "All foreign missionaries must leave Europe immediately. They have absolutely no business being there. Europe is evangelized" (McQuilkin 1994b, 263). This extreme perspective would negate missions in North and South America and in Europe and Africa south of the Sahara. The only valid mission work, therefore, would be within the 10/40 Window.

However, the unreached peoples perspective should not be interpreted so narrowly. Should France be considered reached even though only one half of one percent are conservative, Bible-believing Christians? Should France be only a launching pad to convert the Berber of North Africa? Should American missionaries retreat from the receptive areas of Africa south of the Sahara as Muslim missionaries flood the area? Should Nairobi be considered only a launching pad to convert Sudanese and Somalians rather than a mission field in and of itself? Rather than focusing on one geographical area, unreached people must be reached wherever they live in the world.

The third weakness is related to the second. The unreached peoples movement takes upon itself an aura of authority that compels proponents to view Scripture and the world through its own interpretive lens. "Instead of using the Bible to evaluate the movement, the movement is used as an exegetical grid for the Bible" (Efta 1994, 29). For example, the Great Commission is understood as a statement about unreached peoples rather than Jesus' words at the conclusion of Matthew's Gospel compelling the believing Jews (and thus all peoples) to make disciples of all peoples. The words *unevangelized* and *unreached* are used to define the extent to which people groups are in contact with (or have heard) the gospel rather than those who have not been reconciled to God by the saving blood of Christ.

The world is divided by the movement into precise people groups and categorized according to the degree that they have responded to the gospel. Is this the best (or only) way to categorize the world? Is this the only way to strategize for missions? When held as a grid to interpret Scripture and as the only lens to view the world, the theory of unreached people is frequently more limiting than liberating.

The unreached peoples perspective has validity if for no other reason than that Satan's stranglehold in the 10/40 Window must be broken. Far greater resources must be focused on reaching the unreached. No one model, however creatively defined, can adequately describe the needs of all areas of the world.

# Receptivity

Receptivity, the second major perspective of prioritizing mission fields, has always explicitly or implicitly influenced field selection. McGavran's chapter in *Understanding Church Growth* entitled "The Receptivity of Men and Societies" has especially been formative (McGavran 1970, 216–32). This chapter describes the varying receptivity of the world, factors in the fluctuation in receptivity, and the practical ramification of this principle for mission policy. Although this principle has fewer overt adherents during this era in which conviction about reaching unreached peoples has taken center stage, these foundational understandings cannot be easily dismissed.

## The Nature of the World

The concept of receptivity is rooted in an understanding that the world is dynamic, not static. As a consequence, the receptivity of people to the gospel message is always changing. Sometimes the hearing of the eternal message creates no response. It appears as if the people feel no need for the gospel that all humankind needs. At other times the message hits home to a society crying over problems and overwhelmed by fears. With joy a large number of people believe the message in a very short time, seek the Lord in baptism, organize vibrant fellowships, and revitalize their society around the message of Jesus Christ.

Cultures are like individuals: Sometimes they are more receptive than at other times. Young people reared in a Christian home are more receptive at age twelve than at age twenty. If they reach twenty without conversion, they may be inoculated against the Christian message and hardened to it. Individuals are also more receptive when confronted by a crisis. A Kipsigis man of Kenya was led to conversion after the death of his father. His heart was stirred, not only by the power of the Christ to resurrect and bring to himself those who believe, but also by the freedom, given by Christ, from the fear of the dead. He responded to Christ during a time of brokenness and fear.

The world may be thought of as a giant orchard having many fields. Although some fields are ready for harvest, the husbandman is concerned about all fields, for their harvest will come in due time. He sends planters and pruners, grass slashers, and insect sprayers to fields not yet ready for harvest. However, he sends numerous laborers to fields where the fruit is ready. He is concerned lest the fruit fall to the ground and rot before it can be harvested. In this analogy God is the great husbandman, and cultures and cities of the world are the fields. The Lord cares for all the world and sends workers out to all fields. He is concerned, however, that those he has prepared for the harvest be brought into the harvest. Peoples of the world, like the fields of this metaphorical vineyard, go through times of readiness for the gospel and times of being resistant to the gospel. The receptive should be harvested while they are open to the message and the resistant nurtured until they become receptive.

**The ultimate source of receptivity is the mighty acts of God working through the Holy Spirit to convict the world of sin. . . .**

Although it can be studied sociologically, the relative receptivity of world peoples is more than merely a sociological phenomenon. The ultimate source of receptivity is the mighty acts of God working through the Holy Spirit to convict the world of sin and working through his messengers who carefully plant the seeds of the gospel in not-yet-fertile soil. The ever-present God is working to break down walls and create receptivity.

Receptivity, therefore, is *the readiness of people to hear God's Word and accept his sovereignty*. This definition recognizes that the world is ever-changing and that God is active in it.

### Biblical Foundations of Receptivity

Jesus compassionately described the multitudes as "harassed and helpless, like sheep without a shepherd" (Matt. 9:36). Jesus' description implies that the receptive are seekers: The broken are seeking wholeness; the hungry, food; the sick, a physician; the confused, orientation; the lost, a shepherd. Self-satisfied people, conversely, feel no need for change. Jesus, while seeing these crowds, emphasized harvesting. He told his disciples,

"The *harvest* is plentiful but the workers are few. Ask the Lord of the *harvest*, therefore, to send out workers into his *harvest* field" (vv. 37–38). Jesus implied that God wants a harvest, and because he is Lord of the harvest, he can provide both the harvesters and the harvest.

Immediately after speaking on harvesting, Jesus called the Twelve together to send them out on the Limited Commission. They were to enter a village expecting a response: "Whatever town or village you enter, search for some worthy person there and stay at his house until you leave" (Matt. 10:11). If they were not welcomed or if people would not listen to their words, they were to "shake the dust off [their] feet" (v. 14). The unreceptive were not to be badgered into accepting the gospel but left in favor of those who wanted to hear.

Paul applied this teaching to his ministry. Although he was concerned with teaching his own people (Rom. 10:1–2; 9:1–3), Paul turned to the Gentiles when the Jews would not respond in faith. In Antioch of Pisidia Paul and Barnabas taught Jews in their synagogue. But when they became jealous and began talking "abusively against what Paul was saying," Paul and Barnabas "turn[ed] to the Gentiles" (Acts 13:44–48, 51). In Corinth Paul preached to the Jews until they "became abusive." He then "shook out his clothes in protest" and told them, "From now on I will go to the Gentiles" (18:5–6). When the Jews in Rome rejected Paul's message, he announced that "God's salvation has been sent to the Gentiles, and they will listen!" (28:23–28).

The response to Paul's preaching in Athens and Corinth demonstrates a contrast between resistance and receptivity. In Athens Paul met with outspoken hostility and ridicule (Acts 17:18, 32), although a few believed (v. 34). After speaking in the Areopagus he left for Corinth. His departure may have been precipitated by the Athenian court demanding that he leave or by his realization that few would respond to his message in Athens (18:1). In either case, resistance to his message caused Paul to leave suddenly even though he was awaiting the arrival of Silas and Timothy (17:15).

In Corinth Paul went initially to the Jewish synagogue, where he sought to teach both Jews and Greeks about the gospel (Acts 18:5). When Jews rejected his message, he turned to the Gentiles even though some Jews, such as Crispus, were converted. The locality of preaching also changed from the Jewish synagogue to the house of Titus Justus. During this time of transition, it would have been easy for Paul to give up in despair. But God's presence reassured him. God told him in a vision, "Do not be afraid, keep on speaking, do not be silent; . . . because I have many people in this city" (vv. 9–10). As a result, Paul settled in this area for a year and a half (v. 11), and a local fellowship of believers was established.

Paul could have mistaken persecution for lack of receptivity. Frequently such persecution represents exactly the opposite. Persecution is an attempt to suppress the change feared by civic and religious leaders when the need for social and religious change has become evident. If Paul had left Corinth because of initial discouragement, he would have missed a great harvest of souls. Likewise, Bible-believing Christians began to reap God's harvest in Bulgaria during the early 1990s, but the Orthodox church leaders forced political leaders to limit the influence of new religious groups. Courageous religious leaders, standing against the influence of the traditional Orthodox movement, continued to proclaim God's message.

Resistant societies, on the other hand, do not take seriously new ideologies. Ridicule, rather than silent listening or persecution, becomes the rule. This seems to have been the case at Athens, where Paul was sarcastically termed a "babbler" and one who was "advocating foreign gods" (Acts 17:18). Societies cynical about the Christian system are difficult to penetrate.

The parable of the sower (Matt. 13:3–9, 18–23) depicts the receptivity of different sorts of people as they come into contact with the seed of the kingdom. The same seed was sown, but the soils were different. Similarly, the core Christian message is one, but receptivity varies. The parable must be seen from the perspective of the sower, who is wanting a good harvest. As the sower broadcasts the seed, he aims for the soil where he feels he will get the greatest harvest. The desired outcome of sowing is harvest.

In John 4 the woman at the well acknowledged that the one who taught her about living water was the anticipated Messiah (vv. 25–26), and she then proclaimed her faith to the people of the city (vv. 28–29). While these people were coming to Jesus (v. 30), he encouraged his disciples to think in terms of harvesting. They need not wait four months for the harvest but would reap what others had sown. He said, "I tell you, open your eyes and look at the fields! They are ripe for harvest" (v. 35). When the Samaritans came to Jesus, he taught them, and they believed (vv. 39–40). Christ's harvest perspective enabled him to trust that God was using numerous sowers to prepare for eventual harvest.

The Great Commission demonstrates that the goal of preaching is to produce a response, not merely to sow the seed. Those sent were to "make disciples" (Matt. 28:19). They were to "go . . . and preach" so that the lost would "be saved" (Mark 16:15–16). The *going* and *preaching* were not ends in themselves.

### Illustrations of Receptivity

Receptivity and nonreceptivity of cultures can be illustrated by numerous examples.

*Tanzanian Case Study.* The Bob Bentley and Greg Newton families began work among the Sukuma tribe of Tanzania in 1991. This people group was chosen because they were largely unchurched and numbered between three and five million people. While these missionaries were still studying the language, non-Christians began stopping them on the road with petitions signed by fifty to seventy people requesting Christian teaching in their village. By November 1994, eighteen churches had been planted and over one thousand Sukuma baptized. The Sukuma, as a people, are in a time of transition. They are dissatisfied with fear-ladened animistic answers to life's questions and are seeking alternatives on which to base their lives (Newton 1994, 1).

This receptivity of the Sukuma, however, contrasts to the resistance of most urban Muslims of Tanzania. They militantly oppose Christianity in all spheres of life. Christians, they say, have divided the divinity of Allah. "How can God have a son? Is belief in the trinity not polytheism?" Their own growth takes place mainly in urban contexts through economic influences. Muslim wholesalers seldom sell to non-Muslim retailers, particularly those who are Christian. Funds from oil-rich Arabic nations help build mosques and training institutions. Instead of upholding local cultures and vernaculars, they attempt to press all Africans who move to the cities into a developing, Arabic mold.

Missionaries in Tanzania cannot enter every people group and teach all types of peoples. They must prioritize. Proponents of the receptive-peoples perspective suggest that the receptive should be reached while they are still receptive. Once Tanzanians become Muslims, they are much harder to reach.

*Turkish Case Study.* The receptivity of Turks living in Bulgaria and Turkey are greatly dissimilar. Stan Guthrie writes, "For years, evangelistic efforts among the gospel-resistant Turks have had all the momentum of a glitch-plagued Space Shuttle anchored to its launch pad—potentially a lot of power but no movement" (1992, 1). During the communist rule of Bulgaria, many Bulgarian Turks returned to Turkey to escape suppression. They expected wealthy Arab nations to help with their resettlement. This assistance never came. Christian organizations, however, were available to offer assistance in resettlement. These Turks saw God's love in the actions of compassionate Christians. Because of unemployment in Turkey, many of these Turks returned to Bulgaria. When communism was overthrown there in the early 1990s and the Turks began to hear again the gospel story, two thousand became followers of Christ in three years. At the same time the nation of Turkey, with a population of 56.5 million, could claim only one thousand followers of Christ. Steve Hagerman, director of Friends of Turkey, predicts, "We believe that God is preparing one of the greatest harvests in the 20th century among the Turkish people. . . . Every few days I hear of another Turk who's come to Christ outside of Turkey" (Guthrie 1992, 4). Turkish people are more receptive in some places than others. According to "receptive people" thinking, the focus of Turkish evangelization should be among those who are most receptive.

*Case Study of Baptist Missions in Uganda, 1961–1972.* The history of Baptist missions in Uganda also demonstrates a varying degree of receptivity. One Baptist mission, beginning work in Uganda in 1961, concentrated their evangelism in large cities, believing urban converts would then take the gospel to rural areas. In 1972 their fellowship had grown to seven hundred national Christians in 22 churches. Another Baptist group, beginning in 1962 with a similar-sized workforce, assigned part of their group the task of urban evangelism while others engaged in rural evangelism. In 1972 this group claimed five thousand Christians in 112 churches, with most of their growth coming in rural areas. Probably neither group realized the transient nature of African cities. William Ochieng' described city dwellers this way: "Who is a stranger? A stranger is a guy whose home is elsewhere. That is what most people in Nairobi are—strangers. Give them a holiday and they will be heading for their homes, in the bush" (1981, 6). African urbanites call their urban residences their "houses," but their residences in rural areas are their "homes." They *stay* in the city but *live* in their village. People in African cities of the 1960s and 1970s, with their large populations of "strangers," were not as receptive as those in rural areas. But the nature of African cities is changing as new generations are born in the urban context and lose their rural vernaculars and parts of their cultural heritages. Cultural perspectives of *home* and the rootedness of people, therefore, have significant impact on the long-term receptivity of people.

*Case Study of Eastern Europe.* Many church leaders in the United States assumed that the fall of the wall dividing East and West in 1989 would usher in a period of unparalleled receptivity throughout Eastern Europe. In reality, the receptivity has been mixed. Many people in Romania, Ukraine, and parts of Russia have eagerly sought to hear the gospel for a significant period of time. The receptivity of other countries has been relatively low. One Hungarian missionary, expecting receptive soil, wrote:

> The fact is obvious; we are trying to till *hard* soil!! Not what we expected. . . . We'd all like to see the gospel run like a wildfire on a dry prairie. Instead it's like trying to start a burn-barrel after the (Midwest's) '93 flood . . . . When we arrived in 1990, shortly after the barbed wire was cut (May '89), we experienced an ever-increasing sucking sound—the sound of the Hungarians being sucked into the lies of Satan, that worldly junk will satisfy their inward emptiness. **Herrmann 1994, 1**

Originally, the team of which this missionary was a part expected to establish an indigenous church within five years. Thus five-year commitments were made. It soon became evident that establishing a vibrant church in Hungary would be a fifteen-year, rather than a five-year, endeavor. Their supporting church in the United States, after much consultation with workers on the field, decided to extend their commitment but downsize the church-planting team according to God's call in team members' lives (Herrmann 1994, 2). Thus, new "open" doors may not necessarily mean high receptivity.

The concept of receptivity is not a rejection of missions in whole continents or geographical areas that appear to be unreceptive. The Lord's command to "go into all the world and preach the good news to all creation" (Mark 16:15) clearly negates such an orientation. No area of the world should be neglected. However, those that are not bearing fruit should be held lightly until signs of a possible harvest are evident. When such signs become evident, workers should be called into the harvest in concentrated numbers (McGavran 1970, 230). Joe Betts, long-term Japanese missionary, expressed this perspective:

> Satan still has this country in his grip but we keep pecking away with the unchangeable Word and winning a soul now and then. There will come a day when he will have to turn loose and we want to be here to guide the people in God's truth. **1982, 2**

A missionary in the Netherlands wrote to a friend in Africa: "There you plan on establishing eight churches in a year. Here we are glad when we convert about eight people per year." This man is "lightly holding" his area until it becomes receptive. In order to know which areas should be aggressively harvested and which should be "held lightly," church leaders should be sensitive to the historical, cultural, and psychological trends of a variety of ethnic groups and cities.

## Factors Affecting Receptivity

Many factors influence receptivity. Some factors are specific to certain locations whereas others are universal in application. The three universal factors include (1) worldview dissonance, (2) uprooted populations, and (3) competition with other Christian groups.

*Worldview Dissonance.* Worldview dissonance occurs when people no longer accept as plausible the traditional beliefs and assumptions of their culture. In some cases a new generation arises that does not accept the conceptions of its forefathers; in other circumstances rapid change induces dissonance to occur during one generation. In animistic cultures extreme tension leading to worldview dissonance occurs when old gods and traditional magic seem to have lost their power. In secular societies anxiety arises when the secular answers of science do not adequately explain the pain and evil of the world and life after death.

In many parts of the world the equilibrium of the culture has been shattered by the introduction of formal education. This training equips an educated elite who challenge traditional authority structures and desire to put together a new way of life more in line with their new ways of thinking.

Sometimes rapid political and social changes create worldview dissonance. The fall of the Berlin Wall in 1989 and the eventual demise of Soviet communism shook the plausibility structures of much of the world and created ideological vacuums. Resistant areas of Russia, Ukraine, and Romania have become receptive to the gospel. Three African countries who had Marxists governments—Benin, Mozambique, and Angola—became exceptionally open to the gospel. The demise of communism has also stunned many of the educated elite of Latin America who held to Marxism as a philosophical alternative to capitalism, thereby heightening the receptivity of Latin America. In the mid-1990s the force of change is crouching at the door of Fidel Castro's Cuba, creating intense cultural pressure.

Thus receptivity is greatly determined by political and related philosophical changes occurring in the world. Mission planners must anticipate world changes and prepare evangelists to enter areas that will eventually become receptive.

**Mission planners must anticipate world changes and prepare evangelists to enter areas that will eventually become receptive.**

*Uprooted Populations.* Because old associations have been broken and new patterns have not yet become fixed, uprooted people are generally receptive to the gospel. When the Churches of Christ began working among the Kipsigis tribe in Kenya, the greatest response during the early evangelistic period came in newly settled areas. In Latin America poor peasants migrating to the cities in hopes of improving their fortunes have been exceptionally receptive. In North America hundreds of the suburban churches were begun as people moved from the city to the suburbs.

Some uprooted peoples, however, are not putting down new, permanent roots. They are transients whose roots are elsewhere. They are strangers in a new area, but they plan to return "home." In such contexts numerous converts may result without a long-term community of believers being formed. In 1973-74 I evangelized extensively in the large tea estates of the Kericho District of Kenya. Three small churches were established and 150 adults baptized. Within three years almost all the converts had returned to their original homes. Initially I felt that these converts would return to their home areas and establish new local churches. But the workers were young and had little influence in their extended families. When they returned home, most were pressured either to fit into religious groups with roots in their areas or to return to traditional ways. While churches among the Kipsigis became permanent fellowships with their own leaders, the tea estate churches could establish no such continuity.

*Competition with Other Christian Groups.* A third factor affecting receptivity is competition with other Christian religious groups. Non-Christians frequently are unable to differentiate the subtle differences between Christian religious groups. A multiplicity of these groups confuses them. In societies where numerous religious groups are working, the ones that are distinctive tend to grow faster than the others.

Obviously, it is easier to evangelize a receptive people without competition from other religious groups. Several religious groups evangelizing in a receptive area will result in numerous small groups. Donald McGavran credits this to the fact that different religious groups approach people differently. While one group might fail to influence some, another group might succeed.

This factor is illustrated by the Southern Baptists and the Pentecostal Assemblies of God in Uganda. New missions in Uganda usually focused their work in Kampala, the capital city. This city had been the hub of evangelistic activity since the Anglicans (1877) and Catholics (1879) arrived in the country. Between 1960 and 1972 ten new religious groups began concentrated efforts in this highly Christianized city. Many of these groups experienced minimal growth. The Southern Baptists and the Pentecostal Assemblies of God, however, focused their work in relatively untouched societies. With little or no competition, they became the fastest-growing religious groups in Uganda (Van Rheenen 1976, 116–17). Likewise, missionaries working in the Kipsigis tribe of Kenya have seen more rapid growth in areas that are untouched by other religious groups or where these religious groups were relatively weak. Growth occurred where there were vacuums of Christian influence rather than where denominations were strong.

### Strengths and Limitations of Prioritizing Receptive Peoples

Targeting receptive people has a number of strengths. First, the receptive peoples' perspective prioritizes those most willing to hear the gospel. Second, it acknowledges the world to be ever changing and dynamic rather than static and unchanging. Certain peoples are continually becoming more receptive to the gospel while the receptivity of others fades. Third, this perspective correctly recognizes that God in his Holy Spirit convicts the world of sin and thus prepares unbelievers to hear his message. God works unexpectedly, as demonstrated in 1989 by the fall of the wall between East and West. Four, because this perspective recognizes that there are different levels of readiness to receive the gospel, mission leaders are better able to place mission personnel most strategically for greater harvest. Some areas are held lightly while others are aggressively evangelized.

This theory of reaching the receptive while they are still receptive, however, has one major limitation. God frequently uses missionaries to unreached peoples as the primers to create receptivity. God uses missionaries from other cultures to sow the seed among unreached peoples as well as working through the indigenous people. For example, some of the greatest growth of God's kingdom in our generation is taking place in China. In many parts of China God is working without the direct influence of any cross-cultural missionaries. But nonresidential missionaries are also being used by God to help sow the seeds of the kingdom in various areas. Among the 6.5 million Yi people of South China one nonresidential missionary is recruiting, mentoring, and placing one hundred Christian teachers, doctors, agriculturists, and other professionals to minister vocationally as they also carry the gospel message. In setting priorities, therefore, a balance needs to be established between receptive peoples and unreached peoples. When the unreached are also receptive, such as many among the Sukuma of Tanzania, there is an ideal but atypical mix.

Finally, I present a challenge to mission agencies and research organizations to (1) rethink their almost total focus on unreached peoples and their neglect of those who are receptive, and (2) initiate research to determine when resistant societies become receptive. What if these two primary prongs of prioritizing fields were somewhat equally held and researched with various strategies developed for different areas of the world? When might these two criteria overlap? In what contexts of the world is one more valid than the other? How might these two criteria be used together rather than held separately? Mission agencies and research institutes must find a balance between researching only the unreached or only the receptive.

# Personal Preference

While targeting unreached and receptive peoples are two primary criteria for the selection of areas of mission service, two secondary criteria must also be discussed. The first of these secondary criteria is, in reality, the one that most frequently determines where missionaries are placed. When given the freedom to select their own areas of ministries, missionaries most frequently base their decisions on personal preference.

Personal preference is frequently based on *personal relationships with people from a particular field*. During the 1980s hundreds of Thai students studied at Abilene Christian University and influenced missionary candidates to serve in Thailand. J. M. McCaleb, pioneer Church of Christ missionary to Japan, became acquainted with Japanese who were receiving their education in the United States. Personal relationships are also frequently formed with missionaries on furlough who encourage missionary candidates to join them. Amos Allen, Stephen Meeks, and Oneal Tankersley were my students during my 1977-78 teaching furlough at Harding University. After doing internships under me among the Kipsigis people of Kenya, they became part of a new team working among related tribes of Kenya. Personal relationships might form through military and business assignments in other lands. Harold Paden, an American paratrooper in Italy during World War II, decided to return to help rebuild the country around the gospel of Jesus Christ. Mike Martin, a two-year apprentice to Recife, Brazil, returned to the United States to form a missionary team to plant an urban church in Natal, Brazil.

Personal preference might also take the form of *personal likes and dislikes*. One family sought to go to Australia because they would not have to learn a totally new language. A great outdoorsman was attracted to Alaska, and a surfer to Hawaii. The presence of Western conveniences attracted many to the great urban centers of Africa such as Nairobi, Abidjan, and Harare. One team investigated two equally receptive African peoples and selected the area with the healthiest climate.

When local church leaders send out their own missionaries, *geographic proximity* becomes another type of personal preference. Some local church leaders prefer to support mission work "within a day's drive of home." Nearness allows overseeing churches to be involved in the activities of the mission church. Close proximity also allows the local church to know what is occurring in the mission church and to encourage it in its various struggles.

The strength of personal preference is that missionaries and sending churches make their own decisions about areas and develop commitments to these areas. The rationales that stand behind the selection, however, are frequently nebulous, not specifically defined. Contextual and global concerns (the readiness of people to hear the gospel and reaching those who have little chance to hear the gospel) are likely to be peripheral. Although camouflaged under many other explanations, personal preference is frequently the dominant reason for field selection.

# Urban Expansion

Targeting the largest cities of the world because of their influence and population is a final criterion for field selection. Some mission strategists say that since the city is the wave of the future, mission work should focus on the largest world-class cities in the world, then spread to smaller cities, and finally to rural areas. David Barrett claims that "communicating the good news of Jesus Christ effectively has always been closely associated with the world's cities" (1986, 7).

**Without question, the world is quickly urbanizing, and the Christian missionary movement must urgently seek to win the urban masses.**

Without question, the world is quickly urbanizing, and the Christian missionary movement must urgently seek to win the urban masses. World urbanization is largely a twentieth-century phenomenon. The urban population accounted for only 4 percent of the world's population by 1800 and 14.4 percent by 1900. Urban population swelled to 28.9 percent of the world's population in 1950, 37.4 percent in 1970, 45.7 percent in 1990, and a projected 51.2 percent in the year 2000 (Barrett 1986, 16).

Christianity, however, is losing the battle to win the cities. The percentage of Christians in world cities reached 69 percent in 1900 but significantly declined to 46 percent in 1986 and is projected to continue to decline to 44 percent by A.D. 2000 and 38 percent by A.D. 2050. Christianity is losing the cities "at the rate of 29.5 million new urban non-Christians every year—which is 80,700 a day, or one every second" according to trends in 1986 (1986, 10–11). This decline can be attributed to secular influences in cities and massive population increase in many Two-thirds World contexts where non-Christian world religions are strongly entrenched. Barrett (1986, 11–12) suggests that "the proportion of Christians in a city reflects, to some extent, the amount of relative effectiveness of Christian presence" and suggests that global evangelization should focus on "supercities" (over four million) and from the year A.D. 2000 "urban supergiants" (over ten million).

The strength of this methodology of area selection is that the most rapidly growing sector of the world's population is targeted. Strategizing for cities is imperative because half of the world's population will shortly live in urban centers. It is naive, however, to prioritize cities because they are cities, without considering social and contextual factors. Which cities are receptive to the gospel? Which cities are unreached? In the social configuration, how are cities related to other cities and rural areas? What are migration patterns? Are rural-to-urban migration patterns permanent or temporary? An urban focus should never stand by itself but should be coupled with other criteria.

# Conclusion

Because of limited resources, mission agencies and churches cannot send missionaries to all parts of the world. Decisions to do mission work in certain places will negate proclamation in other places. Developing priorities is therefore imperative. How, then, should mission agencies and churches channel their resources for world evangelization? This chapter suggests two primary perspectives—unreached peoples and receptivity—and two secondary considerations—personal preference and urban expansion. Using these criteria, each agency and church must set priorities, realizing that each perspective has strengths and weaknesses and that God is the ultimate sovereign who works through his people as they make decisions. Prioritizing areas of mission service intentionally helps overcome the fads that so often drive the mission endeavor.

Jim Slack of the Foreign Mission Board of the Southern Baptist Church speaks of the board's two-tiered mission effort. Significant finances are used both to evangelize areas of the world considered receptive and to penetrate World A, where the gospel essentially has never been presented. Slack comments:

> We're harvesting where it's harvestable, and we're planting churches where people have never heard. We're successful at both. We're juggling two balls and neither has fallen. **1995, 5**

For example, 437 new churches were started in Nigeria during 1994, the most in any country in the board's history. In addition, the number of churches planted in World A increased from 37 in 1993 to 144 in 1994 (Slack 1995, 5). This Southern Baptist plan intentionally focuses on winning the receptive while also attempting to open the more resistant areas of the world where the gospel has not yet been proclaimed.

# BUILDING ON THE PERSPECTIVES OF FIELD SELECTION

## QUESTIONS:

1. Contrast World A, B, and C according to the writings of David Williard and David Barrett. Where are most missionaries located? To whom are most of our mission resources directed?
2. What is meant by the term *unreached people*? From your reading or personal experience give an example of some unreached people.
3. Describe *the 10/40 Window*. Besides defining the area of unreached, people, what are other characteristics of the 10/40 Window?
4. What are strengths and limitations of prioritizing unreached peoples? Be thorough and specific in your answer.
5. Define the term *receptivity*. In this discussion how is the world like a giant orchard having many fields? How should laborers farm the various fields?
6. What is the role of the Holy Spirit in changing receptivity? How is receptivity related to the dynamic working of God in the world?
7. Use the comments of Jesus in the "limited commission" of Matthew 9:35–10:14 to describe receptivity.

8. From your reading or personal experience give an example of some receptive people.
9. List *and* describe three general factors affecting receptivity.
10. What are strengths and limitations of prioritizing receptive peoples? Be thorough and specific in your answer.
11. What is meant by *personal preference* as a criteria of field selection? What types of personal preferences are described by the author of this chapter?
12. What are strengths and limitations of personal preference as a primary criterion of field selection? Be thorough and specific in your answer. Why does this criterion so frequently determine where missionaries are placed?
13. Identify the strengths and limitations of the following statement: "Since the city is the wave of the future, mission work should focus on the largest world-class cities in the world, then spread to smaller cities, and finally to rural areas."
14. Discuss the two-tiered effort of the Foreign Mission Board of the Southern Baptists in missions.

## Case Study:

You have recently become the chief executive officer of World Christian Broadcasting and desire to use your position to partner with local churches and agencies to evangelize the world. You have just read this chapter and have decided to convene a missionary strategy meeting of local church and agency leaders of your fellowship to strategize for world evangelization. How should you as a church fellowship prioritize areas for evangelism? What are the major questions to be asked in the strategy conference?

# WORKS CITED

Adeyemo, Tokunboh. 1994. Categories of partnership. In Appendix 1 of *Kingdom Partnerships for Synergy in Missions*, 245–46. Pasadena, Calif.: William Carey Library.

Allen, Roland. 1962. *Missionary Methods: St. Paul's or Ours*. Grand Rapids: Eerdmans.

Allison, Fielden. 1983. The effects of kinship on church growth in the Kipsigis churches. In *Church Growth Among the Kipsigis of Southwest Kenya*, 56–67 (photocopy).

Ambrozic, A. M. 1972. The hidden kingdom: A redaction critical study of the references to the kingdom of God in Mark's Gospel. *Catholic Biblical Quarterly*. Monograph Series 2. Washington, D.C.: Catholic Biblical Quarterly.

Anderson, Gerald A. 1961. *The Theology of Christian Mission*. New York: McGraw-Hill.

Anderson, Rufus. 1856. *Outline of Missionary Policy*. Boston: American Board of Commissioners.

Araujo, Alex. 1993. Retooling for the future. *Evangelical Missions Quarterly* 29 (October): 362–70.

Aulen, Gustav. 1931. *Christus Victor*. Trans. A. G. Hebert. New York: Macmillan.

Austin, Clyde N. 1986. *Cross-Cultural Reentry: A Book of Readings*. Abilene, Tex.: A.C.U. Press.

Barnett, Betty. 1991. *Friend Raising*. Seattle: YWAM Publishing.

Barrett, David B. 1986. *World-Class Cities and World Evangelization*. The AD 2000 Series. Birmingham, Ala.: New Hope.

_____. 1990. *Our Globe and How to Reach It: Seeing the World Evangelized by AD 2000 and Beyond*. The AD 2000 Series. Birmingham, Ala.: New Hope.

Barrett, David B., and Harley Schreck. 1987. *Unreached Peoples: Clarifying the Task*. Birmingham, Ala.: New Hope.

Beasley-Murray, G. R. 1986. *Jesus and the Kingdom of God*. Grand Rapids: Eerdmans.

_____. 1992. The kingdom of God in the teaching of Jesus. *Journal of the Evangelical Theological Society* 35:19–30.

Beckham, William A. 1995. *The Second Reformation: Reshaping the Church for the 21st Century*. Houston: Touch Publications.

Bennett, William J. 1994. American's cultural decline must be reversed. *AFA Journal* (April): 16–17.

Betts, Joe. 1982. Missions newsletter. *The Marcher* 5 (August): 2.

Beyerhaus, Peter. 1979. The three selves formula: Is it built on biblical foundations? In *Readings in Dynamic Indigeneity*. Ed. Charles Kraft, 15–30. Pasadena, Calif.: William Carey Library.

Bonk, Jonathan J. 1989. *The Theory and Practice of Missionary Identification 1860–1920*. Studies in the History of Mission. Vol. 2. Lewiston, N.Y.: Edwin Mellen Press.

Broom, Wendell. 1976. Church growth principles. In *Guidelines for World Evangelism*, ed. George Gurganus, 81–104. Abilene, Tex.: Biblical Research Press.

Bush, Luis. n.d. *Getting to the Core of the Core: The 10/40 Window*. San Jose, Calif.: Partners International.

————. 1994. Global consultation on world evangelization. *Global Church Growth* 21 (Spring): 1–8.

Bush, Luis, and L. Lutz. 1990. *Partnering in Ministry: The Direction of World Evangelism*. Downers Grove, Ill.: InterVarsity Press.

Butler, Phill. 1991. Why strategic partnerships? A look at new strategies for evangelizing. In *Partners in the Gospel*. Wheaton, Ill.: Billy Graham Center.

Butler, Phillip. 1994. Kindgom partnerships in the '90s: Is there a new way forward? In *Kingdom Partnerships for Synergy in Missions*, 9–30. Pasadena, Calif.: William Carey Library.

Chao, Jonathan. 1989. *The China Mission Handbook*. Hong Kong: Chinese Church Research Center.

Chaze, William L. 1983. Our big cities go ethnic. *U.S. News & World Report* 21 (March): 49–53.

Chiang, Samuel E. 1992. Partnership at the crossroads: Red, yellow or green light? *Evangelical Mission Quarterly* (July): 284–89.

Cho, Paul Yonggi. 1984. How the world's largest church got that way. *Christianity Today* 28 (May 18): 50–56, 59–60.

Clinton, J. Robert. 1988. *The Making of a Leader*. Colorado Springs: NavPress.

Coggins, Wade. 1988. The risks of sending our dollars only. *Evangelical Mission Quarterly* 24 (July): 204–6.

Congdon, G. Dal. 1985. An investigation into the current Zulu worldview and its relevance to missionary work. *Evangelical Missions Quarterly* 21 (July): 296–99.

Cox, Susan. 1990. Application paper for missionary principles and practices, BMIS 346, Abilene Christian University.

Darrow, Ken, and Brad Palmquist, eds. 1977. *Trans-Cultural Study Guide*. Stanford, Calif.: Volunteers in Asia Publications.

Davies, Stanley. 1994. Responding to Butler: Reflections from Europe. In *Kingdom Partnerships for Synergy in Missions*, 43–48. Pasadena, Calif.: William Carey Library.

Dayton, Edward R., and David A. Fraser. 1990. *Planning Strategies for World Evangelization*. Grand Rapids: Eerdmans.

Diles, Allen. 1993. Interview by author, 5 May.

Dyrness, William. 1990. *Learning About Theology from the Third World*. Grand Rapids: Zondervan.

————. 1992. *Invitation to Cross-Cultural Theology*. Grand Rapids: Zondervan.

Efta, Damian. 1994. Who are the unreached? *Evangelical Missions Quarterly* 30 (January): 28–32.

Elkins, Philip. 1965. *Toward a More Effective Mission Work*. Dallas, Tex.: Christian Publishing Co.

Elliston, Edgar J. 1988. Designing leadership education. *Missiology* 16 (April): 203–15.

————. 1992. *Home Grown Leaders*. Pasadena, Calif.: William Carey Library.

Escobar, Samuel. 1992. The elements of style in crafting new international mission leaders. *Evangelical Missions Quarterly* 28 (January): 6–15.

Ferguson, Everett. 1989. *The Everlasting Kingdom*. Abilene, Tex.: A.C.U. Press.

Footlick, Jerrold K. 1990. What happened to the family? *Newsweek Special Edition* Winter/Spring:14–34.

Friedrich, Otto. 1987. New Age harmonies. *Time* 7 (December): 62–72.

Garrison, David V. 1990. *The Nonresidential Missionary: A New Strategy and the People It Serves*. Monrovia, Calif.: MARC.

George, Carl F. 1991. *Prepare Your Church for the Future*. Tarrytown, N.Y.: Revell.

Getz, Gene A. 1978. *Sharpening the Focus of the Church*. Chicago: Moody Press.

Green, Michael. 1970. *Evangelism in the Early Church*. Grand Rapids: Eerdmans.

Grigg, Viv. 1990. *Companion to the Poor*. Monrovia, Calif.: MARC.

Groothuis, Douglas R. 1986. *Unmasking the New Age*. Downers Grove, Ill.: InterVarsity Press.

Grunlan, Stephen A., and Marvin K. Mayers. 1979. *Cultural Anthropology—A Christian Perspective*. Grand Rapids: Zondervan.

Gunther, Walther, and Hans-Georg Link. 1986. Love. In *The New International Dictionary of New Testament Theology*. Vol. 2. Ed. Colin Brown. Grand Rapids: Zondervan.

Gurganus, George. 1976. *Guidelines for World Evangelism*. Abilene, Tex.: Biblical Research Press.

Guthrie, Donald. 1970. *The New Bible Commentary Revised*. London: Inter-Varsity Press.

Guthrie, Stan. 1992. Conversions among Turks suggest gospel lift-off near. *World Pulse* 27 (March 6): 1, 4.

_____. 1995. Tentmaking: putting down stakes in mission movement. *Christianity Today* (November 13): 80–81.

Hall, Arthur. 1986. Book Review. *City Watch* 1 (October): 2.

Hamm, Peter. 1983. Breaking the power habit: Imperatives for multinational mission. *Evangelical Missions Quarterly* 19 (July):180–89.

Harrell, Pat Edwin. 1969. *The Letter of Paul to the Philippians*. The Living Word Commentary. Austin, Tex.: R. B. Sweet.

Hauerwas, Stanley, and William H. Willimon. 1989. *Resident Aliens: Life in the Christian Colony*. Nashville: Abingdon.

_____. 1991. Why *Resident Aliens* struck a cord. *Missiology* 19 (October): 419–29.

Haviland, William. 1987. *Cultural Anthropology*. 5th ed. New York: Holt, Rinehart and Winston.

Heard, Renee. 1988. Reading report for missionary anthropology, BMIS 445, Abilene Christian University, September 20.

Hedlund, Roger. 1990. Cheaper by the dozen? Indigenous missionaries vs. partnership. *Evangelical Missions Quarterly* 26 (July): 274–79.

Herrmann, Steve and Lidia. 1994. *The Herrmann Family Newsletter*. Missionary Newsletter (November): 1–2.

Hesselgrave, David J. 1978. *Communicating Christ Cross-Culturally*. Grand Rapids: Zondervan.

_____. 1978. Dimensions of cross-cultural communications. In *Readings in Missionary Anthropology II*. Ed. William A. Smalley, 615–26. Pasadena, Calif.: William Carey Library.

_____. 1988. *Today's Choices for Tomorrow's Mission: An Evangelical Perspective on Trends and Issues in Missions*. Grand Rapids: Zondervan.

Hestenes, Roberta. 1983. *Using the Bible in Groups*. Philadelphia: Westminster.

Hicks, David. 1993. *Globalizing Missions: The Operation Mobilization Experience*. Tyrone, Ga.: Operation Mobilization.

Hiebert, Paul G. 1983. *Cultural Anthropology*. 2d ed. Grand Rapids: Baker.

_____. 1986. *Anthropological Insights for Missionaries*. Grand Rapids: Baker.

_____. 1993. De-theologizing missiology: A response. *Trinity World Forum* 19 (Fall): 4.

Hinton, Keith. 1985. *Growing Churches Singapore Style: Ministry in an Urban Context*. Singapore: Overseas Missionary Fellowship.

Hodges, Melvin L. 1953. *On the Mission Field: The Indigenous Church*. Chicago: Moody Press.

Hutton, J. H. 1961. *Caste in India: Its Nature, Function, and Origin*. 3d ed. London: Oxford University Press.

Icenogle, Gareth Weldon. 1994. *Biblical Foundations for Small Group Ministry*. Downers Grove, Ill.: InterVarsity Press.

Johnstone, Patrick. 1986. *Operational World*. Waynesboro, Ga.: STL Books.

Kasdorf, Hans. 1979. Indigenous church principles: A survey of origin and development. In *Readings in Dynamic Indigeneity*. Ed. Charles Kraft, 71–86. Pasadena, Calif.: William Carey Library.

Keineetse, Keineetse. 1989. Is Shakawe now a spy centre? *The Guardian* 18 (August).

Keyes, Larry. 1994. OC International in an Indian partnership. In *Kingdom Partnerships for Synergy in Missions*. Ed. William D. Taylor, 229–35. Pasadena, Calif.: William Carey Library.

Kipling, Rudyard. 1924. The ballad of east and west. In *Rudyard Kipling's Verse: Inclusive Edition 1885–1918*, 268–72. Garden City: Doubleday.

Kivengere, Festo. 1962. Personal revival. In *Commission, Conflict, Commitment*. Ed. Eric Fife and Arthur F. Glasser. Chicago: InterVarsity Press.

Kluck, P. A. 1985. Social systems. In *India: A Country Study*. Ed. Richard F. Nyrop, 217–72. Area Handbook Series. Washington: American University.

Kraakevik, James. H., and Dotsey Welliver. 1991. *Partners in the Gospel: The Strategic Role of Partnerships in World Evangelization*. Wheaton, Ill.: Billy Graham Center.

Kraft, Charles H. 1976. Mimeographed classroom notes for anthropology, Fuller Theological Seminary.

Kraft, Charles H., and Tom N. Wisley, eds. 1979. *Readings in Dynamic Indigeneity*. Pasadena, Calif.: William Carey Library.

Kure, Maikudi. 1994. A Nigerian response to Patrick Sookhdeo. In *Kingdom Partnerships for Synergy in Missions*, 89–92. Pasadena, Calif.: William Carey Library.

Lamascus, R. Scott. 1989. To understand homeless, minister lives on street. *Christian Chronicle* 46 (August): 1, 10.

Lewis, Jonathon, ed. 1993. *Working Your Way to the Nations: A Guide to Effective Tentmaking*. Pasadena, Calif.: William Carey Library.

Lindsell, Harold. 1949. *A Christian Philosophy of Missions*. Wheaton, Ill.: Van Kampen Press.

Little, Alicia. 1987. Reading report for missionary anthropology, BMIS 346, Abilene Christian University, 26 June.

_____. 1988. Diary kept in Yugoslavia. February 10.

Little, Michael. 1994. Praying through the window II: The 100 gateway cities. News Release from the United Prayer Track of the AD 2000 and Beyond Movement. September 14.

Luzbetak, Louis, J. 1970. *The Church and Cultures*. Pasadena, Calif.: William Carey Library.

Mathews, Ed. 1976. Leadership training in missions. In *Guidelines for World Evangelism*. Ed. George P. Gurganus. Abilene, Tex.: Biblical Research Press.

Mbiti, John S. 1971. *New Testament Eschatology in an African Background*. London: Oxford University Press.

Mbiti, John S., and others. 1980. *The Thailand Report on People of African Traditional Religions*. Wheaton, Ill.: Lausanne Committee for World Evangelization.

McGavran, Donald A. 1970. *Understanding Church Growth*. Grand Rapids: Eerdmans.

―――――. 1990. *Understanding Church Growth*. 3d ed. Grand Rapids: Eerdmans.

McKaughan, Paul. 1994. A North American response to Patrick Sookhdeo. In *Kingdom Partnerships for Synergy in Missions*, 67–88. Pasadena, Calif.: William Carey Library.

McKinney, Lois. 1980. Training leaders. In *Discipline Through Theological Education by Extension*. Ed. Virgil Gerber. Chicago: Moody Press.

McQuilkin, Robertson. 1994a. Six inflammatory questions. *Evangelical Missions Quarterly* 30 (April): 130–34.

―――――. 1994b. Six inflammatory questions—part 2. *Evangelical Missions Quarterly* 30 (July): 258–64.

Merritt, Hilton. 1980. Kisumu—a team effort. In *Church Planting, Watering, and Increasing in Kenya*. Ed. Kenya Mission Team, 39–46. Austin, Tex.: Firm Foundation.

*Minneapolis Tribune*. 1973. Crowd mistakes rescue, attacks police. November 23.

Moltmann, Jürgen. 1981. *The Trinity and the Kingdom*. San Francisco: Harper & Row.

Myers, Bryant L. 1989. Where are the poor and lost? In *Target Earth*. Pasadena, Calif.: Global Mapping.

―――――. 1991, MARC Newsletter (June). 5.

―――――. 1993. *The Changing Shape of World Mission*. Monrovia, Calif.: MARC.

Neighbour, Ralph W. 1990. *Where Do We Go From Here? A Guidebook for the Cell Based Church*. Houston: Touch Publications.

Newbigin, Lesslie. 1989. *The Gospel in a Pluralist Society*. Grand Rapids: Eerdmans.

Newton, Greg. 1994. *Reaching the Sukuma of Tanzania*. Missionary Newsletter (April): 1.

―――――. 1994. *Reaching the Sukuma of Tanzania*. Missionary Newsletter (November):1.

Nida, Eugene. 1990. *Message and Mission*. Rev. ed. Pasadena, Calif.: William Carey Library.

Nyrop, Richard F., ed. 1985. *India: A Country Study*. Area Handbook Series. Washington: American University.

Oberg, Kalervo. 1960. Cultural shock: Adjustment to new cultural environments. *Practical Anthropology* 7 (July-August): 77–82.

Ochieng', William. 1981. City empties for holiday. *Sunday Nation* (December 27): 6.

Ohmae, Kenichi. 1990. *The Borderless World: Power and Strategy in the Interlinked Economy*. New York: Harper Business.

Orchardson, Ian Q. 1961. *The Kipsigis*. Nairobi, Kenya: East African Literature Bureau.

Pate, Larry D. 1991. The changing balance in global mission. *International Bulletin of Missionary Research* 15 (April): 56–61.

Pate, Larry D., and Lawrence E. Keyes. 1986. Emerging missions in a global church. *International Bulletin of Missionary Research* 10 (October): 156–61.

Posterski, Donald C. 1989. *Reinventing Evangelism: New Strategies for Presenting Christ in Today's World*. Downers Grove, Ill.: InterVarsity Press.

Rommen, Edward. 1993. The de-theologizing of missiology. *Trinity World Forum* 19 (Fall): 1–4.

*Russian Good News.* 1990. Published by Hunter Station Church of Christ, Montgomery, Ala. (May): 1.

Schipper, Gary. 1988. Non-Western missionaries: Our newest challenge. *Evangelical Missions Quarterly* 24 (July): 198–202.

Slack, Jim. 1995. Baptisms top 300,000 in 1994, a banner missions year. *The Commission* (March-April): 5.

Smalley, William A. 1958. Cultural implications of an indigenous church. *Practical Anthropology* 5:51–65.

_____. 1967. Proximity or neighborliness? In *Readings in Missionary Anthropology.* Ed. William A. Smalley, 302–6. New York: Practical Anthropology.

_____. 1978. Cultural implications of an indigenous church. In *Readings in Missionary Anthropology II.* Ed. William A. Smalley, 147–56. Pasadena, Calif.: William Carey Library.

Smalley, William A., ed. 1978. *Readings in Missionary Anthropology II.* Pasadena, Calif.: William Carey Library.

Sookhdeo, Patrick. 1994. Cultural issues in partnership in mission. In *Kingdom Partnerships for Synergy in Missions,* 49–66. Pasadena, Calif.: William Carey Library.

Steffen, Tom A. 1993. *Passing the Baton: Church Planting That Empowers.* La Habra, Calif.: Center for Organizational and Ministry Development.

Sundkler, Bengt. 1965. *The World of Mission.* Grand Rapids: Eerdmans.

Taylor, William D., ed. 1994. *Kingdom Partnership for Synergy in Missions.* Pasadena, Calif.: William Carey Library.

Tebbe, James, and Robin Thomson. 1994. Challenges of partnership: Interserve's history, positives and negatives. In *Kingdom Partnerships for Synergy in Missions,* 131–52. Pasadena, Calif.: William Carey Library.

Terpstra, Gerard H. 1996. Interview.

Thompson, LaNette W. 1992. Furlough meets reality. *The Commission* (October-November): 52.

Tippett, A. R. 1969. *Verdict Theology in Missionary Theory.* Lincoln, Ill.: Lincoln Christian College Press.

_____. 1973. *Verdict Theology in Missionary Theory.* Pasadena, Calif.: William Carey Library.

Towns, Elmer L., John N. Vaughan, and David J. Seifert. 1982. *The Complete Book of Church Growth.* Wheaton, Ill.: Tyndale House.

Van Rheenen, Gailyn. 1976. *Church Planting in Uganda.* Pasadena, Calif.: William Carey Library.

_____. 1983a. *Biblically Anchored Missions.* Austin, Tex.: Firm Foundation Publishing House.

_____. 1983b. Leadership training. In *Church Growth Among the Kipsigis of Southwest Kenya,* 37–55. Sotik, Kenya: Privately printed.

_____. 1991. *Communicating Christ in Animistic Contexts.* Grand Rapids: Baker.

Verkuyl, Johannes. 1978. *Contemporary Missiology: An Introduction.* Trans. and ed. Dale Cooper. Grand Rapids: Eerdmans.

Vicedom, George F. 1965. *The Mission of God.* Trans. Gilbert A. Thiele and Dennie Hilgendorf. St. Louis: Concordia.

Wagner, C. Peter. 1973. *Look Out! The Pentecostals Are Coming*. Carol Stream, Ill.: Creation.

Walker, Wimon. 1989. Is Shakawe now a spy center? *Ngamiland Mission Team Report* (Fall): 1–2.

Wallace, Anthony F. C. 1956. Revitalization movements. *American Anthropologist* 5:264–81.

_____. 1966. *Religion: An Anthropological View*. New York: Random House.

Wells, David F. 1989. *Turning to God*. Grand Rapids: Baker.

_____. 1992. The de-min-ization of the ministry. In *No God but God*. Ed. Os Guinness and John Seel, 186. Chicago: Moody Press.

Williard, David. 1993. *World A: A world apart*. Richmond, Va.: Foreign Mission Board of the Southern Baptist Convention.

Wilson, J. Christy. 1979. *Today's Tentmakers*. Wheaton, Ill.: Tyndale House.

Winter, Ralph D. 1992. The new Macedonia: A revolutionary new era in missions begins. In *Perspectives of the World Christian Movement*. Ed. Ralph D. Winter and Steven C. Hawthorne, B–157–75. Pasadena, Calif.: William Carey Library.

_____. 1994. India: Is it the greatest challenge to finishing the task? *Mission Frontiers* 16:10–42.

Winter, Ralph D., and Steven C. Hawthorne, eds. 1992. *Perspectives of the World Christian Movement. Revised Edition*. Pasadena, Calif.: William Carey Library.

Yohannan, K. P. 1986. *The Coming Revolution in World Missions*. Altamonte Springs, Fla.: Creation House.

# SCRIPTURE INDEX

# INDEX OF MODERN
# AUTHORS AND SOURCES

# SUBJECT INDEX